THE ROCK WHERE WE STAND

An Ethnography of Women's Activism in Newfoundland

Bay St George in western Newfoundland is a region shaped by the establishment of the Earnest Harmon American Air Force Base and a boom-and-bust economy. This ethnography explores how women at the Bay St George Women's Council deal specifically with the issues of poverty, single motherhood, child sexual abuse, and domestic violence, and examines the interplay of feminist and Newfoundland identification among these individuals.

Drawing on fourteen months of observation and interviews with women at the council, Glynis George provides a much needed, specifically Canadian, contribution to ethnocultural and feminist studies. The research situates the particular concerns and political activism of these women in this rural region of Canada within the larger context of economic restructuring and neo-liberal economic and social policies that continue to marginalize women in Canada and around the world. Avoiding the common pitfall of folklorization in rural ethnographic studies, *The Rock Where We Stand* represents a unique and innovative contribution to the field.

(Anthropological Horizons)

GLYNIS GEORGE is Assistant Professor, Department of Sociology and Anthropology, University of Windsor.

The Rock Where We Stand

An Ethnography of Women's Activism in Newfoundland

GLYNIS GEORGE

UNIVERSITY OF TORONTO PRESS
Toronto Buffalo London

ISBN 978-0-8020-4764-9 (cloth)
ISBN 978-0-8020-8317-3 (paper)

Printed on acid-free paper

Canadian Cataloguing in Publication Data

George, Glynis R. (Glynis Rosamonde), 1964–
The rock where we stand: an ethnography of women's activism in Newfoundland

Includes bibliographical references and index.
ISBN 978-0-8020-4764-9 (bound) ISBN 978-0-8020-8317-3 (pbk.)

1. Feminism – Newfoundland – Bay St. George. 2. Women political activists – Newfoundland – Bay St. George. 3. Women social reformers – Newfoundland – Bay St. George. I. Title.

HQ1236.5.C2G46 2000 305.42'09718 C99-933077-2

The University of Toronto Press acknowledges the financial assistance to its publishing program of the Canada Council for the Arts and the Ontario Arts Council.

This book has been published with the help of a grant from the Humanities and Social Sciences Federation of Canada, using funds provided by the Social Sciences and Humanities Research Council of Canada.

The University of Toronto Press acknowledges the financial support for its publishing activities of the Government of Canada through the Book Publishing Industry Development Program (BPIDP).

Contents

Acknowledgments

This book and the field research I conducted for it benefited from the sustained support and interest of numerous people. I extend my gratitude to Dorothy Inglis and Gordon Inglis for their hospitality in St John's and for directing me westward, to Bay St George, and facilitating my introduction to members of the Bay St George Women's Council. I am indebted to residents of Bay St George for sharing their experiences and insights with me and particularly to members of the Women's Council, who included me in all activities. Two council members, Joyce Hancock and Peg Jones, whose insights are woven throughout this book, ensured my integration within the community and included me in their own family. Council members were extremely helpful, patient, and open to ongoing dialogue with me, in particular, Sarah Ogletree, Sharon Whalen, Michelle Skinner, Yvonne Gillingham, Rita Greene, Maria Renouf, Stella Campbell, Cindy O'Neil, and Susan Fowlow. I also thank Gilbert Higgins for providing me access to local archives and for his sustained interest in my project. In St John's, Marilyn Porter, Peter Sinclair, and Rex Clark offered helpful advice and I was welcomed by members of the Anthropology Department at Memorial University.

In Toronto, numerous people have provided ongoing interest in and support of my research, including faculty in the Department of Anthropology: Gavin Smith, Krystyna Sieciechowicz, Michael Lambek, Richard Lee, Bonnie McElhinney, Janice Boddy, and Peter Carstens. Janice Boddy insightfully pointed to the importance of 'home' in my study, and Gavin Smith drew attention both to the social and economic context in which ideas and activities are situated and to the significance of place and regional economies. My discussions with Gavin Smith over the last several years greatly influenced my intellectual development and have challenged me to maintain a rigorous and theoretical engagement with political and social realities. My debates with Gordon Inglis and Dorothy Inglis were important in developing and rethinking my understanding of the importance of Newfoundland 'distinctness.' I had invigorating and challenging arguments with Gerald Sider, who helped me to develop a 'voice' for the themes I address here. My discussions with Bonnie McElhinney were useful for situating my work within a larger context of feminist scholarship. I also thank anonymous reviewers for their useful comments. Funding for this research was provided by the Social Sciences and Humanities Research Council of Canada.

I am especially grateful for the personal support of friends: June Larkin, Fatima Correia, Christabelle Sethna, Pauline Aucoin, Albert Schrauwers, and Nick Harney. Members of the political-economy working group (in particular, Belinda Leach, Winnie Lem, Claudia Vicencio) provided an important context for me to develop this study.

I am most grateful to my former thesis supervisor, Professor Stuart B. Philpott, whose friendship and wisdom I value greatly, for his persistent reminder to 'tell the story.' I owe as much to him as to the women of Bay St George for generating the spirit behind this ethnographic study. He made himself available to listen and, along with Diana Philpott, provided much needed support and comfort while I wrote this book.

Finally, my family deserves thanks for their various contributions: I thank my mother, Patricia, for her detailed editing; my brother, Tom, for his computer 'know-how'; my sister Meredith for allowing me to 'borrow' her computer without too much complaint; and, for general support, my sister Mickey, my sister-in-law Eileen, and my father, Michael. Together, they cleaned out the cabin at our cottage on a warm summer's day, so that my writing would not be too interrupted by the boundless enthusiasm of my nieces and nephew.

THE ROCK WHERE WE STAND

An Ethnography of Women's Activism in Newfoundland

CHAPTER ONE

Between Home and Field: Feminist Activism at the Grass Roots

I never heard tell of the Women's Movement before ... then they had a meeting and there was an election of officers like, and I never went. I figure, well that's not for me, right? And when they moved down there to the Women's Centre and when I went there I got to know more what a nice atmosphere and everything it was – in the place like. It's the best thing that ever happened, was for Stephenville to have a place like this. It was like a really, really comfortable home. (Jenny, age forty)

When I arrived in Stephenville, a town on Newfoundland's west coast, in 1992, I lived in the women's shelter, an apartment in the Bay St George Women's Centre. Also resident there were two women who, for different reasons, had no other place to live. Like Jenny, quoted above, I was impressed by the centre's comforting atmosphere and the integration of activism with lunchtime conversation and the everyday management of a household. Yet, for my roommates, whose stories conveyed family conflict and parental addiction, this was not a home away from *their* home. It was a place to imagine what a home could be. For me – an anthropologist, who had come from Toronto to study women's activism – this temporary 'home' provided a window on a particular historical moment, when the women's movement in western Newfoundland was in the ascendant.

The association of home and family with women's subordination was prevalent in academic feminist analysis until women coming from more diverse class, racialized, and regional backgrounds pointed to the importance of the domestic domain for the expression of female authority and to the family's role as a site of support in a hierarchical public sphere. Yet the experiences of wage-working women throughout North America demonstrates how the separation of public and private, and the association of the private, domestic sphere with femininity, forms an ideal construct which few women in recent history have been able to realize (Hareven, 1993:passim). However, it is the hegemony of a masculine public and female private which provides a script for gender identities and forms an ideological backdrop against which normative values regarding sexual practices, parenting, and work are expressed and challenged. Is it, then, surprising that 'home' has figured in the expression of an oppositional feminist culture? How suitable can home be as a location for meaningful cultural production and the expression of critical politics? Is it a trope or the product of a calculated strategy? Does it enhance or inhibit the expression of feminism?

'Home' was the central site for the expression of feminist activism in Bay St George in spite of the ambivalence of numerous women towards the gender roles and identities it housed. And this home was a 'familiar' space to its many visitors, including women from Ontario, Alberta, and Indonesia, for example, whom I met there. Moreover, I was struck by the prominence of 'home' not just at the women's centre but in everyday accounts and the personal narratives of residents in Bay St George. 'Home' referred to one's neighbourhood, community, town, or, in the case of migrants and return visitors, the province itself. Thus, the complex association between home and the families, households and ideologies subsumed within it forms the basis for this book, just as it does it for critical feminist politics in the 1980s and 1990s.

Specifically, how does a grass-roots women's organization establish itself, acquire the necessary resources to make political claims, and generate the moral and social vitality to make women's issues relevant, meaningful, and worthy of attention in the public domain? Why is grass-roots organizing an important focus for study? These questions are particularly significant given the impact of social and economic forces on women's movements and political movements more broadly, and in light of dramatic economic and social crises in the province of Newfoundland and Labrador.

The 1980s and 1990s have been characterized as conservative times in North America and the United Kingdom, a 'historical valley' in the geography of social change, when social movements – women's movements in particular – had to fight to maintain political and social gains achieved in the 1970s (Bashevkin,1998). By the mid 1980s, women's movements had become both institutionalized and jeopardized: by changes in economic policies, by the marginalization of women's issues from political arenas of decision making, and by divisions within these movements themselves.

In Canada, the 1970s was a decade of improvements for women: in family law and womens' reproductive rights, pay equity, and affirmative action, and through greater attention to violence against women in government policy, legislation, and civil society. By the 1990s, these changes were tempered by shifts in government spending and its spin-off effects, including a reduction in the resources available to women's organizations (Bashevkin, 1998). Single mothers, same-sex couples, immigrant women, wage-working wives, and senior women were differently affected by changes in taxation, welfare provision, unemployment insurance, and the offloading of services and moneys from the national government to the provinces (Bashevkin, 1998: 92–3, 117).

The effect of these changes on women, their partners, relations and children has been the subject of debates which can serve to support or marginalize the impact of feminism in political arenas. The issues feminists have addressed have moral and political implications and are contested within civil society: that is, in communities, educational institutions, the media, and households across the country. For example, violence against women; sexual abuse and harassment, and maternity and paternity rights and obligations provoke larger questions regarding the relationship between feminism, women's interests, and the interests of the 'people' as a whole (Brodie, 1998:19).

Moreover, the recognition that women are diverse, and differently situated in terms of class, ethnic background, regional circumstances, and sexual orientation, has generated debate and fragmentation within women's movements (Findley, 1998: 298–303). These tensions could be a sign of growing pains and an indication that feminism is an expanding, influential, and vibrant movement. And yet the way conflicts within women's movements are depicted in mainstream media can also delegitimate or marginalize these movements' political force.

So often in the milieu of civil society, complex politics are reduced to simple questions: Are we living in a post-feminist society? Do feminist organizations represent women in general or merely select and narrow interests? Grass-roots organizing is considered a crucial basis for organizing in this particular climate (Brodie, 1998:20). The focus in this book, is the way women at the grass roots sustain activism in conservative times by negotiating the complex changes which lie beneath the rhetoric.

The Bay St George Women's Council

The subjects of this study are the women I met through the Bay St George Women's Council, and residents I met through numerous other activities. The council is a grass-roots organization with a membership that ranges from 140 to 360 and which is formally operated by a twelve-member executive board and a paid executive director. The organization is housed in a women's centre, which provides services and resources to women in the Bay St George region.

The book situates the Women's Council within the political and economic context of 1980s and 1990s, and examines two timely social problems – the unemployment of single mothers, and sexual abuse and violence against women – to explore how political issues are made locally meaningful and, conversely, to contribute to the analysis of the way experiences become constructed as social problems.

The particular aspects of feminist discourse that I consider in this book are largely, but not solely, derived from those that emerge from local feminist activism, and the issues that I raise are shaped by the field situation and the impassioned concerns of local women. Nowhere is this more evident than in the question of incest and sexual abuse. This is an important issue, yet one that when recounted seems to turn Newfoundlanders into exotics or reaffirm stereotypes. Still, as subsequent chapters show, these social problems have become a socially divisive, culturally contested issue which ultimately tests the power of the Women's Council to direct social change.

My analysis of sexual abuse in particular shows how the emergence of this problem as a social and political issue generates moments of conflict and consent among local residents and reproduces social cleavages that are historically rooted in class, rural, and ethnic relations. That said, the sense of place and commitment to sustained settlement in western Newfoundland remains a unifying force in the region and in the expression of Newfoundland identities. In this sense, the book speaks more broadly, to the way social problems are legitimated and the way women's issues and people's issues connect and diverge.

Hence, women's activism provides a focus for the exploration of regional identities; competing constructions of culture; economic marginalization; and the social, political, and economic constitution of subjects within civil society. This is particularly salient in a setting such as Newfoundland, where the current economic crisis and moratorium on cod fishing are parallelled by cultural and moral ruptures in religious, educational, and sexual norms that provoke new interpretations of the 'traditional' way of life which has typically defined Newfoundland society.

By considering the articulation of dominant discourses of which feminism is a part, I argue that feminism is part of an ongoing process of cultural production and contestation which gives meaning to women's lives and shapes the character of their response. In this sense, it contributes to the expanding anthropological research on the way social movements such as feminism and environmentalism constitute people as political actors and produce political and cultural practices and meaning (Escobar, 1992:395).

The orientation of this book derives from debates in anthropology and feminist studies, a commitment to participatory research, and a constructively critical perspective towards the typologies of change that are available in liberal-democratic societies for women and men to imagine and plan a future. Notions of progress, subversive social practices, and utopian visions, in which social movements like feminism participate, both constitute subordinate groups as political actors and marginalize them from political participation (hooks, 1989; Swindells and Jardine, 1990). Such movements are made meaningful, effective, responsive, and emancipatory with sustained attention to their impact on the complexity of everyday life and to their ability to speak to, from, and beyond the experiences and relationships they represent.

An important part of this process is to situate myself as ethnographer in relation to the research problem and, in this case, to women activists in Bay St George.

Between 'Home and Field'

Newfoundland is an ideal setting to explore women's activism. The province's geographic and cultural location in Canada, my relationship with women in Bay St George, and the favourable reputation of this women's organization provides a timely entry into debates within anthropology and feminist studies. The production of anthropological knowledge has been conventionally rooted in the separation of 'home' from 'the field,' so that one leaves the familiar to encounter the different (Gupta and Ferguson, 1997:8). This is based on the notion that home is located in the west (Euro-North America) and in the academy; and that the anthropologist leaves that home, the familiar, to become an outsider in another cultural setting. The meanings of these dichotomies, 'home' and 'field,' 'insider' and 'outsider,' to name but two, are disrupted by those anthropologists whose experiences and identities reveal the complex relationships that underpin such oppositions. Feminist anthropologists have considered themselves to be outside academia and yet rooted, by cultural definition, in a home; 'halfies' such as Abu-Lughod claim partial membership in both arenas (field, and the Western academy). Indigenous, aboriginal, and native anthropologists are often writing from within the culture they are studying. Hence, their insights complicate the assumption that home and field are separate, that 'home' is situated in the Euro–North American academy. The important point here is that these insights enhance our understanding of culture. They make it difficult to represent cultures as bounded units or to assume that the anthropologist is an outsider to that other, distinct culture (Abu-Lughod, 1992:137).

The problems this poses for feminist anthropologists and those working within their own 'culture' have generated rich insights into the complexity of power, gender relations, the knowledge generated from ethnographic research, and the anthropological narratives that underwrite the representation of others (Limon, 1992; Moore, 1994). So often, this research is cast as partial or subjective (Abu-Lughod, 1992:141), so that the biases and cultural scripts that underlie the pursuit of objective research remain unchallenged. Yet a recognition of the process through which cultures become bounded and fluid, reproduced, and differentiated from within is enhanced by interrogating the insider/

outsider relationship and the political implications of representation and by considering the social location of the ethnographer as a gendered and multiply situated being (Wolf, 1996).

Newfoundland is considered a culturally distinct region within Canada which has a tradition of egalitarian relations and women's involvement in community organizations. At the same time, Newfoundland is often depicted as a 'folk' culture, weighed down by the force of history, parochial in its vision, and marginalized from the processes of economic growth and cultural diversification. As a Toronto-born daughter of a Newfoundland father, I was aware that the flip-side of this distinct culture was the persistent migration of its inhabitants to rural communities and urban centres across Canada. This represented to me the embodiment of a cultural dynamic between region and nation that is replicated throughout the world and forms an important part of anthropological study. The construction of Newfoundland culture and the social and economic problems that Newfoundlanders face is framed by national narratives which marginalize certain regions within Canada. The research process is embedded within these narratives and illustrated by the way in which Bay St George became the focus for my research.

On a preliminary trip, I drove east to St John's, the provincial capital, and was invited to visit Gordon Inglis, an anthropologist, and Dorothy Inglis, a prominent activist in the province at their cabin at Spread Eagle, near the town of Dildo on Trinity Bay, not far from St John's. I arrived at Spread Eagle on a cold, rainy afternoon and spent two days in a large log cabin, modelled by its owners (originally from British Columbia) after a Kwakiutl lodge. Over elegant dinners, I talked non-stop about my work to my captive hosts. Gordon and Dorothy directed me to Stephenville on the island's west coast, where for fourteen months I struggled to follow a single thread in the multifaceted conversations.

On that first visit, I met Joyce Hancock, the coordinator of the Bay St George Women's Council, who occupies an essential place in this story and remains a central figure in feminist activism both in the region and in the province. Joyce welcomed me to a small three-bedroom apartment located over a sports store on Stephenville's Main Street. I was drawn to her enthusiasm and the spirit of this women's council which had already captured the attention of the community and whose mayor proclaimed it to be 'the social conscience' of Bay St George.

At the time, the Bay St George Women's Council was reputed to be the most dynamic of the seven women's councils which have operated in the province since the early 1970s (there are now eight councils). Explicitly feminist, persistently critical, and culturally rooted, the council signified to me a cultural bridge which might challenge hegemonic conceptions of rural women, folk constructions, and the constitution of 'others' within Canadian society.

That I drove eastward from Toronto, to the provincial capital, and retraced my route westward to the opposite coast, exemplifies a centre/periphery relationship that frames my relationship with women in Bay St George, the social and economic issues they address, and the cultural and political context in which these issues may be interpreted. Over time, this would be manifested in complex ways, through an exchange of opinions, heated debate, visits to and from the province, and through the influence this council and its members have on the province. I would like to think that the flow of insights, information, and friendship grew. Certainly, the mentoring process that began on that cold weekend forms a sustained connection between Dorothy, Joyce, and me, which, in my mind, highlights the importance of listening to and drawing upon the experience of elders. But, when I began this research, my understanding of this process was that culture, and the gender identities it constitutes, forms a social glue through which marginalization is both reproduced and contested within and beyond our national boundaries.

Constructions of Culture and Marginalization: Newfoundland in the Canadian Landscape

Although culture occupies a pre-eminent place in anthropological theory, ideas about culture are equally debated elsewhere, in sociology and cultural studies, and within the society of which academia is a part. In academic, political, and social discourse, culture is simultaneously that which we possess, do, and think. It is also a means through which we define and distinguish one group from another in a manner that has political implications and that is produced in a larger context of social and economic change (cf. Handler, 1988; Sider, 1986). Cultural distinctions have shaped the way settlement, immigration, and colonization of aboriginal peoples within Canada and cultural and political domination by Great Britain and, more recently, the United States is expressed. Hence, culture has been a terrain on which debate regarding Canadian identity, diversity, and unity is waged, and the future of Canadian society imagined, in political spheres and within civil society.

The dominant notion of two founding national cultures, French and English, is challenged by the proliferation of cultural diversity that has emerged with the recognition that multi-ethnic peoples inhabit our cities and with the regeneration of aboriginal distinctiveness and polities. Consider, for example, the extent to which culture is invoked in debates regarding Quebec separation, aboriginal rights, and heritage-language education, particularly since the advent of official bilingualism and multiculturalism in the late 1960s (Agnew, 1996). Newfoundland occupies a peculiar place in these constructions because of its late entry into the Canadian state in 1949, the character of Newfoundland society, and its location within a wider political economy.

Newfoundland is frequently cast as the exemplary 'have-not' province in national narratives, which shapes its location as marginal in political and economic discourses of change. If debates about whether we have one, two, many, or no cultures at all are very much framed in terms of mapping the national future, Newfoundland represents an opposing, anachronistic, but politically meaningful culture of the past. I refer here to narratives of progress, cultural diversity, and adaptability in the context of globalization where the Newfoundland economy and its workers exemplify dependency on the Canadian state. This is buttressed by the distinctness of Newfoundland society which has been constructed within fields of power and is codified in the construction of Newfoundland culture as a bounded, 'folk' entity (Kelly, 1993; Overton, 1995).

Folk cultures such as that of Newfoundland are constituted within a historical political economy and relations of domination which are structured by colonialism and mercantile relations and which in this case are rooted in the production and exchange of the cod fishery (Sider, 1986) and, subsequently, in the development of primary-resource industries and the 'proletarianization' of Newfoundlanders as workers. After Newfoundland's entry into the Canadian confederation, the growth of economic development programs and social and economic welfare policies across the province attempted to redress regional disparities and adapt the normative character of living on 'the Rock' to processes of modernization – in which the nuclear family and individualized waged labour figured prominently. The prominence of the Canadian state in this phase of Newfoundland history provides a sharp contrast to the formation of Newfoundland outports rooted in a mercantile fishery.

Although the relationship between Newfoundland and Labrador and the Canadian state is peculiar because of its late entry into Confederation, its economy shares much with that of Atlantic Canada. The Atlantic region's marginalization in the historical development of our national political economy[1] intersects with the differential placement of its male and female[2] residents in the labour market so that the geographic and historical 'peripheralization' of the area and the exclusion of women in the structures of 'mainstream society' (Porter, 1985a:44) coalesce. The relationship between margin and periphery is not, however, monolithic, and because 'capitalist development involves pressures towards centralization and dispersal of capital' (Felt and Sinclair, 1996:5), the proximity of markets, labour supply, the character of state intervention, and socio-cultural relations are central in understanding the location of capitalist production and economic 'growth' in certain regions over others, especially if one finely parses regions within Atlantic Canada and within Newfoundland and Labrador particularly.

Given the complexity of these dynamics, anthropology is useful here. Our analysis increasingly considers culture as means by which processes of exclusion and peripheralization are reproduced and contested. It is this notion of culture, as a historically contested terrain, rife with disjunctions, contradictions, and shared meanings (Sider, 1986:7), that permits multiple interpretations of Newfoundland culture and expressions of Newfoundland identity through which social problems, economic disparities, and gender relations are constituted.

The particular location of individual women's councils makes them an important site to capture a range of political expressions – (everyday, formal, extra-parliamentary, and negotiative) and to assess the impact of women's activism on effecting changes. A more sustained analysis of these varied forms of political of activism and their articulation is crucial given the marginalization of women's issues at the national level over the last fifteen years (Bashevkin, 1998:189) and populist claims that we are living in a post-feminist society.

The Bay St George Women's Council is exemplary in its attempts to balance two dimensions of political organizing – in its creation of an 'alternate' social space, and in its sustained engagement with 'government' – institutions such as, health, welfare, justice, education, and development – as they bear upon women's lives. Bay St George does not conform to conventional and national depictions of Newfoundland culture (Overton, 1988; Kelly, 1993). The Bay St George Women's Council is recognized throughout the province for its extensive engagement with local issues and residents living in the region.

The Bay St George Region

Bay St George is a self-contained region of 24,824 people (1996 Census) which is situated north of Port aux Basques and south of Corner Brook, thirty-five kilometres off the Trans-Canada Highway, on Newfoundland's west coast (see maps 1 and 2). With a population of 7,764 (1996 Census), Stephenville is the major commercial and service centre for the southwest coast although two very small towns, Stephenville Crossing and Lourdes, provide some services for rural communities on St George's Bay and Port au Port Bay respectively. The flat terrain on which Stephenville is situated offers a marked contrast to the rocky coastline of the Port au Port peninsula and the aging mountains which stretch along the the west coast from Gros Morne National Park on the northern peninsula to Port aux Basque. Unlike the island's east coast, this region is characterized by cool, dry, sunny summers and snowy, cold winters.

The Women's Centre, owned and operated by the Bay St George Women's Council, is situated in a residential neighbourhood in the town of Stephenville and is distinguishable from other homes on the street by the large feminist symbol that is suspended by the front door. The house is just two blocks from the town's commercial district, which begins at the bridge over Blanche Brook and continues seaward for several blocks where it meets the shoreline road that leads to the Port au Port peninsula. The peninsula is the locus of the francophone communities which occupy a significant place in this study.

On the other side of this bridge, beyond the narrow river, lie the numerous buildings that once comprised a United States Air Force base, which operated in Stephenville from 1941 until 1966. The houses on the Ernest Harmon base, as it was known, are pastel blue and yellow boxes, organized in tidy rows and loops which bear the imprint of American hegemony through names like Montana Drive and Oregon Avenue. Their uniformity forms a sharp contrast to the diverse styles of homes 'in town,' some of which were built before legal standards were imposed.

These architectural distinctions are visual reminders that the town owes much of its infrastructure to American hegemony, and that, for twenty-five years, American military life co-existed alongside Newfoundland civilian life. Although a few buildings 'on base' remain empty, most have been converted for government, commercial and residential purposes. It is here, on base, that much of the community's infrastructure – courthouse, movie theatre, college, men's and women's correctional centres, arts centre – located.

The south service road, which leads from the Trans-Canada highway to Stephenville proper, by-passes Flat Bay and St Georges, two of the oldest fishing communities in the area. The road continues along St George's Bay through Stephenville Crossing, a small town of about 2000. The railcars parked at one end of town betray its former importance as the major railway depot for the area, from 1915 until the suspension of provincial rail service in 1988. The service road follows the bay over the hills and passes the Abitibi-Price paper mill, a massive, bright blue structure that emits steady billows of white steam which disperse across the flat outskirts of town. Today, each community and the town of Stephenville itself constitute discrete entities bounded geographically and politically through local governments, family land, and intimate histories. At the same time, the past is, in part, shared, through prolonged economic interdependency, flexible borders, and the movement of residents through marriage and work.

I arrived in Stephenville in May 1992, at the opening of the lobster fishery and when Russian and Japanese factory boats parked in the bay to harvest and pack herring for their commercial markets. For the first six weeks, as a 'wayward women from Toronto.' I lived in the shelter of the Women's Centre and was quickly absorbed into the council activities. There, I met members of the Women's Council who eventually provided me the necessary furnishings for the apartment I soon found on base.

As an anthropologist working with a feminist organization, I draw in my research on debates within feminism itself to 'problematize' the insider/outsider relationships in which anthropological knowledge is conventionally constituted. This is exemplified in my relationship with council members and in the insights we shared and debated, a process that began soon after my arrival in Stephenville, once I began to attend council meetings.

'If she gets it, can she write us?' Locating the Anthropologist: Feminisms and Representation

I was invited to the Women's Council monthly meeting where I was introduced, with mocking formality, as a 'woman from Toronto, who has come all the way from the mainland, to study us.' The events of this meeting were then duly ritualized. Meeting protocol was 'analysed' aloud, to clarify this exotic behaviour for the visiting anthropologist. The gravity and formality of the proceedings were exaggerated as the gavel was pounded with additional force and the meeting called to order in a brazen command. Participants, however, soon lapsed into more typical behaviour, characterized by speedy repartee. Women completed a lengthy agenda while venturing off-topic, issuing asides to neighbours, injecting satirical remarks, and completing each other's sentences. As the meeting adjourned, members left the living room to drink tea and banter, seated around the kitchen table.

The ritualization of this process perhaps underscored their new position, as objects of interest and subjects of study, while it mocked the status of the anthropologist and signalled to me that 'airs of superiority' would not be tolerated. Moreover, the contradictory position of participant-observer and the social tensions between observer and observed were reinforced at many council meetings that I subsequently attended. Once involved in council activities, I was considered an outsider who had slipped, rather remarkably it was noted, to the 'inside.' The consequences of my entry, however, were that my behaviour was scrutinized, as was my apparent and occasional re-entry to the 'outside.' On many occasions, I was chastized and accusingly reprimanded for a nod of my head, a hand gesture, a 'squinty-eyed' glance, or a gaze around the room, which signalled to them an attitude of distancing. 'She's switching – there she goes,' one would cry as all eyes glanced in my direction and a few attempted to recall recent statements that might have initiated my repositioning from insider participant to analytical observer. 'What's she thinking? What did we just say? Oh, Glynis didn't like that!' Such tensions were manifested more clearly within the Women's Centre (where meetings were held), by the keen, and at times unabated, observations of certain council members who were never completely comfortable with my ambiguous position. I was a feminist with some claim to Newfoundland heritage. Yet I was an academic from central Ontario, both indicators of my privilege and difference.

This tension was manifested in debates between council members and the academic analysis I brought with me to the field. I was ridiculed for wanting to consider a situation for some time from numerous angles, before providing an interpretation or affirming a particular strategy. This often cast me as 'indecisive,' 'like all academics' who reflect on their navel while the opportunity for action quickly passes. Towards the year's end, I proudly accepted as a compliment the observation that I 'acted like I didn't know anything' – unlike most 'experts' and 'academics' who dropped by to impose their knowledge upon this community. A few decided I was so 'shy and quiet,' a 'poor thing,' that I would never get my PhD without their help. Over tea and numerous Sunday dinners I was well fed and then dragged into lengthy arguments with a few friends over my right to represent them on paper, to become what they viewed as an 'instant expert' on their lives, on the issues and changes they had lived for decades.

This ambivalence was also rooted in a Newfoundland identity distinct from that of central Canada. At times they marvelled that I, a 'woman from Toronto,' seemed to fit so easily into 'their ways' of understanding, their humour, and their view of the world. This fact, along with my other 'good points,' was to them a reflection of the Newfoundland heritage that I clearly possessed. Other times, however, I exuded an air of Toronto, an urban sensibility that was duly noted, in the way I laughed (too quietly), the way I spoke (too slowly), and the way I sat (prim and proper). There were, moreover, a few areas of understanding that I failed, in the view of some, to comprehend. As a 'non-believer' raised outside 'the church,' I could, from their perspective, never understand the impact of religion on their lives – its pervasiveness and the contradictory meanings and emotions it engendered. At times my comments were incurably 'secular'; or if I failed to understand a particular element of religion, I was 'just stunned.' In the words of my most rigorous critic, the question was, 'does she get it?' – 'it' being the totality and sensibility that comprises a way of life. And then, 'if she gets it, can she write us?'

Situating Narratives and Ethnographic Representations

My attempts to 'write' the lives of these women are informed by particular debates and methodologies within anthropology and feminist studies, which coalesce in my analysis and the way these issues are depicted. In many way, my attempts to 'write' the lives of women in Newfoundland are mediated and, in places, overdetermined by the pre-existing constructions of a Newfoundland 'way of life' which pervades these discourses. For instance, current media depictions focus almost exclusively on the demise of the cod fishery and outport community life. Although this is a serious economic crisis for the entire province, it does not characterize my ethnographic setting or form a focus for women's activism in the Bay St George region.

Moreover, anthropologists and social scientists have contributed to making peoples into 'others' through their representation of cultures as distinct, undifferentiated entities. In this way, anthropologists potentially reproduce constructions of marginality by assigning difference to a group of peoples or maintaining a construction of them as different within a wider hegemonic process (Abu-Lughod, 1993:14).[3] Our representations of a people might reinscribe them as marginal within hegemonic discourses (Lowenhaupt-Tsing, 1993:5–7). To write of Newfoundland culture in academia and, by extension, in this book, is consciously or inadvertently to 'write against' stereotypes or reaffirm them (Abu-Lughod, 1993:7).

Personal narratives are one means to explore the dynamics of gender, power, and differentiation without reproducing essentialist notions of femininity or creating homogeneous depictions of women and local or national cultures (Abu-Lughod, 1993:14). This book explores two forms of personal narratives in particular, both of which are informed by feminist discourses which have political implications. Many of the experiences recounted in this book are 'transformation narratives' (Ginsburg, 1989) which recount moments of self-understanding, when women relate personal experience to political events or situate themselves within relations of power in varied and culturally specific ways and to provide an interpretation of their current identification with issues and experiences that comprise feminist practice and politics.

Chapter 5 – devoted to the subject of sexual abuse – narrows the focus of transformation narratives to 'survivor discourse.' And, by situating women's stories within particular social contexts, I consider the articulation of feminist discourse with medical, therapeutic, and bureaucratic fields. Further by distinguishing narration from experience, I try to draw attention to the importance of recounting an experience over and over, to numerous people, as a process in which identities are refashioned and changes in one's life effected and legitimated (Behar, 1992:229; Bauer, 1993:520). This is crucial in understanding consciousness-raising, a key feature of local feminism. A focus on the narration of experience also draws attention to the position of the speaker and audience and potential relations of power between them (Abu-Lughod, 1993:15). Hence, taken together, these narratives reflect, in varied ways, the intersection of feminist discourse, political practices, and lived experiences.

A few key words emerge in the chapters that follow – dependency, recovery, and abuse – which I examine not only as discursive constructs but also as realities that frame and are lived in social relations and articulated in experience. This orientation shares much with Raymond Williams, who argues that the terms used to describe social reality are active in the process of shaping it (Williams, 1976). There is a potential in anthropology to write against the overdetermination of subjects and, at the same time, to capture the ongoing process through which structures of power and the codification of meanings are lived and challenged.

As I demonstrate in chapters 3, 4, and 5, however, a focus on narrative as text should not displace our analysis of the context of power in which experiences and our stories of them unfold (Roseberry, 1989:24). To understand the complexity of identity and the specificity of political practice, it is crucial to recognize the 'constructedness' of experiences and, at the same time, to contextualize 'narratives of transformation' and 'survivor discourses' within particular sites of action which are socially and historically situated. This includes experiences of numerous 'places' that are recorded in personal memories, against which current sites of power are understood and evaluated in relation to women's work and the practices which sustain activism on a daily basis. Women's stories reveal the incongruities between lived experiences, historical transformations, and gender expectations (Ginsburg, 1989:140). And, if we examine them as social constructions, they reveal the 'subjective mapping of personal experience,' the way social identities are created and refashioned in the narration of lived experiences (Behar, 1990:223–6).

Hence, following the lead of feminist ethnographers (Cole, 1991; Lowentaupt-Tsing, 1993), this book interweaves personal narratives and ethnographic descriptions. This draws attention to the ethnographic context in which women's experiences are narrated and their experiences interpreted. It also permits an examination of the way ideologies of family are framed through local narratives of reproduction which give meaning to changes as women live them. These narratives are measured against the realities of making a living and generational changes. Ethnographic studies of women's social spheres and female-centred cultural domains demonstrate the connections between feminist practice and historically embedded social relations and reciprocities. Rather than reify women's culture, they illustrate the 'historically, economically, geographically, and culturally contingent' (di Leonardo, 1991:231) character of women's experiences and gendered and political identities.

Thus, my analysis emerges from everyday activity at the Women's Centre and my participation in numerous Women's Council and related events, including all monthly meetings of the council, all-day seminars in 'Feminist Counselling,' and a 'Feminist Retreat.' I facilitated a workshop on 'Feminist Organization' at the annual Provincial Conference of Status of Women Councils. The participation of the Bay St George Women's Council in the national 'Future of Work' study sponsored by the National Action Committee on the Status of Women allowed me to attend their 'Consultation' conference in Toronto in November 1994. Afterwards, back in Newfoundland, council members kindly took me along on the area tour of their show, 'Our Lives Our Issues,' and I joined their activities at the men's and women's correctional centres. Other events included participation in a 'community-based' 'Anti-Violence Coalition' and all-day seminars on 'Social Issues' and 'Gender Issues' at four area schools.

Once settled in my own apartment, I was able to broaden my social networks, in order to examine the wider social and historical context and meet women and men who were not necessarily connected with the Women's Council. While I met and interviewed many male residents, my relationship to them was considerably more circumscribed by gender prescriptions and a gender division of labour and social spheres. As a single, childless woman I was considered somewhat of an anomaly by both women and men. My connection to men, therefore, was informed by this perceived social status, and thus it took place through formal interviews in their specific roles in the workplace or through my female relationships.

A local historian provided valuable archival material and introduced me to his more male-dominant social arena, which opened access to the paper mill, the Lion's Club, the Canadian Legion, and long-time male and female residents. A neighbour and I joined the town's fitness club, which was an everyday focus for leisure activity and drew women and men from a variety of backgrounds. In addition, I participated in the Stephenville Glee Club, a seventy-member choir, which met weekly and performed three concerts that year. I attended numerous cultural events, including the annual Music Fest, bingo nights, the annual Volunteer Awards Dinner, and the annual Stephenville Festival. The last featured numerous plays, one of which was 'The Only Living Father,' a story of Joseph Smallwood and Newfoundland's entry into Confederation.

The issues that occupied council members were initially peace, reproductive rights, and job training and by the 1990s had expanded to include sexual abuse, violence against women, and, most recently, economic development. But how were these issues connected to everyday experiences and the historical consciousness of area women? Moreover, what prompted the formation of the council and what made 'home' an important metaphor and context for activism?

My understanding of the relationship between these issues and the historical development of the town came into sharper focus during the summer, one of the busiest times of year in Stephenville, when annual festivals and various ceremonies draw both tourists and residents to the public arenas in town. It was through these latter activities, which ran throughout the summer season, that I was provided a valuable introduction to the region and a glimpse into the contemporary understandings of history and the cultural terrain on which social issues, gender constructions, and kin and home became socially and politically meaningful. One of these rituals introduces the next chapter, which explores the historical context in which local feminism emerged.

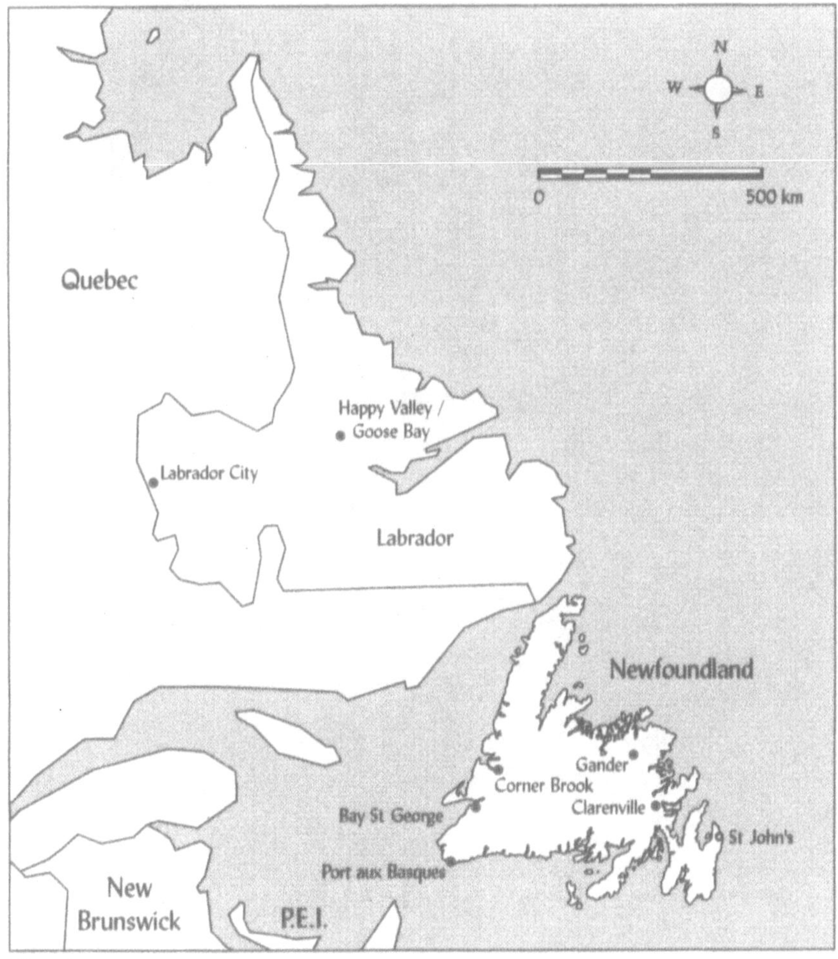

Map 1
Newfoundland

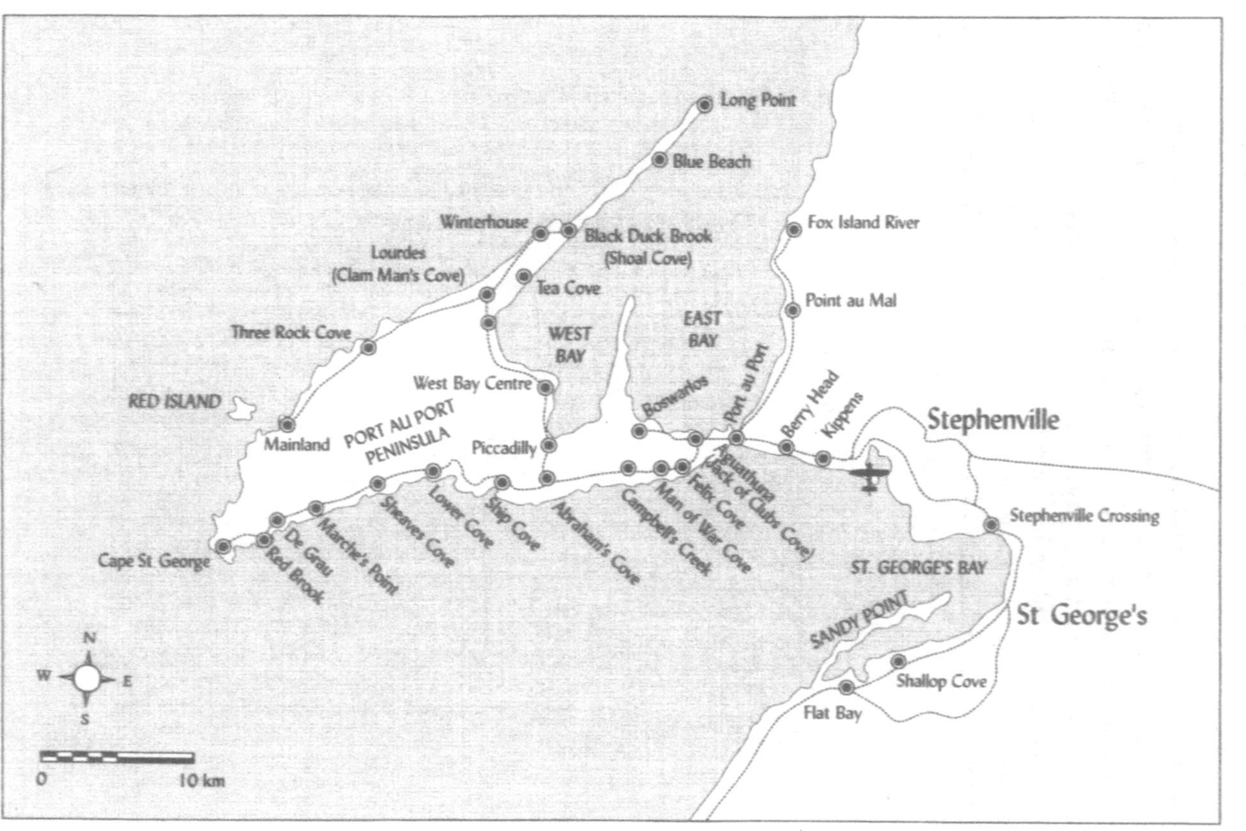

Map 2
Bay St George Region

CHAPTER TWO

Gender, Ethnicity, and Labour before and after the 'Carefree Years'

By the summer of 1992, I had been living in Stephenville for two months and was, by then, accustomed to joining members of the Women's Council in the kitchen at the centre, for lunch, to talk, or, at that time, to design signs for their upcoming walk-a-thon to raise awareness around 'family violence.'

One morning in early July the hum of everyday activity at the centre was disrupted by the deafening arrival of some forty fighter planes, bombers, and freight carriers as they swept, one after another, across town. The planes and the Canadian and American soldiers who flew them were there to participate in Harmon Field Day, a biannual commemoration of the 'carefree years,' a twenty-five-year period when the Harmon Air Force base occupied half of what is now the town of Stephenville. From the kitchen window of the Women's Centre, we could see the planes, painted black or camouflage, land and assemble on the tarmac of the old airfield, overlooking the sea.

The event normally draws a few thousand visitors, residents, and retired and active American soldiers (including those with Newfoundland wives) to Stephenville for a weekend of musical entertainment and bar hopping. It evokes a prosperous era in Bay St George when the extensive settlement of the region was framed by an ideology of freedom-through-might and achieved through the peaceful cooperation of soldier and civilian. Moreover, it is a time when Stephenville applauds its own tenacity in spite of more recent proposed cutbacks and persistent threats to dismantle its airport.

As I would discover, the Women's Council concurs with this right to settlement and commitment to community. Yet it challenges the militaristic terms in which freedom is symbolized and effected by holding an annual peace march and through its display of hospitality. On the surface, Harmon Field Day symbolizes the masculine and militaristic character of public space and forms an opposition to the domestic space in which the Women's Centre is situated. Because of women's historical association with the private domain in western industrial societies (DeVolt, 1991:95), it occurred to me that the Women's centre, modelled on a home, might reflect that history. Yet, as I would learn, the centre housed activities and understandings that resonated with a more complex past – where class, kin, and ethnic relations intersect in the way residents reproduce families and make their living in a boom-and-bust economy.

The biannual event does, however, signify the importance of the air base in the formation of the region; narratives of modernity and tradition generated locally meaningful differences on the basis of ethnicity and rural and urban settlement. The event reinforces a common local assumption – that Stephenville's character as a town has been defined by this military presence. And it reproduces a particular sense of community that informs the participation of women and men in local politics.

This is reflected through an ideology of American-style democracy and the reproduction of enduring livelihood and kin relationships which coalesce to create a region that is open to the possibilities of change and yet reliant on skills, values, and relations that the past has engendered. These combine to have a direct bearing upon the way social issues are taken up and addressed by the Women's Council and the residents of Bay St George.

This chapter examines four major changes in local history which structured the formation and transformation of community, family, and gendered relationships in Bay St George. I argue that the transformation of this region from a cluster of rural villages to an enclave containing the town of Stephenville and outlying communities was largely structured by decisions imposed from provincial, national, and international sources of power. It is within this changing context that overlapping and distinct sets of gender relations emerged to produce ruptures and continuities in the reproduction of families and communities.

In the last thirty years, residents have recognized and responded to the importance of the state in structuring local livelihood by directing their political activism towards the existing political system and the 'government.' Today, social and economic divisions in this largely working-class town are manifested through local relations of power which reproduce gender and ethnic-based differences and rural versus urban traditions (cf Sider, 1991:229). It is this changing context of power that underpins contemporary cultural processes and the character of the Bay St George Women's Council.

European Settlement on the 'French Shore': Bay St George from the 1800s to 1941

> You would be greatly surprised at the peculiar circumstances of this strange place: they are unlike any other even in Newfoundland. There is a great deal of abject poverty, mixed up with a fondness for dress and appearance, that is very painful. White veils and parasols adorn females who are seen at the herring pickling; indeed, there is scarcely an idea of any distinction in society, and it is almost impossible to impress the folly ... yet these ladies are found at the balls, to which they are so much attached, mixed up with Indians, Acadians, French ... and an indiscriminate collection of all sorts ... (de Toque, 1878:250)

This observation of St George's Bay in 1846 by a visiting missionary named Meeks relates key features of the emergent culture of the Acadian, French, English, and Mi'kmaq families who settled the area to fish and trade salmon, herring, lobster, and cod from the 1830s. Meek's disdainful tone reveals the social distance that distinguished colonial elites from the early immigrants who were compelled to transform European cultural norms and, in this case, feminine prescriptions in their adaptation to the hardships of life in this remote and nascent colonial settlement.

In his study of settlement on the western shores of Newfoundland, John Mannion argues that the demands of an unpredictable livelihood and the exchange of subsistence goods and service through kin and neighbourhood ties informed a generalized reciprocity of social relations in spite of ethnic, racial, and linguistic differences (1977:249). From the sixteenth to the nineteenth centuries, settlement on the island was structured and restricted by the British government and merchant interests, which together sought to maintain political and economic control over the seasonal fishery and, subsequently, other material resources (Neary, 1988).

Unlike the island's other shores, the early settlement of Bay St George was structured by political relations and treaties between France and Great Britain. French ships were granted offshore fishing rights although that coast was claimed by Great Britain. Known as the 'the French shore' until 1904, when the French relinquished these rights, the area was sparsely and informally settled (Mannion, 1977:266). The distinct status of this shore fostered the heterogeneous settlement of Acadian, French, English, and Mi'kmaq fishers, particularly in the area of Sandy Point, St George's, and Stephenville Crossing. On the other side of the bay, near present-day Stephenville, a French-speaking majority settled in villages as far as the Port au Port peninsula (see map 2). Of a total population of 772 in 1857, 500 were French-speaking Roman Catholics.[1] The population of the Port au Port peninsula, although sparse until the 1870s, grew to 1600 in 1871 with the influx of Acadians from Cape Breton and French fishermen stationed on nearby Red Island and Long Point, who jumped ship to escape servitude and/or military service and married local Acadian women (Mannion, 1977:37; Thomas, 1983:29).

A disregard for the trappings of power is evidenced in historical accounts and affirms the characterization of Newfoundland outport culture as egalitarian and severed from its sources of exploitation. The colonial state and merchant elites operated in urban centres, far away from these contexts of poverty (Sider, 1986). Capitalist production and subsistence reproduction constituted the essential feature of pre-Confederation outport society, generating an egalitarian ethos within communities across the island (Porter, 1985a:45). The persistence of nor-mative egalitarianism was, moreover, facilitated by the absence of any large monopoly of merchant elites on the west coast (Mannion, 1977:264). Yet, in Bay St George, markers of difference were imposed from above through prevailing constructions of race and British chauvinism that still have resonance today.

On his visit to St George's Bay in 1852, Captain S.H. Ramsay of the HMS *Alarm* reported that little cod fishing was carried on and that salmon were fished by long-time settlers whose rights to salmon coves passed through the male line. Moreover,

> there is a great quantity of eels and lobsters caught here and in the winter the Jack-o-tars chiefly subsist on eels. They are a lazy, indolent people and I am told addicted to thieving. In the winter and spring they are frequently in very destitute circumstances. They are looked upon by the English and French as a degraded race; thence styled Jack-o-tars, or run-aways. They live entirely separate from the English, who are the most respectable portions of the inhabitants and are, in my opinion, very stupid and ignorant (Morris, 1988:3)

'Jack-o-tars,' a label associated with the entire region today, refers to those residents with mixed ethnic/racial heritage, particularly French and Mi'kmaq. English settlers have been positioned at the apex of this colonial hierarchy, followed by French, natives, and the racially mixed.

Gender Relations: Familial Patriarchy and Rough-and-Ready Equality

Marilyn Porter emphasizes the difficulty in generalizing women's relations with men across the island. Her own and other's research conveys the contradictory character of gender relations rooted in pre-capitalist Newfoundland society. Patriarchal legal institutions organized the production and exchange of fish through the legal system and conferred privileges onto men who represented their family-based households to merchants, church, and state (Porter, 1987:25). Within this framework, women found domains of power specifically through their extensive work and the recognition that husband and wife were mutually dependent. Moreover, as the comments by the Reverend Meeks cited above suggest, women did abrogate feminine proscriptions under pioneer conditions.

The overwhelming theme of academic research and individual accounts is the extensive, arduous, and necessary character of women's work in remote outport communities where the threat of destitution and the absence of basic infrastructure meant a daily struggle to make ends meet. The experience of women in Bay St George is not extensively documented, but numerous accounts and local reflections convey mutual dependence and hardships for women and men.

Cecilia Benoit argues, however, that French-speaking families in Stephenville were structured by patriarchal institutions of family and church which exercized control over women through a gender-coded system. An ideology of family-fostered male dominance and control over women, manifested in proscriptions against premarital sex on the part of women and in the celebration of large families, supported women's submission to the authority of priest and father (Benoit, 1990:passim). This was reflected in a sexual double standard which tended to blame and shame women for pre-marital pregnancy (Benoit, 1990:178).

In spite of this structure, Benoit argues that arenas of power granted women autonomy and a valued social identity in the family and villages. Moreover, Bay St George was not homogeneously Catholic and accounts from Anglican women place less emphasis on the restrictions imposed by religion.

Anne: 'The women were hard workers'

The narrative of Anne, a ninety-year-old Anglican woman whose life story I collected, conveys the extent of women's work. Anne, a former teacher and fisherman's widow, describes a rigid division of labour which positioned women as subsistence workers on Sandy Point alongside their brothers, husbands, and fathers.

> In Sandy Point, the women were hard workers. They looked after their families and cooked and looked after the sheep. They made drawers and sweaters and socks. You would have spinning wheels and cards – first you picked and then you carded and then you spun. You'd have a picking spree, say if you had 5 or 6 sheep to shear, and you'd ask your neighbour to come in for a picking spree and you'd feed them well and they'd pick your wool before they'd send it up to the mill in Codroy valley. I can see them in the rectory, sitting and talking and carding and knitting. And we had hooking sprees. They all hooked their own rugs. We'd buy 98 pound bags of flour and I made shirts for my husband from those bags. I made all my children's clothes.

Work was structured by seasonal demands and organized through kin ties which connected households through the exchange of goods and services.

We all had a rhubarb patch and onion patch, and many would go up to Stephenville for their vegetables. It was a farming area before the Americans came so we went over there in a boat in the fall and brought back our vegetables. The ship from Halifax brought most of our groceries; we didn't get them by train. Most people would buy a tierce of molasses or in the older days when they went up with the herring (in boats to Halifax) they brought back their provisions – 5 or 6 barrels of flour, a tierce of molasses, a barrel of salt pork and a one of salt beef.

Then, when I had my own house, I used to help my brother. I sowed seeds for my brother to plant potatoes and my husband would dig them in the fall because in the spring of the year he'd be very busy. I had my own little garden and my own lettuce and radishes. We'd go to St George's to pick blueberries and we'd get bake apples and raspberries and we'd camp, me, Molly and Bill (her sister and brother). I used to bake twice a week, four loaves each time.

Women's subsistence production was crucial to household livelihood. It complemented mens' subsistence and commodity production, which was structured by the demands of the seasonal fishery.

The husbands were mostly fishermen. They caught the herring in the spring and they packed that. It was a big thing at one time. I suppose a lot must have missed schooling then. When I was a little girl – some families stayed in the fish stores near the beach and I thought it was lovely. They had their beds upstairs and they cooked downstairs and the men went out in the front packing herring. Each man had a 100 barrels or more of salt herring, and they'd take them up to Halifax. Some of the men had their own schooners. My husband's grandfather did. The men made their own barrels and packed them in salt. Then there was the salmon. Salmon had to be put in boxes with ice, which meant you had to cut ice in the winter. My husband caught salmon, then smelts in September – in the water and then on the ice.

Sometimes the smelt fishing would take him up to Jobbers Island and they had a tent up there and they'd pack a lunch box with pies. And they went in wintertime and got their moose or caribou. For caribou, they'd go into George the IV Lake on dog team and there'd be a nice crusty snow on the barrens. They did everything with dog team, including cutting wood.

> There was a fishermen's woodlot where they'd cut wood and leave it on the shore to bring home in June.

Anne's narrative suggests a balanced reciprocity between women and men and the work they contributed to maintaining households. It reinforces Porter's argument that the domain of 'production' engendered egalitarian relations within households and between them.

The social context of biological reproduction and the character of conjugal relations were also structured by the establishment of churches in the area by the mid-nineteenth century. In Anne's memory, women, at least Anglican women, used forms of birth control, including abstinence and a herb grown in the garden which was thought to produce miscarriages. Anne details women's participation in community activities, particularly as church workers and midwives. Yet her narrative suggests that the clergy and church institutions played a role in distinguishing men and women's contribution in a hierarchical manner: 'Women rule their homes. But, they didn't seem to rule the church or the organization. Take the Orange Hall. The women were the workers. They made the money for the church. It was the husband's money they were spending, I suppose. But women were the backbone of the family.'

The character of household livelihood and responsibilities within the family was transformed by the introduction of male waged labour, which intensified women's work and fostered their domestication within an emergent dichotomy of public and private domains.

The Emergence of the Jack-of-All-Trades

Transformations in local family-based households from the turn-of-the century fostered the development and entrenchment of the male's role as a jack-of-all-trades, a term widely applied to the male labour force across the island. Divisions of labour that characterized fishing households were modified with the introduction of male waged labour. Women's responsibilities in subsistence work and domestic caregiving intensified as men left the area to work on a seasonal or long-term basis.

These changes altered gender relations in the household and the domains of male and female power. On the one hand, the new order gave men access to cash. On the other, it necessitated their absence for weeks and months at a time, which fostered women's autonomy in daily decision making over childcare. It also increased the burden of their responsibilities, particularly in households with several children. Benoit shows that, while men worked away from home, women worked extensively in the household and the surrounding neighbourhood as mothers, primary caregivers, midwives, and subsistence workers. The absence of men, and reciprocities between women within neighbourhoods and the extended family, generated a feminine social sphere which valued female authority within and between households during mens' absences (Benoit, 1990:175).

Attempts to diversify the economy through the exploitation of other natural resources prompted the introduction of forestry and mining industries around 1900, transformed the social organization of a few communities, and precipitated the growth of towns such as Grand Falls, Belle Island, and Corner Brook (Alexander, 1988:14). Low prices for cod during this period initiated a large flow of emigration, and 30 per cent of those who remained on the island left the fishery. Still, during this period, half of the male labour force across Newfoundland was employed in fishing and logging industries (Alexander, 1988).

By 1901 Stephenville's population had grown to 643, most of whom were Roman Catholic families who made a living through fishing and small-scale farming. Men entered the waged labour force slowly and on a seasonal basis through work in lumber camps, saw mills, and construction, which took them away from home for varied periods of time. The introduction of saw mills, lobster factories, a limestone quarry, and a mill in Corner Brook in 1920 increased working opportunities. Lobster production on the west coast grew as factories increased in number from 12 to 76 by 1887 and employed 700 men in family-based and larger-scale operations (Mannion 1977:251). Paid work was rare for Stephenville women, who produced very large families well into the twentieth century. Census records do register 348 women at work in 1921, curing fish throughout the small villages across Bay St George. However, only those women engaged in paid work, mostly as domestics and teachers, are recorded in 1935 census records.[2]

The Assimilation of Francophones

By 1935 Bay St George was incorporated as a town and the region's population had grown to 6483, the majority of whom were French speaking. At this time Stephenville consisted of 926 people who were settled in three distinct village clusters.[3] A male labour force of 2302 worked predominantly as loggers, farmers, cod fishermen, and labourers.[4] Once the French government ceded fishing rights in 1904, the Newfoundland government sought to assimilate the local francophone population under English-speaking rule. Assimilation was facilitated by Irish Catholic nuns and priests who gradually replaced French-speaking priests from the late nineteenth century. Religious services and education, which were administered through the church and thus denominationally structured, were carried out in English. Francophone names were anglicized on baptismal records, with Aucoin becoming O'Quinn, Benoit becoming Bennet, and LeBlanc becoming White, to name a few. Assimilation was further promoted through the resettlement of English-speaking settlers from Fortune Bay, who were relocated to the Port au Port peninsula in 1934 and settled in the growing town of Lourdes (Thomas, 1983:46). Francophone communities at the tip of the Port au Port peninsula were economically disadvantaged and somewhat isolated geographically and linguistically from other more ethnically heterogeneous communities across Bay St George.

Depression Years: The Commission Government

Unemployment and poverty in Newfoundland outports and towns were exacerbated by the Great Depression, which bankrupted the Newfoundland state and led to its replacement by a British-appointed commission of government. This crisis had been foreshadowed by earlier economic calamities, such as the failure of the colony's financial institutions in 1894 and the fall in export prices for cod in the 1880s, 1890s, and early 1920s, all of which underscored the difficulties of sustaining an export-based economy when, as in Newfoundland's case, 75 per cent of government revenues came from customs taxes and revenues that went towards paying interest on an ever-increasing debt (Neary, 1988:9).

The poverty in Newfoundland communities was reflected in high levels of tuberculosis, high infant mortality rates, and an increased demand for government relief (Alexander, 1977:18). A somewhat detached St John's government, which claimed to have little revenue because of the financial crisis, implemented a threadbare relief program, which was unevenly administered and subject to corruption by appointees from the capital (Neary, 1988:10). About 25 per cent of the island population was on relief in 1931 (Godfrey, 1985:39). Unemployed workers, primary producers subjected to market fluctuations and low catches, and widows were particularly destitute.

Bay St George was no exception. Although ethnic and racial distinctions were significant, families shared a common class base. Moreover, their limited access to education and the difficulties of making a living had inhibited the growth of social and economic inequalities. A federal economic-development report described the Port au Port peninsula as having the potential for a subsistence-livelihood economy based on farming and fishing. But it also pointed out that, in 1937, 200 of its 600 families were destitute and reliant on government relief.[5] There were, however, a few merchant families in the area whose social and economic prominence and privileged position in the fishery trade are well remembered by residents today. These incipient class divisions later intensified with the arrival of the American military and the elite officer class.

American Hegemony and the Carefree Years: 1941 to 1966

> We came to Stephenville from Deer Lake in 1944. I remember arriving in Stephenville Crossing on the train and we had to find a way into Stephenville along the dirt roads. My husband came to get work on the base, and jobs were already getting scarce in other places. Everybody knew about Stephenville and the base and it helped a lot of people. When we first came there was only one grocery store 'in town' and the post office was in Kippens, so you had to walk there from the gate (that separated the military base from the town) where we lived. The theatre was just on the other side of the gate. When we first arrived the people were a bit standoffish. They had been there a long time and they had their name on the pews and we newcomers had to sit or stand at the back of the church. The town was just getting started then and it was on the same scale as Deer Lake; both towns were just getting started. (Loretta, age seventy)

The establishment of an American base in Stephenville transformed the social fabric of Bay St George, established new social and economic hierarchies, and lay economic foundations for secondary and tertiary industry. This process stretched unevenly across the region, creating an urban centre from which emanated rural and underdeveloped communities, a rural/urban formation that persists today. Fishing and farming villages were altered by the influx of women and men from across the island and by the establishment of an extensive urban infrastructure. These changes intensified the privatization of women's work and their insertion into the capitalist economy as secondary workers and, primarily, consumers. While many women found work on base, households shifted from units of production to private enclaves of consumption, which gave primacy to women's roles as domestic workers, mothers, and caregivers.

Newfoundland's political-economic dependence was reflected in the exclusion of the commission of government from the American-British consultations that led to the creation of military bases at Stephenville and elsewhere on the island. Still, the militarization and urbanization of various zones across the province, from St John's westward to Argentia, Gander, Stephenville, and Goose Bay, were largely welcomed. Military bases provided increased revenue to the Newfoundland government, decreased its debt, and initiated infrastructural development and the introduction of compulsory education (Mackenzie, 1986:69–72). Unemployment declined across the island as 25 per cent of the labour force was employed in military bases at the height of construction (Wadel, 1973:6).

Specifically, the development of Stephenville proceeded according to the needs of military expansion during the Second World War. American military planners chose 8195 acres of farmland 'back of the pond' to build their air-force base, which it leased from the British government for ninety-nine years. Dispossessed farmers were given paltry sums for their land. While some left the area, others bought new farm land and some found work as unskilled labourers in the construction of the base. John, the youngest of seven siblings and currently a manager at the paper mill, recalls a 'cultural clash' between Americans and locals: 'Imagine, we were self sufficient, that was our background. An orange and an apple were a big luxury. Then the Americans were very affluent. People descended on you all of a sudden and they could be very critical. But the Newfoundlanders weren't dumb, so there were some fights.

Socially, there were the older, senior officers and some formed good friendships with locals; but there was a lot of competition for girls. Imagine, 2 or 3000 eligible men, and they came from all over. There was both confrontation and good friendships. My mother made a dozen friends.'

The juxtaposition of rural-outport culture with the dominant culture of an industrial and political world power was noted by locals and Americans. It was articulated through narratives of tradition and modernization, backwardness and sophistication, which were harnessed to strengthen American hegemony and its leadership in the progress of capitalist development, Cold War strategies, and post-war prosperity. These glory days are still evoked in biannual commemorations in Stephenville, twenty-seven years after the base's closure. Listen to the rhetoric of the period: 'Many will recall that only a few years ago the distant isolated sections of the island could be classified almost as far away places. People lived close to nature, a sort of simple, uncomplicated life ... Here [in Stephenville] we find people from practically every part of North America ... It tells a story ... how we work, play, eat together, belong to the same society ... It speaks of a common cause, the common good and most of all ... it speaks of the free world' (Moss, 1956:34).

American hegemony was aided by the creation of employment for civilian Newfoundlanders. Indeed, the base provided much paid work and thus attracted a few thousand women and men from across the island in search of jobs. The population of the region grew from 15,982 in 1951 to 24,185 in 1961. Although initially the U.S. Air Force employed 200 civilians, it employed 700 during its second round of construction from 1951 to 1957 and 1300 at its peak. During this time, 367 buildings – including 8 dormitories, a 600-seat theatre, two dining halls seating 1000, 4 civilian dormitories, hangars, and a hospital – as well as a deep water port were constructed (Decks Awash, 1984:10). Jobs could be found in construction, truck driving, machine operation, plumbing, electrical work, waitressing, and clerical work. Men and women who worked on the base during these years recall that the wages were good by Newfoundland standards. In 1960 the annual payroll of $18 million was second only to the Bowaters paper mill in the province.[6]

'You are a partner of our men in uniform'[7]

The prosperity of employment and American visions of progress shaped the character of urban life by engendering a spirit of cooperation between soldiers and civilians. A civilian advisory council was established to 'build a co-operative and productive workforce and to communicate between management and employees' (Moss, 1956:26). This economic activity and the settlement of new residents created housing shortages, commercial development, and jobs in spin-off industries while also initiating the rapid development of Stephenville, which had had unpaved roads and no electricity before the base was constructed. The town, which grew to 6043 by 1961, was comparable to a company town until its incorporation in 1952. The American government acted as owner, providing employment and leisure activities. At the same time, the U.S. air force created a dominant local culture which celebrated militarism, cooperation between soldiers and civilians, and American democratic and social values. Social life was punctuated by parades, theatrical entertainment, clean-up initiatives, and open houses. Some of these activities were organized through the Stephenville Harmon Community Relations Council, which sought to foster 'good will between townspeople and members of the base' (Moss, 1956:33).

> On base you had to be signed in and go through the checkpoint. I had I.D. because I worked there, but you could sneak in. Dorms were cheap; eating out was cheap, there was the NCO club and no charge and the off-broadway shows were no-charge. We had the Inkspots, the Platters ... (Maureen, age fifty-five).

> Everyone had at least one friend who worked on base. My husband and I, we'd go out dancing and to the taverns, once or twice a week. Beer was 10 cents and a 40 ouncer cost $1.50, which was cheap even in those days. (Elizabeth, age sixty)

These halcyon days of glamour and revelry are evoked by older residents who fondly recall dances on base and performances of visiting entertainers such as Frank Sinatra, Bob Hope, Elvis Presley, and Marlene Dietrich and the arrival of various dignitaries such as presidents Eisenhower, Roosevelt, and Kennedy, Prime Minister Nehru of India, and Queen Elizabeth.

The Expansion of Women's Choices and the Reproduction of Femininity

Stephenville was like a wild west town. My first impression when I came was that it was like Dodge City. There were lotsa taverns and money on the go, and a lot of nightlife and government money too. (Bill, a millworker)

The base also introduced the excesses of militarism, including a few thousand men in uniform and a military culture that celebrated masculine bravado and alcoholic and sexual abandon. Family and community life was dramatically and unevenly altered throughout the area. The base provided women with new choices, the consequences of which were somewhat determined by their relationships to men. Many women came from across the island and found work on base as clerical workers; others married American soldiers and now reside in the United States. American servicemen were stationed there for a few years at a time, 'long enough for them to get acquainted with Newfoundland girls and for many years, one of Stephenville's greatest exports was its women' (Cardoulis, 1985:11). According to Cardoulis, over 25,000 Newfoundland women married American servicemen stationed across the island during this period (Cardoulis, 1985:72). Marriage records from St Stephens, the Roman Catholic church in Stephenville, show that from 1944 to 1966 the percentage of marriages between Newfoundland women and American servicemen ranged from 11 per cent of total marriages in 1945 to 37 per cent in 1948. The average for the 1950s was 25 per cent.[8]

Numerous women whose stories I gathered have one or more sisters who married American soldiers and are now scattered across the United States. One francophone woman recalled: 'Oh Stephenville was very different. There was a lot more work for one thing. If there was any work in Stephenville, the Americans made it happen. I have two sisters married with Americans. One is in Indiana, one in Pennsylvania. They met their husbands there. They were working as housekeepers – serving girls.' However, Doris, a sixty-two-year-old resident who moved with her family to Stephenville at age sixteen, expresses ambivalence towards the American presence:

> We moved from Deer Lake to Stephenville later, and it was a whole different way of life; well, the main religion was Catholic and we were Salvation Army. I worked on base in the offices, filing and ordering and it was easy to pick up a job then, especially if you had grade 11. There were good and bad employers, and some were really snotty! There were a lot of women from everywhere and in 1955, the pay was better than working in the store. It seems that everywhere you went, everyone drank. Liquor was dirt cheap! There were lots of clubs and bars; it's still that way. When I was young and working, I'd go out dancing but I wasn't after the American soldiers – especially when you worked with them – they were a pain in the neck! They thought they were God's gift to women. I remember going on a date with one and he had more hands than an octopus. Some of the girls made themselves so available. My husband always said of that time, 'the only way to get a girl was to wear a uniform'! Its not that girls were more promiscuous, some were really straitlaced – there was a real variety.

Some of these women later divorced; others remained and mothered children fathered by American soldiers. It is difficult to ascertain through written documents the number of children born out of wedlock and, in particular, through liaisons with American soldiers. Dorothy, who became a foster parent during this period, recalled that some of these children were a result of liaisons with American soldiers.

Households formerly structured through combined subsistence and non-capitalist exchange were transformed into units of consumption and reproduction as men in the area found work on base or as unskilled labourers in spin-off industries. Exposure to American luxury items and consumer goods increased local demand for consumer products, items that had previously been made in the household. The presence of the air base is described by many as the crucial factor in the assimilation of French-speaking Newfoundlanders, who were required to learn English if they sought a job in town or on base.

Deborah, whose grandfather worked on base, was born in Kippens to a French-speaking family. She emphasizes how impressed she was with American culture:

> I grew up with American children because the next house to us was an apartment-type house where people would come and go all the time. I was lucky that I got to meet people with a different culture and different nationalities. We had a coloured family move in and I'd be friends with their kids. The next family was of German descent. They were working with the base, one was a piano player and he entertained in the pubs. I learned about new foods, like broccoli and apple butter – all kinds of things we didn't have in our supermarkets.

Women's narratives also tell of unwanted pregnancies and the contradictions that young women faced. Feminine prescriptions dictated respectability, chastity, and motherhood within marriage. At the same time, the social superiority of American soldiers, whose masculinity symbolized American military power and cultural dominance, was a strong attraction that held the potential for escape from a remote and economically impoverished family life. Deborah is ambivalent about the impact of American soldiers on her sister's life:

> My sister had seven kids altogether, more than one with an American solder. Then, they would just leave. These men were attractive because there were more females around in the community than males and they (the Americans) were available and good looking. I suppose they had some magic and some money. And it was kind of exciting if you got to the base and the nice clubs that weren't in the community. And you'd be shown a good time. My sister did a lot of domestic work in other people's houses and she worked a lot for Americans. She worked for a Sergeant. When you look at the lumberjacks we had here mostly, I guess they would stand out as being handsome and wealthy.

Joan moved to Georgia with her husband, an American soldier, and returned to Stephenville upon her divorce. As she puts it, 'It was the uniform I think. They were so handsome, and they were clean!'

In spite of the economic development sparked by the construction of the air base, long-held values and prescriptions for womanly behaviour persisted, and many rural families continued to rely on subsistence activity. Elizabeth, who was raised in Port au Port from 1937 to 1957, recalled the immense differences that distinguished life at home from the frenzy of town. Although her father worked at times in the limestone quarry from May to October, she recalled that

> there wasn't any money. We grew our own food and made our own clothes. Mom made our underwear with bleached sack cloth and all our sweaters and the boys pants. We got a lot of supplies in for the winter. At least nobody had more than anyone else. I can still remember the long hungry month of March and I can hear the sound of water dropping on our old wood stove. We had no electricity or running water – I think we got it when I was in grade 10.
>
> I remember when there were only three cars in Port au Port and nothing but dirt road. And sometimes the Americans would come round for a dance on a Saturday night and the whole road would be lined with cars.

Elizabeth was one of twelve children in devout Catholic household. Five of her sisters worked on base and married American soldiers. 'But one of my sisters got pregnant. That was a disgrace back then. She had to stay upstairs for the entire pregancy, the whole nine months, just doing embroidery. Mom raised her [the child] until she died. And then my sister came back from the States to get her.'

Changes in American military strategy prompted the gradual withdrawal of the U.S. military from Atlantic Canada. In Stephenville, 'the carefree days' were abruptly ended by the decision of the United States government to close the base in the mid-1960s. By 1966, the civilian workforce of 1200 had been reduced to a handful. The provincial minister of mines and resources promised that the area 'would not die with a whimper.' Rather, he envisioned a 'great industrial complex that will assure a better future for the district than was ever known in the past and greater than what most Newfoundlanders could have hoped for.'[9] The Canadian state, whose dominance in the region had been somewhat pre-empted by its American counterpart, would now exercise increasing influence.

Boom and Bust: The Rise of Canadian State Intervention, 1966–93

> When the base died all the liquor and cigarettes were suddenly bought out all over Stephenville! Lots of families moved out – the town just died. My brother

had no job and it took a number of years to get one. My other brother moved to Labrador. I was lucky I guess. I found a job pretty quick. (John, age fifty-three, mill manager)

The closure of the base precipitated an exodus of residents and signalled the initiation of new industrialization and social policies to redirect the economy of Bay St George and maintain employment levels. Stephenville was targeted as a potential growth area and urban centre for the government's large-scale resettlement scheme, which was intended to proletarianize rural Newfoundlanders and urbanize the economy for industrial diversification (Copes, 1972:15). At the same time, residents who had arrived during the air-base years and established families and, in particular, businesses lobbied the provincial government to redevelop the region.

Douglas Fowlow recalls that, when he left his teaching position in Labrador City to take up residence in Stephenville, the base had just closed and it resembled a 'ghost town.' He remembers a pervasive emptiness in which 485 or more apartments on base lay empty and houses and buildings were boarded up. Still, the parlous conditions enhanced the 'sense of mission' that he and fellow teachers had regarding economic development through education. Moreover, as a result of the base, the town had inherited a range of recreational and service facilities, 'a more cosmopolitan air, and a less developed sense of social strata.' At the same time, the wild west sensibility lingered along with the false fronts and numerous taverns that lined Main Street, evidence of the extensive underbelly of booze, parties, and social problems that would be increasingly exposed and confronted.

Optimism characterized the final years of Smallwood's provincial government, which viewed economic development as a possibility once the basic foundations of education and industry were established through the cooperative efforts of government and private enterprise. From the late 1960s, various industrial and commercial schemes were initiated through federal, provincial, and local community structures. The government promised a new industry to replace the air base, an adult educational centre to provide training, and the coordination of job-creation schemes among federal, provincial, and local organizations. Although most industrial initiatives failed, the general impact was the establishment of Stephenville as a service and commercial centre for the southwest coast. The base had spawned numerous small businesses in secondary production, particularly construction and the commercial-service sector, and some of these remained viable throughout the period of boom and bust.

The construction of a linerboard mill in Stephenville typified Smallwood's ambitious approach to joint government-private ventures. While it intially provided direct employment for 1300 (including Labrador loggers), this mill workforce shrank to 550 after the mill went into operation in 1973. It was taken over as a crown corporation by the new Conservative government in 1972, and it continued to lose money until its closure in 1977.

The failure of the mill has been variously attributed to poor government management, corrupt private interests, unfavourable market shifts, and, particularly, high costs of pulpwood from Labrador. Yet the loss mirrors that of most large-scale industrial schemes in the province at that time, including the Come-By-Chance oil refinery. In addition to the mill, attempts to develop a commercial-industrial base in fibre-optics, fishmeal, fibreglass longliners, and fish plants, for example, all failed. Briefs to the Royal Commission on Employment and Unemployment underline the naivety of the provincial government, which, in its desperate attempts to attract business through concessions and loans, allowed entrepreneurs to make immediate gain at the expense of long-term economic development.[10]

During the union consolidation of the 1970s, the media discourse, reflected in the local news weekly, centred on labour disputes both locally and across the province. Shut-downs at the Stephenville mill were frequent and gained extensive media coverage, as did the strikes that occurred at mills in Corner Brook and Grand Falls. When the Stephenville mill finally closed, the media gave considerable attention to the plight of mill families, indebted through mortgages and credit purchases. Moderately attended rallies demanded a 'family wage.' Millworkers, especially skilled workers, left in search of jobs across Canada.

With a $2-million tax concession, Abitibi-Price acquired mills in Grand Falls and Stephenville. The latter was converted for newsprint production in 1981 (Goulding, 1982:220). This mill has thus far proved to be a more stable provider of tax dollars for the municipality. It employs 300 men in its papermaking and wood-harvesting sectors and a handful of women in its clerical department; it has also generated employment for small business contractors who employ woodcutters on a seasonal basis. In 1992 the starting hourly wage for these unionized workers was $18.50 and, because of opportunities for overtime work, annual incomes range from $40,000 to as high as $90,000 for the most skilled papermakers. Not surprisingly, today, an ambition among younger men is to get a job at the mill.

The growth of the welfare state nationally, and the government sector provincially, fostered the development of Stephenville as a commercial and public-service centre for the southwest coast and signalled the increased role of government in regulating and mediating forces of capital, labour, and family (Armstrong and Armstrong, 1988:72). Although the participation of women in the labour force grew unevenly, and somewhat behind national averages, by the late 1980s, numerous women were employed throughout the area, in full-time, part-time, and contractually limited positions in government and the commercial sector. These positions ranged from unionized, relatively well-paid government-sector occupations to low-paid, short-term commerical work. While many professional occupations were filled by women who came from elsewhere across the island, young area women began to acquire the necessary education and some of these jobs (Brown, 1982:21).

Specifically, an increase in jobs filled by women was achieved through the opening and growth of assorted government institutions, including the community college, founded in 1971, social services, the local Canada Employment Centre, and the male and female correctional centres, opened in the late 1970s. For example, in the early 1990s, approximately 100 women were employed as nurses in the hospital and in the nursing home. Three hundred women were employed, mostly as teachers, by the Roman Catholic Appalachia School Board. The community college, with 199 employees, employed 88 women as teachers and support staff. In addition, the opening of a mall in the 1980s created assorted and lower-paid, part-time service jobs in the commercial sector.

Numerous women I interviewed over the age of forty found paid work once their children reached adolescence. Indeed, whether they returned to school for 'upgrading' or not (and some did), most of these women found paid work in government and the commercial sector, jobs that mirrored or, in their view, complemented their caregiving roles in the domestic arena. Their identities as mothers and caregivers were not displaced by paid work; rather, their gendered identity expanded to embrace new relations and new meanings. For example, Jane, a fifty-two year old mother of three, recounts her decision to become a probation officer. She had accompanied her husband as he found various jobs across Canada and occupied herself with domestic work and childrearing, sewing all her children's clothes, participating in Brownies and Girl Guides, and taking courses in typing, accounting, bookkeeping, and French in the evening. When they returned to Stephenville, she decided to apply to the prison as a corrections officer after visiting a friend who was incarcerated: 'All my girls were gone from home and I had time on my hands. When I went to the prison, I thought, "I bet they could use me in prison; I could sew and crochet; they'd be happy for me to help out." I really wanted to work with these girls and to help them.' Although Elaine worked as a cashier while her children were growing up, she was able to find work in the growing Department of Social Services, after retraining to upgrade her clerical skills at the college. The increase in public-sector jobs and the entry of women into the labour force were instrumental in providing area women with access to bureaucratic networks and arenas of power within the public domain from which they had been excluded. This newly acquired access facilitated the formation of the Women's Council in 1985 and ultimately shapes its current character.

Yet the entry of women into the labour market was uneven. The increase of women in the paid workforce was greatest in Stephenville proper and the numbers declined progressively from the surrounding area to the most isolated rural communities where paid work was less available. In 1986, for instance, the female labour-force participation rate for Stephenville was 49.2 per cent, while, for the more isolated Cape St George, it was 29.9 per cent. However, women's participation rate has increased slightly over the last ten years in both rural and urban areas.[11] This has generated structurally rooted divisions between women which are no longer determined solely by the occupations of their spouses.

Underemployment and Regional Disparity

The closure of the air base caused high unemployment, increased the welfare rolls, and precipitated the increased role of the Canadian state in providing employment and income for the region – a trend that has continued over the past twenty-five years.[12] The introduction of employment schemes through the (now defunct) Canada Assistance Plan and the provincially funded Employment Opportunities Program initiated the creation of 'make-work projects' from 1972. Although these programs were intended to 'provide meaningful training and employment opportunities for social-assistance recipients,' they often did not fulfil their mandate.[13] Rather, they reduced the numbers of welfare recipients and thus the social-assistance costs of the province, allowed workers to qualify for unemployment insurance (acquire 'stamps'), and embedded local development and municipal organizations in the job-creation system.

Although the town of Stephenville had acquired an extensive infrastructure from the air base, for which it paid $1, rural communities on the Port au Port peninsula did not reap the same benefits from the military presence. While residents, including those who were French-speaking at that time, had acquired jobs and an American pension, according to Ralph Matthews, a large population was still attempting to enter the labour force by the mid 1960s (Matthews, 1976:15).

Before introduction of the birth-control pill, and changes in the post-Vatican II era to local values regarding family size and sexual practices, family poverty was exacerbated by the persistence of large families. Indeed, government reports targeted the Bay St George area in particular as one of the most depressed in the province and across the country, with a high infant mortality rate and one of the highest birthrates in Canada in the mid-1960s.[14] Local economic-development associations, organized since the 1960s, developed strategies to gain political representation and access to government funds through assorted federal and provincial programs.[15] The Port au Port Economic Development Association, for example, which was established in 1964, directed economic initiatives towards infrastructural development and education to foster a small-scale fishery, farming, and tourism.[16] After 1971, the association became a key employer and organizer of local 'development' through its involvement in federal government 'make-work' programs, which, in combination with provincial work schemes, have provided funds for infrastructure and wages for the last twenty-five years.[17] Until recently, attempts to create employment have been directed at men and traditionally male occupations.

Theresa, a fifty-six-year-old mother of five who lives in a remote community on the Port au Port peninsula, was able to access such 'project work,' in part because it was designed to draw on her domestic skills. Living in a small community near her four sisters and seven brothers, Theresa remained home for much of the 1970s and was kept occupied with knitting, sewing, baking bread, and 'doing crafts.' Once her five children were 'grown' (in their early teens) she began working as a gas-pump attendant at her brother-in-law's gas station, and later she became a project manager on a government-funded craft program where she taught twenty-one other women from the francophone communities to quilt.

> I got the job through word of mouth because one girl was working down at Social Services and I got a phone call and she asked me if I wanted to go to work and I said, it depends on what kind of work. I'm not qualified to do much. I worked all my life, but not for a paycheque. My husband said, 'Don't be afraid to do what you've been doing all your life.' I taught them how to cut pieces for a quilt. And I bought materials, took inventory. It was really my first job where I had to be in charge. I loved it and I did it for six years.

Attempts to maintain and diversify the local fishery, however, have produced mixed results. A local scallop farm shows promise but has failed to generate many jobs. Fish plants in Stephenville and on the Port au Port pensinsula were closed in 1979 and 1987 respectively.

The Formation of the Francophone Association

The francophone communities whose residents continue to speak or understand French are situated at the tip of the Port au Port peninsula (see map 2). There, roads remained poorly paved and access to commercial goods and services, paid work, and educational opportunities were restricted by the distance of geography and of language. The thrust towards assimilation created a sense of francophone identity which was reinforced at school by the ridicule and coercive treatment meted out by peers (Matthews, 1976:105).

During the 1970s, these experiences resulted in the formation of three community-based francophone associations and struggles to reclaim francophone heritage and language rights. Residents began to lobby for access to public funds in order to maintain and revive their francophone culture, develop a tourist industry, and gain greater access to resources, education, and employment opportunities. Prior to this, the area had classified local 'French culture' as 'folklore,' that is, a vestige of the past. One francophone community, however, was granted bilingual status in 1971 by the provincial government (Waddell, 1983:225). French was largely spoken within the intimate, domestic context of family and among neighbours and relatives so that residents had an uneven knowledge of oral French. Today, with the opening of a school, French-language skills have improved, particularly among youth.

In the last twenty years, volunteers in the francophone associations have collected numerous lifestories and genealogies of residents, who trace the settlement of their ancestors from their origins in northern France and Nova Scotia.[18] Theresa, who was born and raised during the base years, recalls her own childhood and the settlement of her family. Her account illustrates the disparity that emerged during this time, between Stephenville and the outlying rural communities, particularly those farthest from the town, including the francophone communities on the Port au Port peninsula, and a few rural communities south of Stephenville Crossing where residents with native heritage resided.

> My grandfather jumped ship. They were fishermen then, but they were treated like slaves on those boats – they would settle here in summertime and on Red Island, and so my grandfather finally settled for good.
>
> Growing up, it was different than it is today for sure. We were sixteen in our family, so the chores were divided. Well, when you grow your own vegetables, and there's cattle and pigs, and hens, everybody has a chore ... I'd milk the cow or separate the milk to make butter or there was always the garden to weed in summertime. I have eight brothers and seven sisters and the boys did the heavier chores outside. We had an ox that my father

> used to haul wood and bring home. My father was a fisherman, like everyone else then. He was the kindest man ... We always had a church, but not always a priest. We'd share the priest with other communities. Then we got a permanent priest. He was English and when we went to school, our books were English. In the winter we'd go to school with a chunk of wood under our arms and it would take an hour to warm up. And we had to walk, there were no roads then and there were no cars.
>
> The first time I came to Stephenville, I was nine and I'll never forget the lights. We used kerosene and we had no running water, but in Stephenville, they had all these lights. I think we got electricity in 1963 ...

Theresa suggests that learning French today is also a strategy to help children gain employment. In considering changes in the local economy, she weighs the pros and cons of migration and, in so doing, outlines the importance of historically rooted community and family ties in meeting current livelihood needs.

> I got involved in the French Centre from the beginning. There were 15 of us and now there's 250 members. We figured that our French was going and you know, if the French Centre hadn't started when it did there would never have been French in the schools now. It was hard because the government wouldn't recognize that we were French.
>
> Now we have carnivals and walk-a-thons and lots of fund-raisers still because the government doesn't give us much money. Now the kids learn French and it'll help them get jobs. Because you know, the younger generation is going away working and they're not coming back because there's nothing here for them. They got no choice. Whenever there's a job they go maybe to PEI (Prince Edward Island) to dig potatoes or to the tobacco farms. Some went up to Ontario and got good jobs, but the government is cutting jobs everywhere too. And you can't afford life up there [in Ontario]. You know, there, if you're not working it's not like you can bum (money) off your neighbour – you don't even know his name. Not like home. If you come around home and you're hungry and you go to the door, they'll feed you right?

Today, the French associations receive some government funding for specific projects and as operating grants. Theresa describes how women's domestic work and female-centred networks, which together maintained ties between households within the community, are reproduced and transformed to maintain the French Centre:

> We have to raise money and our work is all volunteer, all donated work. I'm responsible to call so-and-so to make a pot of soup for Saturday night. And then, when we have the festival, that's sometimes a thousand or more people we're feeding who come for this event. Then we have dances and you bring your own food. If you want to come with me and share with my pot, then you bring your own. We share the cooking. And I can always count on my sisters and my good friends, 'cause you always have friends who you can depend your life on. Sometimes, my sister will call and ask what I've done all day and I'll say, 'Oh not much' – but I'm after doing laundry, I'm after baking my bread, I'm after cooking supper – and I did nothing. Force of habit, I guess. It's what I'm accustomed to – it's just part of living.

Theresa's interpretation of the past is not only gendered, it is connected to her ethnic identity as a Franco-Terre-Neuvienne. At the same time, her attitude is akin to that of many residents whose perception of place is tied to the contemporary demands of meeting social and economic needs in a boom-and-bust economy and to the understanding that out-migration is the alternative to the vagaries of making a living on 'the Rock.' In this context, 'home' is a powerful and relative idiom which refers to one's neighbourhood, community, or the island itself, and it is part of the moral framework that underwrites community, kin, and gender relations.

Cultural Expressions of Gender, Difference, and Sustained Settlement

Bay St George both manifests and contests popular depictions of Newfoundland culture, especially as national and provincial discourses centre the culture of the outport fishery. The town of Stephenville and the adjacent rural communities exhibit lifestyles that can also be found in other communities scattered across Canada, particularly in areas of primary-resource production in general (not just fisheries) where the permanence of settlement is disrupted and threatened by the distance of power and the depletion of resources (cf. Dunk, 1991:53).

Cultural continuity with regions across Canada may be reinforced by the presence of Newfoundlanders in many of these communities. For example, the genealogical trees of sixty-five residents that I collected show that more than half the siblings in most families (many of which have ten siblings or more) have migrated. These men and women found waged, unionized, or 'unskilled' jobs in places such as Brampton, Ontario, Thompson, Manitoba, or Fort McMurray, Alberta.

In Bay St George, historically rooted lifeways persist and are punctuated by seasonal changes. Long, snowy winters are followed by cool springs and the opening of a brief fishing season. Japanese and Russian factory boats appear in the bay to harvest and process herring. Local fishermen lower nets and set traps for herring and lobster. Small dories and traps, which line the shores in a few rural communities, are signs of an outport way of life which endures through social ties of family and seasonally rooted patterns of work and leisure. Although most residents have long abandoned their reliance on the fishery, it is still an important occupation on the Port au Port peninsula and in Bay St George South. Moreover, throughout the region it is common to see men, women, and children gathered in twos or threes to catch smelts beneath the ice and to fish trout and salmon from the 'ponds' and rivers. The annual moose hunt, a much-anticipated event, is a vivid reminder that subsistence 'resources' in the woods flourish in spite of scarcity beneath the sea.

Daily life is punctuated by the participation of local people in assorted organizations that are common in many rural communities. In addition to the Women's Council and the francophone associations, Kinsmen and Kinettes, Lions and Lionesses, and the Canadian Legion raise funds for community events and children's activities which are often held in their own halls. There are regular bingo nights, sponsored by secular and religious organizations to generate revenue. Women's groups, particularly the women's auxiliaries of the assorted religious denominations, hold annual teas, 'take-out suppers,' and 'sales of work' (craft sales) to supplement revenue. The sale of local, hand-made crafts is also popular in shops, museums, and community centres throughout the region. The Knights of Columbus, the church auxilliaries, and a denominational school system ensure the integration of religion into everyday life.

Residents also participate in various clubs which reflect specific interests, include men and women, and provide a forum for the display of local talent. A drama club performs yearly, and the local Glee Club presents three performances a year. More political issues are channelled through an environmental organization, local branches of political parties, a local Cross-Roads Canada which focuses on 'Third World' issues, a Chamber of Commerce, and the Bay St George Women's Council.

Stephenville is a working town where the expression of elite status and power is not immediately and visibly evident through personal styles, distinct residences, or leisure activities. Residents proudly claim their town to be 'open,' 'friendly,' and 'tolerant,' in contrast to other towns in the province which can be 'snobbish,' 'close-minded,' and 'unfriendly.' This urban spirit is often attributed to the influence of American culture and the social and economic foundations it established. Residents point to assorted amenities like the Golf Club, the skating rink, the swimming pool, and the Arts and Culture Centre – all of which are accessible to everyone – as the legacy of the American presence. Outsiders are welcomed, many argue, because so many residents arrived as outsiders themselves over the last fifty years. As one mill worker put it, 'we're all friendly here, because nobody is really from here. We're all from somewhere else.'

While some residents in town attribute social levelling to American democratic values, I suggest that it is also rooted in historically embedded social practices which are reproduced under contemporary circumstances of unemployment and out-migration in a state-mediated economy (cf. Smith, 1999:187–9). Social and economic divisions are truncated and status differences are minimized by an overall recognition of the necessity of out-migration, the persistence of unemployment, and the reliance of residents on seasonal and part-time work and government-income supplements. Many residents with whom I spoke were raised in outports and rural communities across the island or came with their parents who worked on base. Their memories convey the extensiveness of economic hardship and the cooperative spirit of earlier times.

The social levelling of status distinctions is expressed as 'helping out,' or, in Constance's terms, 'sharing the pot.' 'Helping out' includes the networks of reciprocal ties between extended kin, informal economic exchanges, and volunteerism in local organizations such as the church and community centres. These reciprocities, as I will show in subsequent chapters, cushion family members from the boom-and-bust economy and the insufficient funds the state provides, although they also reproduce gendered social and economic differences.

Hence, the notion that nobody is better than anyone else is commonplace. Yet the normative foundations of generalized reciprocity are cross-cut by expressions of differences which bear directly upon the way social problems are taken up in public and private political arenas: kitchens, community centres, schools, and town councils. The uneven economic development of the region reinforces local narratives of difference that were formed within the context of colonial settlement and intensified with the urbanization of Stephenville. Differences between rural communities and the town, between French-speaking communities and the largely English-speaking population, and between a Catholic majority and a Protestant minority,[19] manifest political and economic divisions although they cannot be reduced to any of these oppositions. Rather, expressions of difference form a normative basis for the expression of certain social values even though many recognize the interdependence between town and rural communities. Furthermore, numerous residents from the town and its most immediate outskirts have memories of a French past and French-speaking grandparents and parents or speak in French-accented English themselves.

However, a sense of urban superiority that emerged during the base years persists within the town and among residents who view the rural communities in general and francophone communities in particular as more 'traditional.'[20] Perceived physical and ethnic differences between French-speaking settlers, those of Mi'kmaq heritage, and the English-speaking majority are dichotomized by locals in narratives which reflect persistent disparities in the region. This is reinforced by the sustained settlement of French-speaking and Mi'kmaq residents in small communities on the most remote edges of the region and their peripheralization within the local and national labour market. However, the formation of two organizations in addition to the Women's Council suggests that historical differences are salient today and reflected through political representation. A Mi'kmaq association[21] for the region of St George's and Flat Bay on the south end of Bay St George, and francophone associations on the tip of the Port au Port peninsula, have generated collective, racialized ethnic identities and provide resources for the peoples they represent.

'Traditions' are reproduced in social and economic spheres: by the 'jack-of-all-trades' who works seasonally nearby or temporarily off-island, returning to haul wood from skidoos to pick-up trucks. On the Port au Port peninsula, for example, a large number of men classify themselves as 'labourers,' and 'carpenters,' appellations that indicate their reliance on 'unskilled,' heterogeneous, seasonal, and often migrant forms of work in fish plants (in Nova Scotia), on farms in Prince Edward Island, and as woodcutters for private contractors.[22]

Long-term unemployment and a sustained reliance on unemployment insurance, 'make-work' projects, and social assistance continue to provide a low and, in many cases, substandard income for residents throughout the region. Although unemployment has hovered at 25 per cent in the last ten years, these levels are spread unevenly throughout the area. In some rural communities, unemployment is considerably higher, reaching even 80 per cent, according to the local Canada Employment Centre. Local educators emphasize that levels of education remain low and call for increased training and education programs. Their position, however, is informed by a recognition that here, as elsewhere across the island, training and education are at best a step towards more successful integration into the national labour market.

These distinctions are, however, relative and largely confined to the region itself. Across the island, older residents with whom I spoke, on the northern peninsula and in Grand Falls, for example, associate the entire region of Bay St George with 'Jacquetars,' a term they use in a derogatory way. My own father's brother married a 'Jacquetar' from Stephenville. His family, who were poor fishers from an island near Corner Brook, frequently spoke in these same tones of superiority. At the same time, Stephenville is viewed elsewhere as a 'wild town,' filled with clubs and rough activity.

These characterizations inform the expression of normative standards of behaviour for men and women to create multiple and contradictory gender scripts. Given the focus of this study on women's experiences and activism, constructions of femininity are examined in greater detail throughout the book. However, femininity is constructed in relation to constructions of masculinity, which display a few predominant forms. While this study does not deal with masculine identities, there are masculine constructs which are locally hegemonic, and historically residual, and which warrant a brief description. Whether men and women accept, contest, or internalize these distinctions varies considerably, as do their interpretations of the way the region itself is characterized.

Masculine Displays

Although personal narratives often indicate that gender identities were historically more fluid than dominant depictions would convey, gender identities have been further transformed and framed in terms of normative changes in the region and in the province – which was increasingly measured by, and hence politically and economically marginalized in relation to, a Canadian and urban norm after Newfoundland's entered Confederation. The nuclear family has increasingly formed the normative means through which making a living, raising children, and evaluating gendered behaviour is interpreted. Yet extended family relations are important in meeting the social, emotional, and material needs of residents, particularly in outlying rural communities; and they form a crucial bridge between incomes determined by the labour market and the demands of reproducing a household in a boom-and-bust economy such as that of Bay St George.

The dominant depiction of Newfoundland culture has been its egalitarian ethos, and this is evoked in the memories and claims of many residents: that women and men are separate but equal in heterosexual, familial relationships. Yet the importance of a patriarchally oriented family conferred considerable power in men over women – through church, state and reproduction – and generated what Henrietta Moore refers to as a 'sub-dominant' (Moore, 1994:59) masculinity in relation to hegemonic displays of male power within a provincial and Canadian context. While the authority of a paternal, responsible male provider is greatly respected and men who conform to this are sought after, it is an ideal construct, which is meaningful for its elusiveness in the context of seasonal employment and temporary migration.

Moreover, this construct is mediated by historical oppositions which are salient today and which correspond to masculine class divisions that distinguish mental and manual labour but are not reduceable to them: 'Townies' – the white-collar worker who is educated and often from away (either the mainland or St John's) – are contrasted with rural Newfoundlanders – the sons of miners, fishers, and loggers whose skills, pride, and sense of self and self-control emerges from their work in dangerous, male-dominated occupations and from the stories of work these men have absorbed.

The division of labour in a primary-resource-based staples economy meant that most men sought a living in outdoor, seasonal, physically demanding, and often dangerous work in fishing, logging, and mining. The construction of masculinity associated with such work celebrates strength, endurance, and even bravado on the job and hard-drinking and toughness off the job. It also embraces a mindset capable of dealing with the vicissitudes of seasonal or boom-and-bust economic cycles: 'I got two-and-a-half more cigarettes and I've still got one more beer,' in the words of a local song, 'Rock-Bottom,' popular during my fieldwork. This notion of manliness is conducive to many men seeking occupations with similar characteristics, such as the armed forces or the police.[23]

In Bay St George, there is some recognition of a dominant masculinity through which Newfoundland men are evaluated and which they both respect and contest. The merchant, the clergy, and the soldier form a triumverate which could be updated to include the bureaucrat. The American soldier – clean, well-dressed, and wealthy – was exemplary of multiple trappings of power: physical displays of masculine strength and skill combined with economic power and status that Newfoundland men did not have. That these distinctions are still relevant for some was reflected, for example, during Harmon Field Day and at the local club on the night of this military commemoration.

Harmon Field Day

My friend Joan and I headed to the old air field on Harmon Field Day, where the celebration of 'the carefree days' was in full swing. Hot dogs and ice cream were for sale on the grassy fields where young children played organized games. Joan and I toured the planes on display with her son, David, who has always wanted to be a Royal Canadian Mounted

Police (RCMP) officer or a soldier and was excited by the opportunity to talk to these young men in uniform. Each plane bore a description that listed the number of soldiers it could carry, the number of bombs it had dropped, and the various armed conflicts in which it had been deployed. There were considerably more men and children who crowded around the pilots stationed by their F15 and F16 jets. David listened as one man explained how they loaded the bombs that they dropped on 'Joe Iraqi' during Operation Desert Storm in the Gulf War. Pilots stationed around a plane called 'The Mad Bolshevik' recounted the amount of training they required to fly various jets as well as the perks that came with the jobs. When one man compared them to Tom Cruise in the film *Top Gun*, the pilot joked, 'Yeah, we're always competing with each other – all the time – but there's plenty of women to go around.'

That evening my friend Debra and I met at the Manhattan, a cavernous tavern that attracts men and women of all ages from town and outlying communities to listen to live bands play 'Newfie jigs' and country and western music. There, shots of liquor are accompanied by equal amounts of mix and the patron who asks for wine quickly marks herself as being from the mainland. On that particular evening, however, the bar was filled with 'outsiders,' especially men in American and Canadian military uniforms who strutted across the floor, patting women like myself on the head.

Raymond, Debra's brother, is a single, twenty-eight-year-old woodcutter who – in his own estimation – is moderately successful in attracting women on Saturday nights. But 'I don't stand a chance with the women tonight!' he quipped. His insight led us into one of many conversations regarding the hierarchies of heterosexual mating and dating that operated in town, the rules of which were dependent on the social status of the parties involved. Hierarchical distinctions were expressed in varied combinations in which education and occupation, place and family of birth, musical tastes (country and western versus pop rock), and clothing and hairstyles figured prominently. Raymond would not even bother himself to approach the few mainland women present, who, in his view, were 'snobs' and distinguishable by their streaked blond bobs, preppy shorts, and glowing tans.

The expression of masculine identities through military power is evidenced by the number of young men who seek careers in the Canadian armed forces and the (RCMP) and through annual commemorations of Newfoundland's participation in the First World War. Ironically, perhaps, Canada Day in Stephenville (as elsewhere in the province) begins with an annual commemoration which evokes the brief era of Newfoundland's independence. In a ceremony at the cenotaph, wreaths are laid to honour the memory of the Newfoundland regiment that was virtually annihilated at Beaumont-Hummel in 1916. The Canadian Legion hosts a luncheon to follow the ceremony. A large memorial at the far side of this relatively opulent hall displays photos of Newfoundland soldiers, many now deceased and some killed in action during both world wars and the Korean War. Legionnaires are happy to recount moments of glory, tragic deaths, and the friendships and kin networks which connect the diners in the room to the hero depicted on the wall.

Moreover, the expression of a latent national identity surfaced on several occasions during the summer in Bay St George, notably in the portrayal of Joey Smallwood and the Confederation battle in the play 'The Only Living Father.' Some residents in Bay St George, as elsewhere, had preferred either to join the United States or to remain tied to Great Britain, and this was noted in the performance and greeted with commentary by the audience.

Military events are the most dramatic indicators that public space in Stephenville is gendered insofar as it reflects the intersection of military power and dominant constructions of masculinity. Yet the participation of women in community life suggests that the formation of a women's council within a domestic space does not simply reflect the expression of a feminine opposition – located in the private domain. Women's roles as mothers, caregivers, subsistence workers, and, more recently, paid workers embrace both domains. Moreover, by 1985, gendered roles had shifted across this changing rural and urban landscape. Women have absorbed this history of shifting gender roles in such a way that numerous contradictions between female power and dependence pervade everyday life and provoke ambiguous cultural interpretations of 'womanly' behaviour (Abu-Lughod, 1989). These transformations structure the experiences of women and the context in which local feminist activism was both formed and implemented over the last ten years.

By the time the Women's Council was formed in 1985, this history was manifested in the multiple meanings of home and the composite character of families and gender roles subsumed within it. In the next chapter, by exploring the reciprocities and networks in which women have been involved, I assess the way activists created what they perceived to be a common basis for the expression of local feminism in its earliest years.

CHAPTER THREE

Re-creating Home: The Local Construction of Feminist Practice

I was working on the peninsula for the federal government doing work programs and projects to train women for the labour force and I discovered that these courses had little meaning to them. So I would put on my own workshops to talk about all aspects of their lives and I would hear quite horrible stories about women's lives. They certainly had no power, even in the family, in the community, and I started to feel the work I was doing was really useless. (Joyce, coordinator, Bay St George Women's Council, 1986–96)

By the time the Women's Council was formed in 1985, women's participation in the paid workforce was on the rise, particularly in the public sector as nurses, social workers, teachers, and white-collar staff. And by this time Stephenville had emerged as a commercial and service sector for the entire southwest coast, having benefited from the extensive infrastructure which the American military had left behind. The uneven character of the local economy was manifested in high rates of unemployment, particularly in rural communities, and a recognition of economic and social differences between women informed the character of the Women's Council and the insights of its founders, as Joyce (quoted above) conveys. In these circumstances, there was debate among the 'founding mothers' regarding the kind of social space they sought to create. Since they chose to house their council within a home-like setting, what did a 'domestic' setting offer to area women and to grassroots activism?

On the one hand, it is not uncommon for North American women to refashion 'home' or domestic settings as the spatial and ideological basis for the expression of a distinct feminist culture (Martin and Mohanty, 1986:192) These spaces foster the creation of utopian visions, alternate political practices, and woman-centred consciousness by drawing upon women's work and celebrating feminine identities (Echols, 1983: passim; Popkin, 1990:198).

On the other hand, as critics have pointed out, the creation of such 'home-like solidarities' (Ginsburg and Tsing, 1990:8) calls into question two enduring concerns within feminism. The expansion of feminist analysis from a women-centred focus to a consideration of the relations of difference – regional, class, and ethnic relations, for example – in which women are situated points to the exclusion of different women from these utopian visions, a topic I introduce here but consider more fully in subsequent chapters.

Secondly, the focusing of activism on a home may reproduce essentialist notions of womanhood. How does a grass-roots movement treat 'women' as a social and political basis for collective and individual action without reproducing gender essentialism? Does the association of women with 'home' convey that women are naturally associated with particular behaviours, cognitive processes, practices, and emotions (Alcoff, 1988) which are gendered as feminine and attached to stereotyped images of domestic life?

I suggest that in Bay St George the hegemony of a masculine public and a feminine private intersects with the expression of Newfoundland identities and socially embedded labour (paid and unpaid) to make this 'home' both widely accessible and locally meaningful. In other words, it is the relative, overlapping, and locally meaningful character of 'home' and the social relations subsumed within it that renders this space both comfortable and provocative.

As I have suggested, 'home' and 'community' are locally meaningful terms which give meaning to the material contexts in which women's work and reciprocities are embedded. Spheres of family, workplace, and community constitute key discursive arenas through which women's identities and social relations are reproduced; these social spaces form the loci for their evaluation of and response to daily crises and specific struggles (Parr, 1990:9).

It is noteworthy that many founding mothers of the council were engaged in paid work, and yet a substantial component of feminist organizing in the early years drew upon activities associated with the unpaid domestic sphere and the historical context of mothering. It is the intersection of paid and unpaid domains that forms the basis for activism and the character of local activism, as subsequent chapters illustrate.

This chapter begins my examination of the significance of home as a site for activism and the expression of feminist, feminine, and Newfoundland identities. I focus on the way social labour, particularly women's unpaid domestic work and the context of mothering, intersects with key elements of feminist practice – consciousness raising, reciprocities, and reproductive rights – to show how feminist issues such as peace and a pro-choice position on abortion were locally meaningful.

Specifically, I show how the Women's Council creates a feminist home by transforming key symbols and social practices that comprise women's experiences and social identities which derive from the domestic arena. 'Kin work' (di Leonardo, 1987:440) and the female-centred networks in which labour is embedded integrates feminist discourse into everyday life at the centre and is translated into explicitly feminist practice.

The personal narratives that are integrated here show how women contest distinct configurations of power and reinterpret personal experiences within this feminist domain. At the same time, they expose the way women internalize and contest local constructions of femininity which are shaped by institutional and normative structures – notably, church, family, and community. Feminine identities intersect within one's location as a resident of Bay St George and as members of a feminist organization to create affinities and disagreement with neighbours, kin, and the values and practices that are locally espoused

The Formation of the Bay St George Women's Council

In the early 1980s Joyce, one of the founding mothers of the Bay St George Women's Council, was frustrated by the limitations of her work as an employment counsellor. Along with twenty or more women, she took up the 'challenge' from feminists in Corner Brook to form a Women's Council in Stephenville in 1985. A meeting organized at the local college drew a crowd of women, twelve of whom became 'founding mothers.' Many of these women were public-sector employees, who had gained knowledge of, and access to, the private lives of area women and the domains of power within government.

Some of these women worked within a bureaucratic apparatus in which particular experiences, including addictions, lack of education, child neglect, and poverty, were categorized into discrete 'problems' (Smith, 1990:15). As counsellors, social workers, and teachers, these front-line workers came to recognize the intersection of these problems in women's lives and sought to establish an organization that would embrace an integrative perspective and develop services for experiences that had not yet been locally named or recognized. At the same time, these women brought with them personal crises, childhood memories, and a nascent understanding of feminist practice and gender inequalities. Their experiences, combined with women's historical roles in the family, were central in shaping the character of local feminism.

Drawing on their own skills and networks, as well as lessons from feminists across the province, the council 'hammered out' what it now calls a 'feminist vision,' one that combined critical activism with a sensitivity to the particular problems, relationships, and values that comprise local experiences. 'Equality,' 'Peace,' and 'Justice' are the key components of their 'feminist principles,' which, they argue, cannot be attained without the empowerment of women and the redistribution of power this process would inevitably engender. Firmly rooted in Enlightenment traditions, local feminists view 'choice' as a key manifestation of female agency which can be acheived only through a balance of collective action and individual realization. The question that concerned the founding mothers, was 'how these ideas were to be put into action.

The scope of their vision included a structured organization through which members could formally interact with local residents and institutional representatives, and a social space that would permit the self-conscious construction and expression of an alternate set of practices, values, and feminist identities. Although membership vacilates from 140 to 360 members, the Bay St George Women's Council, as noted earlier, is formally operated by a twelve-member executive board and a paid executive director who meet monthly and make most decisions by consensus. The number of participants is considerably widened through the operation of the Women's Centre and the involvement of council members in numerous local organizations and institutions.

The formation of the Women's Council in 1985 was quickly followed by the establishment of the Women's Centre, a decision that provoked one of the first debates in local feminist history. Members sought a place that would embody the character of feminism in Bay St George and where women's experiences could be shared. A few women favoured a small office space on the main street 'in town' to depict an organization of 'professional' women; others preferred a five-room apartment situated above a store. Joyce explains that she wanted to create a less hierarchical environment than the office she used as an employment counsellor:

> When women would come to my office I always felt like I didn't want to have chairs there and people waiting to see 'Joyce Hancock.' I wanted them to feel they were coming to see Joyce. But I felt a centre should be a place women felt they should own. It should be like a sense of community, like a women's community. I remember when we were looking for a place to have the centre and there were some women who wanted to have an office. But a few of us went to this dirty, filthy, old apartment on top of a store and some described that what they saw beyond the dirt and beyond the grease and the stinky toilet and beer bottles was what we could do with it. And I said, 'Oh – there's a kitchen where we could bake, and there's room where someone might work, and you could make that into a toyroom.' We just didn't picture a women's centre being an office.
>
> We scrubbed the toilet and we made curtains. We had a 'shower' so we could give dishes to ourselves, and as time went on, we got women on the Cape [Cape St George] to make quilts and donate them. And that atmosphere – it wasn't orchestrated – I think it was a part of our vision of the centre. That any woman who came in off the street could say, 'That's the women's centre and it has to be comfortable for me.' And no matter who's here, you feel a sense of home.

The Women's Centre

Several years after its formation, the Women's Council purchased a larger, four-bedroom home which contained a basement apartment that could serve as a women's shelter. The council is now housed within a domestic setting that seems to recognize, by its very design, the history that most area women share. Indeed, in a region where women's employment can be infrequent or temporary, the domestic context is perhaps the only setting in which women are guaranteed to have some experience. It is within this social context that the ideas of feminist practice and alternate visions unfold through female-centred networks and socially embedded reciprocities.

A large television and quilt-covered sofas create a comfortable space in the living room where most meetings are held. Quilts and white-lace curtains sewn and donated by francophone women from 'the Cape' convey a well-cared-for domestic space which is embellished by symbols of feminist culture. A poster of Nellie McClung hangs upon one wall, and a poster of a peace dove on another. Assorted newsletters, from the National Action Committee and provincial organizations, and reports are scattered on coffee tables. A large feminist symbol adorns a banner over the long wooden dinner table which faces an open, well-stocked kitchen.

Four offices and a 'resource library' are located in the four rooms (former bedrooms) which are tucked away at the back of the house. These rear rooms are joined by a hallway which is decorated with a wall-sized tree from whose branches are found a hundred or more feminist symbols, each commemorating, by name, one or several people who have made some contribution to the feminist movement through their involvement in the centre and council. Surrounding the tree are clusters of photos, carefully labelled, depicting various dinners, celebrations, demonstrations, and training sessions in Ottawa, Stephenville, St John's, and elsewhere.

And yet 'home' is a context that inspires ambivalence: comfort and conflict are themes that are replayed in many interviews I conducted with council members, including Dora, a founding mother and one of the most senior council members whose experiences and responsibilities largely unfolded within a domestic setting. Listen to Dora, to appreciate how the creation of a local feminist space is informed by her understanding of home as a place where one's relationships and personal history are embedded.

Dora: 'Some women won't say boo – but I never kept my mouth shut!'

Dora is a sixty-year-old mother of five who, when her children entered adolescence, returned to the paid workforce as a fish-plant worker, a store clerk, and a 'respite worker' at the halfway house for ex-prison inmates. Much of her story, however, focuses on the experiences that preceded her entry into the paid workforce. Normative expectations of womanly behaviour and a gender division of labour combined to inhibit her autonomy, to narrow the range of choices available to her and to confine her to a caregiving role. Dora suggests that girls were brought up to be subservient to boys and men through a gender division of labour within households that were structured by the demands of migrant work.

> I was born in Deer Lake which was a company town; it had the power plant for Bowaters and everyone was involved in the same operations; my dad worked in the woods, others worked on the plant. Dad was away for weeks at a time, from spring until winter – then home for three or four months. He didn't get UI [unemployment insurance] then. We were never hungry, but there were times when there wasn't a lot to eat. We bought supplies and charged them to the store to last the winter. My parents pushed me on into school, but other parents would say, 'What do ya need school for, you're only going to get married.' They had no use for it, not like today.
>
> In our first house, there was no running water. My brother and Dad got the wood, but I can tell you all about chores. I had to do the ironing, scrub floors on Saturday, do dishes. When I was eleven, my brother was only sixteen months and my mom had the twins and I was the oldest girl. The males in my family were tended on hand and foot! We got their dinner, served their tea, ironed their shirts. I really resented that. Mom and I talk about it now and she knows how I feel – she feels different now too, but then that was the right way to rear a family. The men were always going away and when they were home everybody would give them a free ride. I always resented having to look after my brothers. It's not 'cause they couldn't do it. My brother now is a better housekeeper than me! It was just

> taken for granted. I had more chores, 'cause there were more of them. I had to do all the dishes, whereas the boys could share bringing in the wood ...
>
> I remember I wanted to join the Armed Forces and Mom and me, we had really big fights about that – you have to remember it was during the Korean conflict, and she thought it would be dangerous. I don't know why the Armed forces, it was something I got on my mind; in Deer Lake, we had a lot of men doing it, or maybe it was my brothers – I wanted to learn to give them a big smack! [She laughs.] We had big fights home; we're a real family of argument.

Dora worked as a clerk for the American air-force base until pregnancy compelled her to quit and marry John, whom she had met on base. She describes how his employment shaped the terms of her own domestic work and the community context in which she was expected to raise her children. Her husband worked from the late 1960s to the late 1970s, in plumbing and construction, and he was away from home for long stretches of time, living elsewhere on the island and in Nova Scotia and Alberta. Dora says: 'I never minded my husband being away. There was no time to sit and brood and there were advantages – I had more control over my home. There were no disagreements over decisions. I got used to that. When he returned, everything was all upset, all hectic and you knew he was only there a short while and people would all come in to visit. You learned to make your own decisions and take responsibility and when the kids would ask "Mom can I do this?" he would feel left out.'

They moved as a family to a rural community some two hundred kilometres away in 1960, when jobs were few in Stephenville. John found work in the woods there. Dora notes how women's practices within this rural community shaped her experiences as mother and wife and her performance was evaluated by local standards of femininity:

> I hated —. It's beautiful – but I hated it. It is the most male-dominated place I'd ever been in! You see, I'd been into my own home and I had to live with that behaviour growing up. I was trying to get out of that kind of dominated home; but I was pushed back in there in —. There was pressure to keep a super clean house, pressure to get your husband

> everything from dinner to tea. I hate housework and you couldn't even talk about that! Men drank when they felt like it – you weren't supposed to open your mouth ... some of us have come a long way!
>
> I always spoke my mind and I was known there as 'the bitch.' I resented doing things 'cause of where I was at, and what was expected. Neighbours were very judgmental and everyone knew everything. If John and I had a big fight, everyone knew! But I never kept my mouth shut, not like other women there, that's what they do. Some women won't say boo. Right through my generation, we still have ideas about what's male and female. Now, we got to rear our children differently.

Dora emphasizes the discrepancy between her own character and the feminine norms that silenced and judged her. These norms were enforced through the gaze of neighbours and their persistent definition of feminine expectations, which imposed upon her a subvervient role that seemed to contradict her own assertive personality and her will. Like other women her age with whom I spoke, Dora enjoyed the increased friendships and personal satisfaction that paid work granted, in spite of its regimes and the additional demands it placed on her time, which included caring for a son with cerebral palsy.

Dora is aware that most of her life at home and in workplaces has been devoted in some way to caring for and communicating with other people. These activities have engendered in her character traits that make her very diffrent from her husband, a very quiet, 'private' man. She values his manual skills immensely but sighs that he views the display of 'emotions' as 'womanly' and, therefore, unacceptable behaviour for a man. Dora recalls her decision to get involved with the Women's Council just when her son was placed in a group home and her husband's illness, which kept her home, left her with time to reflect.

> I realized I had lost my individuality. I had no choices. It seemed that all my life all the choices had already been made. I was somebody's wife, somebody's daughter. Everybody knew me around town, but only as John's wife. I was searching for something for myself. I was feeling guilty about leaving George in the group home. He demanded my whole attention for twenty years. I didn't want an organization that was the offspring of men like the Lionesses. I wanted something for women. And

> I was really concerned about pornography and the peace issues ... Everybody said, 'now you'll be burning your bra!' – but I'm not radical. You have to realize my generation, women weren't always valued. I'm a feminist if it's a point of equality but I don't put men down. We created a nice atmosphere there – it really felt like home.

By attending the initial meeting to form a Women's Council, Dora sought a place where the value she placed on her work and social contributions would be recognized. Relations of caring, female-centred, and domestic networks have comprised social relationships in Dora's life and inform her sense of identity. The Women's Council incorporates and celebrates the skills that women's historical roles have engendered. But these roles are also transformed by the context of feminist organizing.

Bridging Home and Community: Social Labour

The centre conveys the spirit of a home, not just in appearance, but in the use of women's work (some of it paid) and the female-centred social networks that are necessary to maintain it. Like any home, it had to be tidied by the unpaid efforts of regular visitors or hired workers, both of whom gained satisfaction from having a role that draws on their own skills. As di Leonardo demonstrates, an extensive amount of women's unpaid work is focused on maintaining and ritually celebrating kin ties between households (di Leonardo, 1987:442). This work draws women into female-centred networks and provides them with some autonomy as well as emotional fulfilment. In a similar vein, the Women's Council draws on the unpaid work of area women. In so doing, it gives political meaning to social practices which historically surround kin work, thereby transforming women's kin work into political activity.

Domestic work in the Women's Centre is a necessary form of household maintenance which integrates area women with each other and incorporates feminist discourse into everyday activity. On a daily and weekly basis, dishes must be washed, lunches prepared, groceries bought, and floors swept. Council members peruse the weekly advertisements for sales on toilet paper and photocopy paper; they compare prices and buy in bulk when possible. The fridge is well stocked with lunch foods, desserts, and juices for whenever children might be around. Although the job of household management is often assumed by women who are paid to work at the centre, it passes to a core group of volunteers when money for paid workers is not available. The more arduous task of cleaning the entire house, including vacuuming, floor and bathroom washing, in both the centre and the basement shelter, takes one day every few weeks. A few women focus on this job, for which they are paid if money is available; if there is no money, they do the work on a volunteer basis.

Household maintenance, moreover, requires sporadic and seasonal outside work such as fence repair, extensive snow shovelling, lawn mowing, and painting. A few women at the centre are particularly skilled at these kinds of work; at other times, men who are part of the social network of the women, particularly those who are unemployed, are paid for particular skilled work, such as installing locks, plumbing, and carpentry. The net effect is the creation of a home that has the feel of being lived in, used, and cleaned throughout the week, like any home.

Cultural traditions and domestic activities that historically have comprised women's domestic work are reshaped to embrace a public domain within terms set by council members. Residents are invited to numerous dinners and parties; seasonal celebrations such as Thanksgiving, Easter, and Christmas are acknowledged with a dinner. These celebrations are devoid of religious overtones; rather, the traditional religious occasion seems to provide the social context for the display of feminist hospitality under what appears to be politically neutral circumstances. In 1993, for example, an Easter dinner followed the work of compiling the quarterly newsletter. There is also a yearly Christmas party in which area residents fill the entire house for an elaborate meal. On these occasions, continuity of women's roles is most apparent in the amount and variety of work that underlies the success of centre activities, such as the production of the newsletter and the dinners. During the newsletter compilation/Easter dinner, I counted at least sixty hours of work, shared by ten or more women, apart from the actual writing of the articles. The Christmas party took at least eighty woman-hours of actual preparation, spread over three days.

Just as women's household work includes childcare, so, too, is this facilitated at the Women's Centre, which is well stocked with children's videos and numerous toys and games and has a large playroom in the basement. On any given day, it is common to see a child or two playing downstairs or joining us at lunch while their mothers or caregivers pass by to visit or perform a particular task. The celebration of family life is implicit in the way children are easily integrated into the deadline work of compiling a newsletter, for example, by re-arranging the living room to allow them to watch a video. At the same time, the family as an institution, and its concomitant ideal form, are challenged by the recognition of the diverse family forms that are represented here. At Easter, several women arrived with children in tow. Some are single mothers; two others, one of whom works in the evening, bring their children along while husbands work; another babysits two children while their parents are at work.

Domestic work and the gender division of labour from which it stems is also channelled into explicitly feminist and political activity. The maintenance of a traditional gender division of labour is exemplified in a 'white ribbon campaign' which takes place on 6 December, in commemoration of the 'Montreal Massacre' when a man shot fourteen female engineering students. During that week, several volunteers took up to sixteen hours each buying, cutting, and pinning over 250 purple and white ribbons which were to be distributed in the local mall and at the college. A few men volunteered to sit at a booth in the mall for a few days to hand out white ribbons to men. While some applauded the volunteer efforts of these men, others pointed out that it reinforced traditional images whereby men gain public recognition in passing out the ribbons and announcing their support, while the immense work that went into making the ribbons remains the hidden work of women. The following year, the council changed this practice and the men made their own ribbons.

The informal atmosphere lends itself to extensive and diverse discussion in which feminist perspectives are injected between a laugh and a story. At Easter, for example, a few women complained that the unemployment insurance and GST cheques were late. Mary, a single mother, complained, 'Never mind chocolate bunnies, I can't even afford groceries – there'll be a riot at the Post Office!' Stereotypes of single mothers, for example, are challenged through rowdy joking and running commentaries on the sexist comments made by local male community leaders. 'Safe sex' is a popular topic. How to broach this topic before passion overcomes reason? 'Hang a condom around your neck – then he'll get the message!' Attempts to educate or raise the awareness of women are rarely raised in lecture format. Rather, there seem to be ongoing discussions regarding sexuality, health, and political issues in which women, usually engaged in some other activity, are encouraged to form opinions. More controversial, perhaps, are playful attempts to talk about female sexuality in a way that highlights female pleasure. Women are encouraged to educate themselves about their bodies, and there are books available in their resource room.

Female-Centred Networks and Community Reciprocities

The everyday organization of council activities is informed by local configurations of work, reciprocity, and the proximity of residents in a semi-rural context. Like the communities that make up the region, the council is a permeable entity that connects area women in diverse ways. Feminist practice unfolds in a local context in which women live, work, and socialize as residents, daughters, workers, and wives. The council is embedded in local reciprocities through informal networks, the structure of the local economy, and the local labour market. In this way, the council gains access to important social and material resources, which are produced and exchanged in exclusive spheres and mediated through local mechanisms of power.

Many items in the centre, such as furniture, televisions, a VCR, and, occasionally, food are donated by area residents, which indicates the resourcefulness of council members and their reliance on informal networks and face-to-face exchange. This became clear to me soon after I found my apartment on base. I received a couch, a television, a comfortable double bed, a toaster, and curtains from five of the first women I met. At the end of my stay I redistributed the items I had received. One council member is noted for her resourceful skills and ability to collect donations from assorted commercial establishments. Joyce readily called upon family members to transmit messages or take a friend's child for the night. Anna, another part-time worker, would occasionally bring her mother to town 'from the Cape' to shop and to help out at the centre by making cakes. Indeed, a few francophone women from 'the Cape,' who are particularly skilled in sewing, knitting and quilting, are informally reimbursed for their crafts which are often presented as gifts to council visitors and participants.

Occasionally, council members hold a noon-hour dinner which features 'traditional' Newfoundland dishes. On these occasions, Jane fried the baloney, which she served with baked potatoes, pickled beets, and mustard. More elaborate 'Newfoundland dinners,' which feature turnip, potatoes, carrots, greens boiled in salt beef, and peas and partridgeberry puddings, were served for the occasional guest and visitor. On one occasion, scrunchions and 'doughb'ys'[1] were added, in this case, to create authenticity for the visiting anthropologist. A few members who have access to male family members provide moose meat for moose stew, which is a rather coveted item given the limited number of hunting licences permitted each year.

The council regularly employs one to three part-time and full-time workers through contract arrangements with federal and provincial departments such as Health and Welfare Canada, as well as make-work projects through Social Services and the Canada Employment Centre. These women do the bookeeping, payroll, and letter-writing while also coordinating various training projects for local women, usually one or two per year. Arrangements with the local college, and assorted student-training placements, introduce young women to the Women's Council and feminist activism. Numerous council members became involved with the centre, as students, through these educational initiatives.

The Women's Centre receives many residents who come on a one-time or regular basis to use the council's services. These include access to information on health, sexuality, training, and abuse, through limited counselling and a resource library. The Women's shelter, which is located in the basement-level apartment, houses women and their children, who, for numerous reasons, require temporary and relatively safe residence.[2] Upon settling down in the shelter, I was informed that they were accustomed to a woman like me, having provided similar residence to a woman writer who needed a place to stay.

The outside 'community' then, enters this feminist domain both at the invitation of the council and through the work and other outside experiences that various members and visitors bring with them. At dinners and over more informal lunches, women pass through on a break from work or meetings. Social workers, counsellors, nurses, and clergy bring the experiences of other women with them and the knowledge of decisions made within local institutions. Women who are not council members but need personal counselling or information, or are considered to have access to information, are often contacted through these informal networks.

For women living in more remote communities, access to the council, the centre, and its resources is dependent upon transportation, hazardous weather conditions, and the cooperation of family members. Council members attempt to address this through extensive 'out-reach,' such as organizing discussions in nearby schools and community halls and providing ad hoc or planned transportation. Those members who do not actively participate through the board or subcommitties are kept informed of local, national, and occasionally international women's issues through a quarterly newsletter.

A female-centred collectivity is created through a series of networks that are rooted in family, kin relations and locality. I often reeled in confusion when Debra, long a part-time worker, recalled the intimate histories of this or that family. 'Is he still with the Mrs?' ... 'Did she get that job?' ... 'Did so-and-so, Mary's cousin, leave her husband? leave Stephenville? leave Newfoundland?' On a journey with me to the community in which she was raised on the Port au Port peninsula, Kate, a single mother, led me to several homes where conversation inevitably turned towards the location and circumstances of those living around the bay or in Alberta. It is the networks that emanate from families, the personal knowledge of area women and particular communities, that form a crucial component to grass-roots organizing and 'consciousness-raising.' These are the key features of local feminist activism and of the means through which women's experiences were transformed into local feminist issues. What were the issues that occupied the council in its earliest years?

Consciousness Raising: 'It isn't fair that I had to have all those children'

The influence of the broader 'Second Wave Women's Movement' on local activism is reflected in the emphasis on 'consciousness raising,' which forms an integral component of the council's activities. Embodied in the time-worn phrase 'the personal is political,' consciousness-raising attempts to bridge the social and political divide in contemporary Western culture, which severs personal experience from systemic relations of power. By articulating and reflecting upon personal experiences, women are encouraged to recognize their commonality and the systemic relations of power which shape their choices and life experience (Adamson, 1988:204). The local practice of consciousness-raising was exemplified to me in numerous ways which underscore the range of a process that might begin with 'giving voice' and ideally coalesces into political activism. For some area women, the act of narrating experience, of centring themselves in a personal account, is a satisfying and provocative act. This is exemplified in the presentation of 'Our Lives Our Issues,' a performance written by 'Estasy,' a feminist trio, that was commissioned by the council and presented throughout the Bay St George region to celebrate and communicate the experiences of 'senior' women in Bay St George. The show not only depicted a local 'herstory' but encouraged women in small groups to recount personal experiences.

The performance typified projects initiated by the Bay St George Women's Council to promote the sharing of experiences by area women and provide a social context to encourage women's participation, raise female consciousness, and foster the exchange of information. The show was presented in twelve communities in the region through a myriad of sponsorships. It was the featured performance for Community Education Initiatives Day in Port au Port East. The Women's Institute in St George's hosted the performance at the seniors' club across the bay and female inmates enjoyed the show in the small chapel of the Stephenville Correctional Centre. The performance depicts an important continuity in the lives of area women, namely, their shared experiences as primary caregivers in the social reproduction of the family-based household.

I recall accompanying Estasy members one rainy Saturday evening in May to the Francophone Association Centre. Situated along the main road at the tip of the Port au Port peninsula, the centre was sheltered from the sea by clumps of tuckamore and rock. We gathered in the main hall, which was sparsely furnished with stackable chairs, a small stage, a large video screen, and a piano. Miniature woodcarvings of lobster traps, dorys, and fishing stages made by a local artist decorated the room; walls were covered with photos of residents and the names of those who contributed to the Francophone Association through their volunteer efforts.

That evening, tea and cake were served for the audience and performers and conversation moved to and fro: from rowdy joking to weightier reflections on local politics. The show had evoked memories for one member of the audience, Mary, a sixty-year-old widow, whose own life mirrored one of the scenes. Mary distinguished her life from that of women today by recounting her own 'ignorance' and the difficulties of raising sixteen children with a drunken husband whose work in the woods kept him away from home for months at a time: 'I had sixteen children myself. Things were so different back then – we knew nothing about sex or pregnancy. The first time, I didn't know I was pregnant. I didn't know I was having a baby or that it would come out of me like that. I just thought I was getting heavy. I know it's hard to believe. I know I sound stupid. When I was growing up it was all a big secret. Our parents would send us away when the new baby was coming, and when we came home, there it would be, a new baby. They told us that the witch had brought it.' Mary went on to criticize both her husband and the Catholic Church for preventing her from using birth control. She recalled how her 'contrary' husband would blame her for the pregnancies yet refuse to sign the papers that would permit her to take birth control.

> My husband was not a nice man. He was a drunk, even when I first married him. He never helped with the housework or the babies. He was always on a drunk – but he wasn't home anyway; he'd go cutting wood for Bowaters in Deer Lake and he'd be gone for months – all summer long. But he was usually drunk when he was home. He was a cross man. He never hit me, but he called me some awful names, over and over. Believe you me, I know what it's like to have tea in my face. I know what it's like to have a cup of soup thrown at me ...
>
> I heard about the pill in the late '60s, but I was already pregnant with my fourteenth child. But back then, my husband had to sign a paper to let me take it, and he wouldn't sign – he said I was supposed to have babies, I wasn't supposed to prevent pregnancy.

When Mary's husband became ill and died just after the birth of her sixteenth child, she found herself widowed at age forty-five, with a newborn and ten children still living at home: 'I don't know how I got by, especially for those first six weeks before I got welfare. I'd go around to people's houses doing little jobs, getting flour here and sugar there ... I managed, I got by. But it isn't fair that I had to have all those children. It isn't fair that I had to go through a life like that. Now women get their tubes tied and I would have too, if I could have ... I warn my daughters. "If he starts drinkin' by the first baby, get out fast! Because its not going to stop, it'll only get worse."'

In Mary's narrative, the demands of migrant work, the vagaries of personal circumstance and the prescriptions of the church combine to create 'unfairness.' At the same time, she is personally denigrated through the specific behaviour of her husband who, in exercising his privilege as father and household head, translates Catholic doctrine into lived experience and reproduces the male dominance accorded to him. Mary's criticism of the church and her husband is echoed by other older women who produced large families. According to Margaret, a sixty-five-year-old mother of ten children,

> It wasn't my choice to have a lot of children. I kept getting pregnant. I used to burn through them. Then, after I had one, we'd wait six weeks before having sex. I didn't want to get pregnant, but I didn't use birth control. My husband was a faithful churchgoer and that was the message in the church: 'Go forth and multiply.' I wouldn't want a big family now – they get no love and attention when they're born a year apart ...
>
> I heard about the pill five years after I was married. After my tenth child, I went on the pill, but they say you shouldn't stay on it for health reasons and I got pregnant again. I was devastated! I was thirty-six years old and I said, 'no God no!.' I'd been pregnant from nineteen to thirty-seven – one year apart. I lived in maternity clothes! Your body doesn't get back into shape – I was always just one shape.
>
> Abortion is still not an option, not in Catholic families, we're steeped into it. I find with the Catholic church, you're always frightened to death. Something is always going to happen to you, and you're always going to hell; it's frightening!

Performances such as 'Our Lives Our Issues' provoked stories and commentaries from women like Mary and Margaret and form an important contrast to more common and celebrated depictions of 'the past' that tend to emphasize mutual dependence between husband and wife. Women who followed church prescriptions and produced children within marriage were rewarded with reverence, not choices – yet, in spite of their critical perspective towards the church, both Mary and Margaret spoke fondly and proudly not only of their children but of motherhood. For example, Margaret emphasized the importance of her children in helping her adjust to widowhood: 'When my husband died, I had no insurance, no money, only a disability pension which gave me little to rear seven children still at home. I had to do something because I had the kids. So I went back to school. I was forty-five, I had no confidence, but I did really well into it. And the children were wonderful. When I got home, the house would be clean, supper ready. I couldn't have done it without them. Life was never all that lucky for me, but I got lucky with ten children. They're the best. They got me on a pedestal.'

Today, mothers, especially those who raised large families, are honoured through local histories and the more intimate recollections of younger women who cannot imagine surviving such circumstances. Changes in reproductive practices and a general improvement in living standards have generated among young women a strong sense of difference between their lives and those of their mothers. These changes inform the narratives of younger women who measure their own self-worth and convey what raising a family means to them by comparing themselves to their mothers. At the same time, the institutional power of the Catholic Church and the gender scripts it underwrites continue to inform contemporary constructions of femininity against which women evaluate their own behaviour and life choices.

The Local Expression of Catholic Hegemony

Mom was not subservient, no way – but she let Dad have her morning, noon and night – whenever he pleased!

Joan, age thirty-six, the youngest of nineteen siblings

> I was raised in a family of thirteen ... Mom was a quiet person. I don't remember her very well. Now that I think back, we didn't talk much – I don't think she had time to talk. ... Mom never went to church, but she was a Catholic. There were things you didn't talk about and didn't do. Like, no sex talk in the house – and my mother had so many kids, she'd never talk about taking the pill. That wasn't the right thing to do. The priest was always right and the teacher was always right. (Doreen, age thirty-two)

Stories of large families are common in Bay St George, and senior women, many now deceased, are frequently invoked, almost as founding ancestral figures who are revered for their production of numerous progeny. Mrs G—, now deceased, is renowned for the twenty-two children she bore, and stories of various women producing eighteen or more children are told with pride and great respect. The Marian cult in Catholic doctrine provides women with a female model that symbolizes the positive value placed on motherhood. For example, Patricia, a seventy-year-old widow who was unable to have more than two children owing to the onset of polio, cherishes the symbol of Mary. Figurines of Mary in her various incarnations as mother of Christ and queen of heaven are scattered throughout her living and dining room.

This focus on Mary, which is described by a few senior men 'as excessive,' is rivalled by the commemoration of area priests and recollections of their 'good works.' Senior residents recount the miracles of locally revered priests, like Father Joy, under whom the largest wooden church on the island was built on the Port au Port peninsula. His prayers to St Theresa, it is claimed, induced a rose-scented fragrance through the church and protected workers from injury. Priests are remembered, by name, character, and personal tastes, through commemorations in small museums and in everyday conversations. Older residents recall schooldays punctuated by hourly repetitions of the Hail Mary, recitations of 'The Angelus,' regular visits to the church, and extensive testing on the catechisms and the sacraments.

Reverence and fear towards nuns and priests mark the narratives of many who are ambivalent about the power of the church and its functionaries. In the words of one twenty-eight-year-old woman, 'When the priest came into the classroom it was as if God himself had appeared at the door!' Nuns appeared as independent, culturally superior women who performed good works outside marriage and therefore signified a kind of upward mobility and an alternative feminine model. Young women could aspire to feminine goodness and purity. Several women wanted to enter the convent as children. In their words, nuns were 'more genteel' and more 'high class' in their posture and manners. 'I can still tell a nun from a mile away – its the way she walks; the way she talks, the way she carries herself,' another woman recalls.

In spite of the pervasiveness of Catholicism in marking life passages, many Catholics claim that the church is not important in their lives and many cannot explain the meaning of the liturgy or various symbols. Still, the power of the church is evoked by numerous residents who recall flashes of 'fear' that invariably overcame them when on the verge of breaking Catholic doctrine. Moreover, on a walk through the Catholic church one day, a friend of mine who disclaimed the influence of the church on her thinking stopped in astonishment as we passed the altar. Aware of my secular upbringing, she gasped, 'Glynis, you're not saved!' The realization that I would surely go to hell or purgatory aroused in her a frightened empathy.

That women and men might interpret church doctrine differently was conveyed to me in discussion with a couple who debated the influence of the church on their marriage and their world-views. Loretta recalls her quest to obey church doctrine, in spite of the spirit of the late 1960s, when church influence began to decline and notions of 'free love' and premarital sex became popular. The 'fear' and 'stigma' of a premarital pregnancy combined with the realities of pregnancy to make sex and birth control a 'serious' activity and moral preoccupation. In contrast, her husband recalls 'never giving a moment's thought' to birth control or the religious consequences that might result from his amorous adventures. 'I never believed a word of it,' he exclaimed. 'But Loretta, she was the one who was brainwashed.'

While Catholic residents often attribute the influence of the church to the doctrinal ideas they internalized, the church's important role in shaping life experience is primarily due to its institutional power. This is facilitated by those residents – judges, doctors, social workers, nurses – who exercise *de facto* control over women's bodies. Some of those people support catholic values through their counselling and their implementation of legislation and policy regarding women's health and welfare needs. In this way, interpretations of reproduction continue to shape women's experiences and constrain their choices. As one woman recalls, 'I remember when I went to the doctor for a checkup. It was 1974 – and I discovered I was pregnant. I told the doctor I just could not have this child. I had children. I was divorcing – you know, he just looked at me and laughed! Abortion was simply unmentionable; it wasn't even an option that he was prepared to offer – it was unthinkable' (Maureen, mother of two, age fifty).

Although 'Planned Parenthood' was introduced by the Newfoundland government in 1970, and abortion legalized across the country in 1972, the Catholic Church maintains its ban on abortion. A movement to prevent abortions, driven by the Knights of Columbus, resulted in no abortions being performed on Newfoundland's west coast by 1977 (Benoit, 1990:53). Today, there are still no abortions performed on the west coast of Newfoundland. Rather, women must travel across the island to St John's (a twelve-hour bus ride) or to Halifax. Some doctors in the area are reluctant to sign the necessary papers that permit abortion. Government officials, nurses, and doctors do not always offer abortion as an option when counselling pregnant women. While birth-control products are available and widely used, it is more difficult for young women to obtain them and use them effectively. Some doctors have been known to refuse young women's request for birth control. It is difficult, these women say, to purchase over-the-counter contraception in a region where anonymity is not always achievable.

In the era of the denominational school system, which ended only recently, education was taught in both public and religious schools by public-health nurses. These nurses claimed, however, that conditions were applied in Catholic schools, such as the way in which birth-control devices could be demonstrated. Today, students continue to receive education on human reproduction and birth control. Yet the influence of Catholicism persists. The purchase of contraception by the unmarried signals an a priori, conscious intent to engage in sexual relations, a practice that the church discourages. As the narrative below highlights, Catholic prescriptions and the gender scripts that Catholicism teaches inform local constructions of femininity and an ideology of family against which women measure their own behaviour, choices, and self-worth.

Marina: 'I didn't have feminist ideals, I had feminine ones'

Marina is a mother of two who grew up on the outskirts of Stephenville with four siblings. Her father, a boilermaker, welder, pipefitter, and 'jack-of-all-trades,' worked away from home for much of her childhood. Marina grew up 'surrounded by' her father's brothers and cousins. Her recollections are framed by popular psychological discourses on 'dysfunctional families' and health 'disorders' as well as Catholic ideology. In the latter respect, her story conveys the way Catholic dichotomies of purity and sin coalesce with contemporary images of female beauty to frame the aquisition of femininity as an unattainable quest for perfection which is marred by human weakness and inadequacy. Moreover, feminine ideals seem to reinforce a gender division of labour in which women serve the needs of breadwinning husbands and submit to the erratic display of male dominance by maintaining order.

> My dad's an alcoholic and I'm sure you've heard many tales of that here – This affected me greatly, but not knowingly. The one thing about me in the family system was that I was bold, and if anybody ever said anything to Dad's face, it was me. So, we really didn't get along. And I always lived to hear about it when the next drunk came on. He would never do or say anything about what I'd said when he was sober, but when he was drunk! He wasn't physically abusive, it was very much verbal – really ugly, actually.
>
> Now Mom, she had to make sure everything was just so. For one thing, where Dad was away from home a lot, she had to manage the entire home, the finances, and the hyperness of her children. So it was kind of a crazy set-up. Then, when he was home, he'd be drunk, which could be a fair amount of the time. Mom's role was to divy up our roles and make sure that we were quiet and didn't say anything. She was the monitor. But I don't ever remember them fighting.
>
> You didn't know if Dad would be happy and you were going to get money, or contrary and then rowdy and sort of violent. And every once in a while, he decided he was going to rule the roost. There was a dent in our wall from the time he threw a beer bottle and Mom would not let that be

> fixed. That was her silent way, if anything came up, they wouldn't fight, she'd just point at the wall. My parents were very traditional, especially Mom. She thinks women are women ... and she tends on Dad hand and foot, and always has, and she gets disgruntled when I don't jump up to do something for my kids or Dad.

Adult females after whom Marina modelled herself emerged within a Catholic tradition that was reinforced through her extended-family relations and a denominational education system in which nuns figured as prominent, alternate role models to mothers.

> I went to the Catholic school in — as did almost everyone else. It was very much RC [Roman Catholic]. I don't think I knew what a Protestant was. I'd never seen one. I mean, there was no such thing as anyone having married outside of the religion and that included aunts and uncles. My entire life was surrounded by Catholicism. So, if you were going somewhere on Sunday, you were going to church.
>
> I remember saying at school that I wanted to be a nun; I didn't really want to at the time, but that's what people would want to hear. Then I wanted to be a teacher. I grew up very typical in terms of what women could do. I didn't expect or want anything other than that. I didn't have feminist ideals, I had feminine ones. Even today, that's a struggle for me 'cause the idea of equality of the sexes is so different from my family's thinking.

Marina reflects that her decision to join the convent was both a calling and an attempt to acquire a female identity. Convinced that she was not pretty enough to attract a man, she implies that the convent offered another model of femininity, one that would allow her to achieve feminine self-perfection. The relationship between Catholic notions of purity and cleanliness in the construction of ideal femininity is explicit in Marina's understanding of womanhood.

> Now, as a teenager, I was always an obese child. That's technically true; I'm sixty pounds overweight. Anything to do with weight, I know. I really believe that affected my social life. It had a lot to do with my self image. And when I look at pictures of me now, I think, my God! I wasn't

> unattractive. I was attractive. I thought I was huge! I still have this negative self-image, but I'm surviving better today. I believe personality does make a difference. In terms of a disorder, I think it's more of a mental disorder than an eating one.
>
> I dated the guys nobody else would have anything to do with! [she laughs.] I think I had maybe two dates in school. It's really sad when you think of it – 'cause I got out of school and I entered the convent.
>
> Now, others would just scorn me for saying this – people don't believe me – but I truly was called and I don't mean by a ghost in the night! But it was tugging at me constantly. And I question this all through the years, did I do this 'cause I didn't have any dates? 'Cause men didn't show any interest? But I also had this urge, like I always went to church and it was a whole part of growing up. But when I got to the stage where I wanted to and nobody was telling me I should, there was such a sense of security and goodness and purity and cleansing and it's all tied into that calling.

Marina's struggle to acquire a mature, feminine self is a quest for self-perfection that was interpreted by family members as an act of arrogance: 'My parents, when I talked to them I expected more. They said, "Whatever you choose to do." My grandmother shocked me by saying [she imitates], "Who the hell do you think you're going to be? There are other women in this world who struggle day to day to raise children and do you think you're going to be any holier?" I thought she'd say, "Oh the chosen child!" None of that. Even in her grave I'd like to ask her, "Gramma, why did you feel that way?" – because my whole family was very religious. It was a way of life.'

Sexual desire and service to God are expressed in oppositional terms and symbolized through notions of pollution and purity in Marina's account of her days as a postulant. Her vocation director suggested that she wait for a year before taking further vows.

> I was very interested in men. I had a healthy libido, and today, I'm a very sexual person – it just happens to be with myself. I had a great sense of that part. I didn't suppress anything. But I was a virgin. So, I left high school and went to the presentation house in St John's. But, basically, I wasn't convent material. We had constant counselling sessions and our sessions dealt with my vocation director suggesting that I wasn't mature

> enough. We'd go through the journals that I had to write and she kept pointing out that everything I wrote always led toward children and family. She told me that convent life wasn't enough of a family for me, that I wanted more. I stayed there for a year, as a postulant, but then I went to New Brunswick.
>
> I worked in New Brunswick so I wouldn't have to live at home and deal with all the crap that went on there. It was the most rewarding time for me, but it was also unsatisfying because it forced me to realize that I'd made this decision to join the convent and now I had to rethink it. I had also had a sexual experience, a one-night stand. It frightened me to death, and the only reason I did it was that I wanted to experience it. Sex.
>
> I was working at this nuclear-energy plant and there were – oh, 2000 men ... I think I just came into something, like God, I can be a person. I was surprised at the attention I got for that whole year. I couldn't believe that there was anything good about me to look at, to want to be with.
>
> Then, that year, I went on this promiscuous rampage. So, I exited the convent, and entered, I'm not sure – oh God in heaven – and entered harlot street! I stayed in New Brunswick for six months and went on a rampage. Then I went home. So then, I took all that ugliness – that promiscuity – that I saw as ugly and turned it around and became a good girl and came home. So, home, I entered my Catholic area.

Marina's narrative conveys the importance of Catholicism in structuring gender relations and normative practices, which subsumed sexuality within a prescribed context of social and biological reproduction. Reproduction was structured by relations of family, neighbouring kin, and educational institutions and reinforced by an ideology of family that framed the expression of motherhood. For Marina, 'home' is a Catholic social space which compels her to a certain kind of behaviour. At the same time, Marina has, as I think she recognizes, internalized Catholic values which continue to give profound meaning to her everyday life.

It is noteworthy that the choices laid before her, and that would comprise her adult feminine role, were defined in terms of dependence on men for her sexual, emotional, and personal satisfaction. It is a dependence, however, that Marina absorbs, contradicts, and ultimately rejects. Although her narrative emphasizes that her attainment of adult femininity was achieved by becoming an object of male desire, she also conveys the persistence of an autonomous sexuality, one rooted in the pleasures of self-gratification.

Moreover, Marina recounts with some irony that, after her return to Stephenville, she married G—, an Anglican, whom she had met in a nearby 'club.' Their marriage ended a few years later. Marina recognizes the elusiveness of feminine perfection, which is accentuated by the realities of conjugal relations and familial conflicts. While Catholic values and practices remain embedded in her identity as a mother and a woman, she has found ways to address them in her working life.

Women like Marina describe a change in consciousness or understanding which necessitated a rejection of their earlier values and practices. For example, Andrea, Marina, and Katherine state that, growing up, they had absorbed the negative stereotypes of feminism and the Women's Centre as 'man-hating' and 'radical.' They hesitated to join the centre but changed their minds when they got to know a member or went there because of a particular 'crisis' in their life. For Katherine, however, the formation of a feminist identity meant a rejection of many of the values she had acquired growing up, values rooted in contradictory notions of equality and female submission. Katherine was raised in a home where she was not restricted because she was female and was encouraged and expected to establish a career and get a good education. Her awareness of gender issues was triggered not just by a university education but also by the scandal of sexual abuse in Catholic institutions:

> [Mount Cashel] shocked the hell out of me. It really affected me. We were really religious at home – we had prayers every night and we went to church all through my childhood. I haven't been to church since ... Then I started asking questions. Did a priest become that way because of celibacy? Did the Catholic Church attract sex offenders?
>
> When I came home to Stephenville I got involved in a Women's Centre project on homecare and I didn't have strong feminist beliefs. I never believed I wasn't equal. But instead of just telling me I was unequal, Joyce (the coordinator) had me take part in actitivies. It changed my life – the way I saw culture, where I was. And I would never go back. In a workshop at the centre in 1990, I saw the movie 'Killing Us Softly' and that movie

> changed my life. I was a good Catholic girl in terms of sexuality; I was respectful to men as I was supposed to be. I was demure. I was passive and that's how I thought it should be. I thought I would marry and have children. My life was all mapped out.
>
> When I learned I wasn't equal I was shocked! I was always treated equally at home. My Dad would talk with me, make me form opinions, ask me questions. I had a skidoo. I had to chop trees. I had to help make a bridge [verandah].

The formation of feminist identities often contradicts and challenges locally rooted and hegemonic cultural processes. As residents, neighbours, daughters, and wives, women interact within a larger social context in which feminist values are hardly prized. These contradictions are reflected in the ambivalence of council members in expressing a feminist identity or articulating what they perceive to be radical elements of feminist thought.

The Women's Council consists of women raised in both Catholic and Anglican families, although there are more Catholics. I have focused more on women who were raised in Catholic families because the role of the church was more prominent in their narratives and because of its more expressed policy regarding reproductive issues. Moreover, while a few Anglican women in the council also remark on the influence of religion in their upbringing, they do appear to have integrated these Christian principles into their feminism. I have not, however, systematically considered how these two forms of Christianity might have affected women differently. In conversation with council members, it was noted that gender scripts in Catholicism may be more pervasive in the seasonal, liturgical, and life-cycle rituals in which women participated and hence figure more largely in the minds of women interested in defining sexuality and feminine ideals.

Critical Feminist Issues: Pro-Choice

'Mildred the Midwife' is a character Marina plays who claims, 'when the Eucharist contracts, the baby is ready to come out.' Such malapropisms expose the importance of Catholic ideology to local constructions of femininity. It is within the context of Catholic hegemony and, as

Marina implies, against this context that feminists construct distinct interpretations of sexuality, reproduction, and gender scripts. Just as 'reproductive' issues informed the earliest concerns of Second Wave Women's Movements, so were council members quick to establish a public position on issues surrounding reproduction in an effort to, in their words, 'increase choices available to local women.' For this council, a feminist position is one that recognizes women's rights of choice over their bodies and their reproductive functions, a position in which the use of abortion and birth control figure prominently. To appreciate the perceived 'radical' character of this position, note that only two councils in the province, Bay St George and St John's, articulate a public pro-choice position on abortion.

In spite of considerable debate within the council and dissenting voices among members, the council publicly announced its position and engaged in debate with prominent residents through the local media. The council was aware that this might threaten its relationship with otherwise supportive residents and the Catholic school board. A survey taken by the council in 1986 indicated that more than 60 per cent of those interviewed in the region were clearly not in favour of abortion. The council lost support at this time, and today many women who are otherwise sympathetic to Women's Council initiatives keep a social distance from the organization because of the abortion issue in particular. According to one thirty-eight-year-old woman, 'I don't like [the Women's Council's] stance – they want to make abortion too easy, too accessible, so then women will use it as a form of birth control. The Women's Centre publicizes this issue far too much and they fight for it far too much. I can't support them wholeheartedly for something I strongly disagree agree with.'

While the possibility of abortion is now publicly recognized and legally affirmed, the difficulties of terminating a pregnancy remain. As a St John's health worker put it, the bureaucratic and medical protocol surrounding the procedure renders abortion a difficult option for residents throughout the province. The distance of geography, the expense of travel, and cultural assumptions surrounding reproduction make it even less accessible to many female residents of Bay St George. For example, during the Christmas holidays in 1992, a few council members scurried to find a local doctor who would agree to sign the necessary medical papers for a young woman seeking help from the Women's Centre to terminate her pregnancy. After three refusals, they finally succeeded and she made her way to St John's.

Another event in the council's early history shows how members developed methods to address controversial and locally meaningful issues, to encourage debate, and to turn protest into public celebrations.

Public Displays: Violence, Peace, and Military Power

In the late 1980s, during Harmon Day celebrations, a soldier had bragged to the son of a council member that 'we could blow away the entire west coast of Newfoundland in less than fifteen seconds.' His statement provoked the council to expand its annual commemoration of the bombing of Hiroshima and Nagaski on 6 August by inviting local members of the Canadian Legion to join in its march to the cenotaph. The legionnaires replied by criticizing the council for the 'disrespect' this conveyed to soldiers killed in action. On the evening of the council's march, legionnaires blocked off the road with cars. This prevented the marchers from assembling at the cenotaph and they were forced to conclude their celebration in the local school auditorium.

Although council members recognize their naivety in requesting the cooperation of Legionnaires, they argue that the event was a turning point for the council. It prompted a series of debates in the local media and drew provincial media attention. Now each year on 6 August the Women's Council organizes a peace event – much larger than the earlier parades to the cenotoph – in memory of those civilians killed in the nuclear bombing of Hiroshima and Nagasaki. Besides a march, it includes entertainment at the local school. By 1995, the council had gained enough community support from the town to shut down Main Street for the purposes of the march.

While the controversy over the peace event caused a few tensions between council members and some residents, it transformed the local discourse in which the usual commemorations of war were conveyed. Through the news media, council members emphasized the importance of expanding these commemorations to include the memory of civilians and provoked discussion on the nature of war, peace, and social justice. Moreover, they used the example of war to draw attention to the problem of violence against women and children, in the family, in schools, and in religious institutions, an issue that would increasingly occupy council activities from the late 1980s to the present.

To paraphrase their sentiments: violence is not merely the aberrant behaviour of a few uncontrolled husbands or drunken men, but a state-sanctioned form of social control and domination. There is, as council members put it, 'a fine line' between the commemoration of male bravery and the celebration of militarization. Displays of violence, both state-sanctioned or domestic, are dramatic reminders of male dominance that do not even require the participation of most men to reinforce female dependence or subordination. Whatever female display of violence occurs (and it does) is not sanctioned through such state mechanisms or visions of freedom. The flip-side of such masculine displays is the necessity of male protection, a role that both informs and is reinforced by male authority within the family. In this sense the relationship between intimate and institutional violence was a connection that council members make and that characterize their historical consciousness.

Affinity to 'home' and concern with issues of peace does not reflect a simple identification with a nurturing caring ideal or domestic space. Rather, homes are discursive and social sites of power and of personal struggle where autonomy and dependence coalesce. In this sense, the location of the Women's Council in a domestic setting is subsumed within a hegemonic opposition of male public and female private, but to reduce activism to such an opposition would be to ignore the way council members draw upon and transform socially embedded relations that extend beyond the home and involve the unpaid and paid labour of many, so that activism might take root. To what extent, then, is feminist organizing connected to the production of an oppositional, feminine culture and to the reproduction of essentialist notions of womanhood?

Re-creating Home, Culture, and Identity

Micaela di Leonardo has criticized feminists for drawing on her research to exemplify that there is a singular, homogeneous women's culture which has enduring features. She is concerned that, by reifying practices as 'feminine' and harnessing them to a feminist politics, feminists gloss over the differential experiences of women and reproduce essentialist notions of culture and gender (di Leonardo, 1991:248). It may also confine women to the very space and social roles that women like Dora and Marina struggle to resist.

Thus far, I have focused on the way council members in the early years incorporated practices and identities associated with the domestic arena, reproduction, and feminine roles into their feminist politics. This provided a culturally specific frame for activism to take root, which was hardly surprising given that women were, and are, differently situated in the labour market and given the normative context in which women were historically expected to mother and work. As subsequent chapters show, however, this does not mean that differences between women were not woven into the fabric of local feminist practice, or that women's paid work had little impact on feminist practice (a topic I explore in chapter 6).

By focusing on women's social labour, the networks in which they are embedded, and the context in which gender identities have been constructed, I suggest that the Women's Council became meaningful to residents of Bay St George because it drew on images and roles that had historical resonance: the space formed a locus for rural and urban networks; it formed a starting point for local feminists to enter public debate and to introduce issues that gave centrality to the reproductive sphere and women's experiences in domestic and community life. It also provided a context for critical reflection on the character of gender identities as they are situated in Bay St George and for the expression of Newfoundland identities.

I draw attention to the importance of situating women's identities as feminists, as residents of Bay St George, and as Newfoundlanders because it helps to convey the social and political significance of the Women's Centre: it is rooted in local understandings of place that are not fixed but that provide a locus for talking about, drawing upon, and transforming lived experiences in a way that attends to social and economic problems as gendered issues.

In extending Doreen Massey's analysis of place as a 'particular constellation of relations,' Megan Copes suggests that individuals create a 'progressive sense of identity in place' through the personal constellations of power relations which flow between individuals and households and within relations of production (Copes, 1996:180). This is reflected in the significance that women assign to the Women's Centre. By providing a place, not simply an organization, women can maintain skills they have acquired as mothers, daughters, workers, and wives and feel sufficiently comfortable to consider social and personal change. This is particularly important in a context where women have very uneven participation in the paid workforce.

Martha, the mother of a toddler, joined the centre as a student. Raised in a violent environment where her father regularly beat her mother, Martha recalls how she gradually lost 'the chip on her shoulder' when she became involved at the centre. She describes her first visit to the centre: 'I remember when I first came to the centre. We were in the old centre and there was a big flight of stairs and when I went up, there was Sammy the dog and I said 'this is home' ... When I found the Women's Centre I found myself ... I found my little nook in life. I know wherever I go, I'll always have that as my family ... I've never really left the Centre. I came back and did a lot of volunteer work.'

'Home' is, in Martha's case and others, an imaginary place, an idealized setting that may contradict the actual settings in which they were raised. Home is the site where families and narratives of reproduction – of what raising a family and making a living in Bay St George is and should be – are reproduced. It is also, as the account above conveys, both a context of oppression and a source of female control and identity formation. And yet the relationship between home and place is not just located in the imagination; it is also conveyed through activities at the centre which are often referred to in terms of Newfoundland identity.

Although the composition of the council is always in flux, of the active council members, only 10 per cent have lived off-island for one year or more. Still, council members frequently invoked stereotypes of Newfoundland or contrasted their behaviour and activities with life on the 'mainland' (Canada). This may have been enhanced by my presence, but the notion of Newfoundland distinctness is so commonplace and so much a part of local humour and self-parody that this seems unlikely.

As an outsider, I felt that practices that were associated with Newfoundland and its outport history did contribute to the atmosphere at the centre: certain foods, expressions, and a particular sense of humour were emphasized for me, the anthropologist, perhaps to highlight uniqueness, to celebrate difference, or to test the authenticity of my heritage. A few of my greatest sceptics frequently noted how easily I, a Toronto native, fit into the council and rural Newfoundland. On the one hand, I was unfamiliar with some of the local expressions. I felt awkwardly urban on many occasions and was frequently mocked for my intellectual tendencies and my academic vocabulary.

On the other hand, I love the smell of fried baloney and the fatty taste of turnips, potatoes, and carrots which have been simmered in salt beef. Such smells and the ubiquitous tins of evaporated condensed milk evoked memories of my own childhood. At the same time, my feelings of comfort at the Women's Centre were reinforced by a certain style of communication into which I slipped with great ease. Endless bantering, self-effacing postures, mutual putdowns, and pervasive sarcasm are noted features of Newfoundland social relations that reinforce social levelling.

These surface features are embedded in a set of social relations, the enduring participation of many members over several years, and the meaning assigned to these practices, which are then distinguished from those of other towns or of mainland Canada. Jane, the only woman at the centre to have lived away for some time, commented that she learned some of her feminist ideas in Toronto:

> In Toronto, I was carrying out traditional roles in and out of the home, and working to raise two children. I couldn't do it in Toronto ... I had no extended family, no community support ... and the few friends I had, weren't enough ... I needed a place, and it was only here [Stephenville] that I could put my feminist ideas into play. I was looking for an opportunity to find my space and my safety here ... I was at a point to demand a place, and in spite of some rigidity at the centre in terms of behaviour, there was also an acceptance of diverse behaviour.

A strong ethos of interdependence pervades the Women's Council in the social embeddedness of their work and a recognition that individual women participate at particular points in their lives. Local feminism is constructed through the integration of feminism with pre-existing social relations and cultural values which are fostered within the social space of the Women's Centre.[3]

In a sense, then, the council has created a selective tradition by drawing attention to that part of the past which has given women strength and personal power, and by subsuming those practices which reproduce gender asymmetries. Their oppositional discourse, particularly in the early years, shares much with women's movements throughout Western societies. Yet it is generated against, and in relation to, historical narratives of military power and narratives of reproduction which are global in scope but which, at the same time, emerge from the lived experiences of women in Bay St George.

As the following chapters suggest, however, there is an interplay between women's experiences in the the reproductive sphere and their participation in, and exclusion from, the sphere of paid work. This intersection forms a central component of local feminist organizing and underpins their critical perspective. The persistence of an idealized home, in the form of a nuclear-family model, marginalizes women such as single mothers and victims of physical and sexual abuse by reinscribing them into narratives of reproduction as pathologized, deviant, or unfortunate individuals. A focus on their experiences draws attention to the larger socio-economic and political context in which these women are positioned and to the specific social issues which the Women's Council has taken up more recently.

CHAPTER FOUR

Contextualizing Dependency: Single Mothers and Feminist Politics

All the jobs are gone, and the economy's grey,
If I don't get me stamps, I'll have to go away.
I'll take my car and sell her, sell her, sell her, sell her
Keep the collectors away
It's an unemployment nightmare (unemployment nightmare)
On this rock today (on this rock today)

I just needed seven stamps, I went to CEC (went to CEC),[1]
I begged for seven weeks (begged for seven weeks)
so I could get pogey (get pogey)

They said to listen to the jobline, jobline, jobline, jobline,
Contact my MHA.[3] So I asked for a project,
I don't care what it pays (I don't care what it pays) ...

'Unemployment Nightmares' (sung to the tune of 'California Dreaming')[2]

While living in Bay St George, I was fortunate to accompany Estasy, three members of the Women's Council, as they entertained and educated audiences in community centres and schools throughout the region. 'Unemployment Nightmares' was particularly popular because of the way it satirized local lifestyles and at the same time cast blame and responsibility onto broad cultural forces. Although I was an outsider, I understood the keywords in this song, which referred to the dependency of residents on government schemes and financial support. Yet it took several months for me to appreciate how this reflected the way some residents made their living in the region and to understand its significance for local feminist politics.

Across Canada, changes in provincial and federal programs such as unemployment insurance and social assistance in the 1980s and 1990s were buttressed by the increasingly predominant notion that some citizens, Newfoundlanders in particular, had become reliant on these programs. This reliance was often described as a 'tradition' which had to be changed or modernized so that a new ethos would flourish, one that valued labour mobility as a prime adaptation to the boom, bust, growth, and decline that has characterized regions within Canada.[4]

This trend has particular meaning in Bay St George and the province more generally, given the cod moratorium as well as the fact that a committment to place has long been cross-cut by the persistent migration of residents. The resulting ambivalence was reflected in the everyday comments of residents regarding those who drew upon government support, in the programs promoted by the local development organizations, in the attitudes of social workers and employees of the Canada Employment Centre, and in the courses offered at the community college.

On the one hand, residents seemed both to accept and to mock the notion that government 'handouts' had become a tradition – part of a way of life – and one that needed to be transformed. On the other hand, some, who themselves drew upon these schemes to make ends meet, recognized that government assistance had become an important form of adaptation to the boom-and-bust livelihood in the region.

Specific groups of people became the focus for debate – men and women who relied on government handouts – specifically, single mothers; people in certain rural or ethnic-based communities; certain families; people who relied on 'traditional' jobs, such as labourers, carpenters, and woodcutters. These people became the bearers of cultural tradition. Hence, perceptions about their lives, choices, behaviours, attitudes, and strategies became a focus through which ideas about change, blame, responsibility, and solutions could be debated.

As anthropologists have pointed out, there is a tendency to label as 'tradition' those livelihood activities and forms of production that are historically rooted, particularly social labour, kin arrangements, and informal reciprocities. This is problematic in that these practices become viewed as antithetical to 'modern' approaches to change – those that are driven by very uneven processes of capitalist production, labelled as normative, and buttressed by the predominance of certain cultural norms such as labour mobility. Why is it that certain forms of work and certain ideas about women and men's roles are labelled as 'traditions' when they are espoused by residents? After all, historically rooted gender stereotypes also inform government policies and the labour market.

The selective invocation of this dichotomy can distort our understanding of these arrangements – that they are actively recreated in the present context of uneven capitalist development and also by those who are not positioned to define its direction. Hence, they are contemporary and ongoing responses of residents to the difficulties of making a living in changing economies (Smith, 1999:167–90). In moving beyond the dichotomy, it is possible to examine the way gender asymmetries are reproduced and challenged by residents, and the way gender intersects with the exigencies of making a living.

This is particularly relevant for Newfoundland, where households and their individual members have drawn upon kin, subsistence, informal economic arrangments, migration, and unemployment insurance and often social assistance to make ends meet. Changes to government programs have provoked widespread debate across the province regarding an entire way of life, and I return to this issue in subsequent chapters. The focus here, however, is in the way ideas about tradition – family and community and ways of life – inform government programs and form a focus for local feminist organizing.

Unemployment, training, and education are issues that the Women's Council has taken up, in particular as they affect different women at varying stages in their lives. For two reasons, this chapter studies single mothers who rely on state support: they have been a sustained focus for the Women's Council, and they are represented in its membership. Also these women experience a number of difficulties which highlight the cultural and economic constraints that tie some women to family and place and render labour mobility an unlikely adaptation. Hence, a focus on their situation illustrates that the cultural expression of feminist activism, its conflation of home and place, is rooted in and responds to the dilemmas of making a livelihood.

Moreover, such an examination has implications within the wider Canadian context. Single mothers became a focus for debates throughout the 1990s which revolved around the effect of welfare-state policies on Canadian citizens (Bashevkin, 1998:96). Cast as exemplary victims of welfare dependency, single mothers are part of a pathologized citizenry whose experiences are individualized in a way that displaces our focus on the social and economic forces in which they are situated. A focus on the their experiences within an ethnographic locality challenges constructions of dependency as a 'pathology' by demonstrating the way current circumstances arise from a series of life responses and contingencies that unfold within intimate histories of kin-based households. Within this context, men and women are distinguished by divisions of labour, social and domestic responsibilities, and cultural categories of masculine and feminine that define and give meaning to their experience.

Gender, Dependency, Labour Mobility, and the Welfare State

In her study of provincial welfare systems, Jane Ursel characterizes the growth of Canadian state welfare from the 1950s to the present as a transformation from familial to state patriarchy. Just as women were controlled by the historical structuring of reproduction within male-dominated nuclear families, so, too, are women controlled by the state. Mechanisms of reproduction impose responsibilities of motherhood on women and exercise control over them, binding them within a context of dependence (Ursel, 1992:6; Hernes, 1987:passim). The conceptualization of the state as a patriarchal system draws attention to the continuities in reproduction that structure women's oppression through social regulations and gendered divisions of labour. At the same time, it obscures the way in which state policies such as child support, women's participation in state bureaucracies, and feminist activism have expanded women's choices and facilitated their departure from abusive marriages (Dahlerup, 1987:112). Analysis has shifted from a focus on state patriarchy and state typologies (Barrett, 1988:249; Jenson, 1992:213) to more finely parsed explorations of specific mechanisms of power and institutions through which access to government resources and services are organized in the areas of health and social and economic welfare.

For example, in their genealogy of dependency, Nancy Fraser and Linda Gordon uncover the discursive and historically structured 'registers' in which subordinated groups – single mothers among others – are constituted and in which they are increasingly pathologized as 'dependent' in contemporary efforts to transform economic welfare policies. This displaces the focus of responsibility from social forces onto individuals, they argue (Fraser and Gordon, 1994). Moreover, they show that welfare dependency is gendered, for example, in the redistribution of unemployment insurance and social assistance. These policies are inscribed with gendered and racialized stereotypes and normative assmptions which favour the heterosexual, nuclear-family formation and identify women with mothering and caregiving (Fraser, 1989).

Fraser and Gordon examine the way single mothers on social assistance, and black women in particular, are more often singled out in American discourse as possessing character traits of dependency. It is important to locate women within specific and historically rooted relations of power which are culturally inscribed and mediated by national policies, regional histories, and social inequities such as race.

In Canada, discourse on labour-market reform depicts workers as individual actors who are expected to adapt to labour-market demands in the post-industrial era through retraining and resettlement to growth areas. In such a context, dependence on state programs that alleviate regional disparities are viewed as a hindrance to the adaptative abilities of individual workers (Johnson, 1994:8). Included here are programs directed towards eliminating regional disparity through transfer payments and development moneys, as well as those directed towards individuals, such as unemployment insurance and social assistance, which have until recently been framed according to national standards of basic 'rights' and 'needs.' Attempts to foster labour mobility, to inhibit regional dependence, and to dismantle national standards are evidenced in recent changes to 'unemployment' insurance and social assistance and are reflected in media discourse.[5]

The right to mobility intersects with a discourse of dependency to cast Newfoundland and its residents as the exemplary 'have-nots' whose resource-based economy makes them overly 'reliant' on 'handouts' by the federal government. Dependency in Canada is also constructed as a psychological trait, a state of being, or an addiction – not as a social condition or relation of subordination (Fraser and Gordon, 1994:330). One need only glance through papers such as the *Globe and Mail* for illustration. To cite an example from an article on changes to unemployment insurance, Canadians, and Newfoundlanders specifically, who draw on unemployment insurance are depicted as those who have 'succumbed to the ... insidious, addictive nature of unemployment payouts' (*Globe and Mail*: 6 January 1994:6). The article further says that Newfoundlanders, 'like smokers psyching up to quit, speak in terms of the need to break the habit of depending on handouts' (Globe and Mail: 6 January 1994:6).

Fraser and Gordon's focus on 'historical shifts that can rarely be attributed to specific agents' (Fraser and Gordon: 310), however useful, does not capture the complex social relations and localized understandings through which dependencies have been manifested in Bay St George. Nor does it capture the significance of discourses of dependency in the way they are implemented through specific regional social and economic policies and through the work of area residents who are multiply situated: as government agents, neighbours, and family members. It is important to consider local, provincial, and federal intervention in the labour market. Such intervention underlines the dynamics of the local political economy and Canadian state policies in mediating the reproduction of gendered difference.

Gender, Social Assistance, and Unemployment in Bay St George

Although the programs outlined below have been dismantled in the last five years, a summary of them is nonetheless relevant in order to apprehend the interplay between region and gender which continues to shape women's experiences today.

A dual system of income redistribution in which social assistance is distinguished from unemployment insurance has been blurred in Newfoundland by the involvement of provincial and federal governments in short-term job creation over the last thirty years (briefly outlined in chapter 2). Make-work projects provided residents who were receiving social assistance with sufficient weeks of work to gain their unemployment 'stamps.' For example, 34 projects created 591 'jobs' for residents of the western region of Newfoundland in 1978. In 1986, 2675 jobs were created and in 1990, 1096.[6] In addition, the local Canada Employment Centre also provided paid work, known as 'Section 25s,' for those residents who were in receipt of unemployment insurance. The Stephenville office created, on average, sixty projects annually in the early 1990s, which ideally employed at least 180 residents. Community-based agencies, including the Women's Council, economic-development organizations, and municipalities, apply to receive placements to hire workers for specific projects and tasks. These placements did not historically go to the more permanently employed seasonal worker, but to those 'less attached' to a particular employer. 'Section 25s' were used either to 'top-up' a low unemployment-insurance payment or to extend the number of weeks one received unemployment insurance.[7]

Men have had greater access to these programs since their establishment in the early 1970s. The overall greater participation of men in the labour force compared to women suggests they were more often better positioned as recipients of unemployment insurance. Indeed, in a 1980 report, Cheryl Brown noted that single mothers were discriminated against in that they did not receive work through government-sponsored projects in Stephenville even when they applied (Brown, 1982:23). Canada Employment Centre officials agreed that men were the majority recipients of these placements until the mid 1980s, when an 'Employment Equity' policy required at least half of the placements go to women. Since then, women have been increasingly incorporated into make-work jobs through projects targeted specifically at their traditional skills, such as sewing, quilting, and crafts, but more so through their inclusion in traditionally male work such as road building and repair. The slow increase of women in the labour force suggests that growing number of women have drawn on unemployment insurance. This is certainly reflected in the accounts I recorded: eighteen of the thirty-five women whom I interviewed at the council for the National Action Committee 'Futures of Work' project had drawn unemployment insurance at least once, and a few had done so on a more frequent basis.

The Newfoundland government has reproduced the 'dependency'

discourse by emphasizing in its reports the 'dependence' of its workers, 'youth' in particular, on unemployment insurance. Across the province, and in Bay St George specifically, 50 per cent of employed nineteen-year-olds in the early 1990s drew unemployment insurance, which constituted half of their income.[8] Studies on the Port au Port peninsula, for example, indicate that the rate of unemployment is highest in the more remote communities, where 20 per cent claimed to have received employment through make-work projects.[9]

The failure of this study however, to distinguish respondents on the basis of gender skews work identities in favour of male-dominated work and suggests that a traditional gender division of labour informs local attempts to examine and solve unemployment. This is mirrored in the attempt to identify 'academic and career needs.' The majority of respondents who wanted further education indicated an interest in trades such as carpentry, business education, computers, and mechanics, traditionally male-dominated forms of work (although beauty culture, bookkeeping, cooking, nursing and childcare were mentioned).[10]

The gender dichotomy between unemployment insurance and social assistance that Fraser and Gordon note should be situated within this local context in which employment opportunities are spread unevenly throughout the region. This has created large pockets of underemployed men and women, many of whom have maintained themselves through social assistance when their opportunities to gain unemployment insurance are inhibited by sustained unemployment or, in the case of youth, the inability to gain the twenty weeks of work necessary to qualify.[11]

At the same time, the framework in which local 'development' researchers operate is informed by a traditionally rooted gender dichotomy. This brief overview of government interventions is a reminder that low-income single mothers are only a portion of those who require government funds to make a threadbare living. As well, the geographic location of these women within the region may shape their experience of single motherhood and their identities as workers and citizens. Indeed, in a recent Statistics Canada summary of the ten 'incorporated communities' which contain the lowest median 'family' incomes across the country, five are located in Newfoundland and two of these are located within the Bay St George region.[12] Yet my focus here is less on the bare income figures or broad labour-market patterns than on the relationships of dependency that distinguish single mothers and expose the reproduction of gendered differences in a way that 'frees' male labour and subjects women to the social controls they contest.

The effect of these overlapping discourses and policies on single mothers in western Newfoundland is to situate them in a cultural and economic double bind – where the dependency of Newfoundland coincides with their dependence on the state for welfare and employment payments. Yet single mothers are by definition tied – to dependent children – so that the life experiences of single mothers in Bay St George encompass the intersection of these contexts of dependence, namely, region, gender, and family.

The nuclear family, the division of labour subsumed within it, and the gender scripts it underwrites form the normative means by which state policies are implemented and funds redistributed. Mechanisms of redistribution reproduce and codify gender difference, specifically femininity, in a way that favours neither the determinacy of patriarchy nor the capitalist process. Rather, it exposes the differential ways in which women and men are inserted into the labour market and compelled to make and plan a livelihood by embracing, reproducing, and contesting pre-existing relations and structures of family and community. It is within this context that the identities of single mothers are constituted and their behaviour evaluated by other residents.

The Poverty of Single Motherhood: 'Poor is when you say, "I'm going shopping," and it means, to the grocery store'

On Thursday afternoons, at the end of each month, Main Street is a bustling locus of activity. It is the day of shopping, signalled by the call that 'the cheques are in.' Drivers signal their buddies on the street; they patiently give right of way to those making left turns as they creep behind the line of cars headed towards the main intersection in town. Two school buses, privately operated by the largest grocery store in the area, are stationed in the parking lot to chauffeur peninsula residents who spend their day shopping and visiting 'in town.' Inside the well-stocked store, shoppers jostle for space, manoeuvring one or two brimming grocery carts with a child or two in tow. Here, shoppers can choose among a plethora of packaged edibles, shipped all the way from the mainland and the United States. Near the entrance, older men in baseball caps and jackets generate trails of smoke at the coffee bar, where they chat and watch the line of shoppers passing through the check-outs.

The distinguishing features of a long-time culture may be found in large buckets and open steel tubs of salt pork and beef, dried and salted fish (if available), the prominent display of canned, evaporated milk, and Newfoundland's 'own' brands of 'Purity' crackers, butter, lemon-cream biscuits, hard-tack bread, and molasses candies. Long gone are the days when fish were traded in kind, for molasses, salt pork, and a sack of flour. Now, the checkouts move quickly as cashiers tally goods paid for by cash and pension, welfare, and unemployment cheques.

Outside, past the main intersection, upwardly mobile shoppers fill the parking lot of the co-op grocery store, which offers a 'better' selection at competitive prices, to card-carrying members only. One afternoon, my neighbour, Joan, and I walked from Main Street to the mall, listing the items we both needed. Along the way she moaned at the fast-paced growth of her son Matthew and the ranked items in priority of cost and need. 'Sweat pants and T-shirts now on sale, for Matthew, at —. Those will go on lay-away. Socks at the Bi-Way, running shoes at Woolco ...' Can she manage a pair of aerobics tights for herself? Maybe next week.

As we passed the magazine stands, Joan resisted the temptation to buy another romance novel, which, she admits, she would read voraciously and far too quickly to warrant the cost. She prefers the racier novels of Danielle Steel and historical fictions that guarantee a few scenes of raunchy sex. These novels are a luxury that Joan allows herself on occasion, to celebrate the end of a difficult week or to mark the moment when all needs for Matthew, and then for herself, have been met. As we browsed at Reitmans, Joan pointed to assorted blouses and skirts that she would like to buy 'once the weight is off.' After some deliberation, however, she tried on the clothes, in anticipation of her birthday, six months away. 'That's when we'll have a night on the town,' she declared.

For the single mothers who live on less than $15,000 per year, and on whom I focus, cheques from employers, unemployment insurance, social assistance, and/or child-support payments are anxiously awaited moneys that are usually already mentally spent. At a certain level, women who live on such a small income are united by the way livelihood strategies must bridge needs of mother and child in a culture in which basic needs are often 'packaged' and thus mediated by consumer ideology and dictates of the market. Moreover, the importance of government cheques in an economy characterized by high unemployment and migrant and seasonal work is reflected in everyday commercial transactions. Residents demonstrate detailed knowledge of unemployment insurance and the due dates of government moneys. Local understandings of citizenship and individual rights are reflected in a widespread acceptance that government support is part of a way of life. Yet long-term recipients of social assistance, male and female, are somewhat denigrated through dominant local stereotypes, unlike those who draw unemployment insurance.

As individuals, men and women have rights as consumers to purchase and, as citizens, to draw government cheques. Yet for women this is mediated by the historical context in which women were subsumed as dependants within nuclear and extended families (Fraser, 1994:318). The emphasis on the individual in state and market domains coincides with this historical dependency to engender contradictions in the life experiences of single mothers. These unfold throughout their life cycles and the social pathways that link them to residents, neighbours, and extended family.

The Social Construction of Single Mothers

> When I first came here illegitimacy for women was a stigma. It was kept a secret and you were looked down upon. Now it's open and you're still looked down upon – now they say you don't care about 'the family' or responsibility.
>
> (Marilyn, social worker)

Women's life stories are laced with secret births, hidden parenthood, social shaming, and, ironically, a matter-of-fact recognition that 'illegitimacy' has been a way of life. Jane, forty-two, the daughter of a single mother, recalls with some indignity the way nuns would ridicule her status in front of classmates. Julie, who is now forty, and one of ten siblings, did not discover until she was an adult that the girl who was 'reared by her grandmother' was in fact her step-sister. It gave her a new insight into the rigid respectability and propriety that had always been imposed by her mother, who still refuses to speak of the birth of her first child. Joan, thirty-five, insists that her sister, with whom she shared a bed in their teenage years, kept her pregnancy 'a secret' until she was well into her sixth month.

At the same time, Susan, forty, and sister to eleven, recalls with fondness diapering and caring for her older sister's son, whom she grew to treat as a younger brother. Elizabeth, sixty, chuckles that she married her husband only after she became pregnant. Linda, twenty-nine, recalls the baby she bore at age fourteen, who is raised by a cousin and now resides happily in Ontario. One morning I entered the office of a local public-health nurse. She was in the middle of counselling a young woman who had just given birth that morning and sought a discreet adoption. The young woman had, thus far, managed to conceal the pregnancy and delivery from her family and her neighbours.

These life-story fragments reflect continuity in the reproduction of motherhood and family and the contradictory cultural processes that have long deemed the mother sacred and the unwed mother profane. As Stuart Godfrey notes, 'Newfoundland was encumbered with the historic dichotomy between the "deserving" and the "undeserving," the "fit" and the "unfit" mother ... the transition to acceptance of the legal right of unmarried mothers and single-parent families to financial aid would be a slow process' (Godfrey, 1985:85).

The pregnancy of unmarried women has been informed by narratives of promiscuity which convey a double standard for female and male behaviour and which are still meaningful today. The sexual prowess of men is taken-for-granted behaviour that is infrequently noted, while the sexual behaviour of women generates considerable comment and judgment within the family and local institutions. The region, I was told, is noted for its high rate of single motherhood and particularly for the large number of women who never share residence with a child's biological father.

The arrival of American soldiers created ruptures in social and sexual norms. Betrothal to 'clean' and 'civilized' American soldiers promised an escape from the drudgery of extensive subsistence work, provided access to shiny new cars, and offered new gendered stereotypes which rendered Newfoundland men wanting. It is within this context –

of Catholic proscriptions and military hedonism; of secret births, condoms scattered on the beach, and promises of marriage – that single mothers emerged as a significant social category and a serious social problem by the early 1970s. Although some attribute the development of single motherhood to liaisons with American soldiers and the sexual bravado that characterized the base years, others relate the persistence of 'unmarried mothers' in the rural areas to a pre-existing tradition. Although sexual abstinence was preached, a man and a woman were expected to marry after she became pregnant.

Historically, the social stigma attached to unmarried women who became pregnant was mitigated by the reintegration of these women and their children within the extended family. As life stories indicate, women either married the child's father, or another man, raised the baby in the extended family, or gave the child up for adoption. When raised by grandparents, the child's biological parentage may have been concealed or openly acknowledged within the family and surrounding neighbourhood.

The reintegration of these mothers within the larger family underlines their dependency on other breadwinning adults. It shows the economic difficulties that mothers experienced raising children alone in a region subjected to economic boom and bust that offered little employment deemed appropriate for women. The poverty of widows with children is frequently mentioned in government reports when redistribution of 'relief' was poorly administered and recognized as insufficient (Godfrey, 1985:84).

An increase in the number of women who chose or were compelled to raise children alone from the 1970s has been variously attributed to the expansion of government services and systems of redistribution. As well, social workers point to the erosion of the social stigma attached to single motherhood and changes in cultural norms regarding sexual relations and marriage. Women's stories recount their transition to single motherhood through divorce, widowhood, and fluid partnerships. Today, some of these women are able to earn a 'single parent family' wage with a modest but secure income as public-sector managers, teachers, or nurses, for example. Many, however, remain 'dependent' on external sources of income and support to reproduce their family-based households. Indeed, the prevalence of poverty among single mothers is well documented in Newfoundland and across Canada.[13]

Today the secrecy and shame of non-marital pregancy is mitigated by the increase of single mothers since the 1970s and the varied circumstances that make women the exclusive caregivers to their children in contemporary society (Lord, 1994:191). However, the social stigma that shrouded 'unmarried' mothers has in the last twenty-five years shifted onto low-income single mothers in general and, more often, those who live 'on assistance.'

Consider the circumstances of four women who live on incomes that border on the poverty-line annual income of $14,348.[14] The stigma attached to 'assistance' and 'single motherhood' converge to generate labels from which these women measure their own behaviour, construct their self-worth, and make livelihood choices.

Joan, Karen, Beverley, and Bonnie

Joan is a single mother of one ten-year-old boy who makes a yearly income of just over $14,000 from daily 'babysitting' and a relatively high and reliable monthly child support cheque of $500 from her former husband, an RCMP officer. Karen is a thirty-three-year-old 'separated' mother of two boys, one sixteen, the other six. Having left school for the birth of her son at age sixteen, she had few recognized job skills and little training. A part-time job in a local bar allows her to be with her with her young son during the day. While Karen works from 6 p.m. to 4 a.m., twice weekly, her sixteen-year-old babysits his younger brother. Karen receives $400 each month in child support, but her job brings in less than $800 per month, giving her a yearly income of approximately $13,440.

Beverley is a thirty-two-year-old mother of one boy who has received both social assistance and unemployment insurance somewhat steadily over the last few years. Although she has completed college courses in forestry and community studies, she could not find adequate full-time work to gain a living wage. She cannot seem to earn more than $11,000 a year as she transfers somewhat regularly from government-sponsored project work to unemployment insurance and social assistance. Beverley did not receive financial support from the father of her child, a seasonal worker, who is now deceased.

Bonnie is a thirty-four-year-old mother of two who has spent the last four years as a full-time university student. Although she was originally granted child support from her former husband, a self-employed accountant, she relinquished these payments and in return he agreed to share custody and care of their children five days weekly for the 7 1/2-month period she is enrolled in school. During the school term Bonnie lives on a student loan of $6,560 and receives social assistance during the summer when her children are living with her.

As mothers, these women are concerned to provide their children with opportunities that will give them access to jobs in adulthood and permit their social integration with other children. As consumers, they experience similar tensions and difficulties in distinguishing luxury items from basic needs for both themselves and their children. The demands of maintaining family are met only if their own needs are put aside. Moreover, peer pressure among children and the cost of children's social activities make the prioritization of expenses a difficult task against which their virtue as mothers is evaluated. For Joan, this means planning months in advance to purchase hockey equipment, while Beverley, anxious to allow her son to travel with other teammates to a soccer tournament, saves to provide spending money once her son has raised the necessary funds through sponsorships. Karen admits that she has little additional money for 'extras,' particularly computer games and software, yet she finds it difficult to deal with her 'guilt and worry' when she repeatedly refuses her son's requests. Books, movies, and the occasional night out for themselves are organized infrequently, and often months in advance.

Babysitting is an arduous and intensive responsibility for Joan, who is actually paid less than the minimum hourly wage for a forty-hour week. Long, snowy winters and heavy winds that frequently sweep across the bay inhibit mobility and confine Joan and her charges to long days in her small two-bedroom apartment. While Joan enjoys much in her job, she has few adult social contacts and is frequently exhausted when her son arrives home from school. She relishes nights out and regular trips to the aerobics club at the end of the day. Such 'luxuries' for herself are included in her carefully planned budget.

For Karen, working in a bar is an opportunity to maintain contact with an adult social world. The occasional harassment by male patrons and the inebriated state of a few clientele can be tiring by 4 a.m., but Karen accepts these intrusions as hazards of her work. In spite of long nights, she is able to remain home with her six-year-old son during the day. Moreover, these long nightshifts allow Karen to complete her high-school degree through correspondence courses organized at the college.

Beverley anxiously awaits acceptance for government projects which will provide her with at least ten weeks of work and up to forty-two weeks of unemployment insurance. While the income this grants is virtually the same as the money she receives 'on assistance,' Beverley welcomes the freedom and positive status of an unemployment cheque, which signifies her status as a deserving 'worker.' Some women are employed in arduous jobs such as maintaining and renovating churches, community halls, and the local arena. Beverley has in the last few years been fortunate to work at the Women's Centre, which provides for a few placements each year. At the centre, she performs a variety of tasks from housekeeping to preparing campaigns which introduce her to numerous residents and maintain her social and political interests. While women working on government projects can get subsidized daycare, the location of their work and scheduling can be a problem. Flexibility at the centre means that Beverley's son is easily integrated during an occasional lunch or holiday.

It is the experience of social assistance and the cultural devaluation of welfare recipients that Beverley hopes to avoid and that informed the decisions of Joan and Karen to gain waged work. As the daughter of a single mother, Joan remembers an impoverished childhood and the numerous restrictions placed on her mother, who was compelled to receive social assistance. 'Mom was never given enough to live on,' Joan recalls, and social workers monitored her mother's attempts to save money while also expressing disapproval of the occasional moves the family made. Adamant in her quest to 'have control,' Joan proudly recalls divorce proceedings that awarded her child support. Deemed 'unemployable' by the judge because she was now a single mother who had only a grade 6 education, Joan rejected the appellation and was determined to find work. She is critical of the judge, who expected, even encouraged, her to make financial arrangements with Social Services under the assumption that she would be on social assistance.

Karen decided that 'welfare wouldn't be a choice' because she was aware of her sister's experience in that situation. Having heard 'stories of entrapment,' and cognizant of 'the culture attached to it,' she too feared 'losing control over her life' and was concerned that the 'social stigma' of being on welfare would have a negative impact on her children. While Joan and Karen assert that they maintain 'control' over their lives and futures, Beverley is quick to highlight the extent of social restrictions on her own. Although the opinions of both Joan and Karen derive from personal knowledge of local experience, they also reinforce long-held stereotypes of 'welfare culture' as a condition characterized by dependency and lack of control. To what extent do these dominant norms reflect and define the experience of women on social assistance?

Living 'on Assistance'

> The problem with people on welfare is that they don't know how to shop. They live beyond their means. (Store clerk)

> Living on social assistance means a whole way of life. It means buying food on sale, clothes on lay-away and borrowing food at the end of the month before the cheque comes in. (Beverley)

> The best thing for a family is if you're a woman and you've never worked and your husband is disabled – now that's an honourable way to get social assistance. The only time dignity is valued is when you die. You get a fine coffin and its all paid for. (Penney, social worker)

In Bay St George, welfare stories are commonplace and often reinforce dominant depictions of welfare recipients. Many residents have at least a mother or a friend on welfare or have themselves accepted social assistance at some point in their lives. While many residents live on fixed and small incomes, it is welfare recipients who are most often named as individuals who cannot manage their own affairs and who are unable effectively to budget the money they do receive. Yet, as Beverley proclaims, living 'on assistance' can be a job in itself, one that requires considerable organization, planning, and will power to resist the purchase of items most of us take for granted. In this regard, all recipients of assistance – single 'able-bodied,' disabled and single parents, female and male – are united by the difficulties of living on such a restricted income and by the stigma attached to their position as clients of the state.

In Bay St George in 1992, 187 single parents received social assistance, a total that comprised 21 per cent of all client cases.[15] Although Newfoundland has some of highest unemployment rates in Canada, it provides one of the lowest per-capita social-assistance payments in the Atlantic region (Durst, 1994:207). Consider, for example, the basic allowance of a single mother with one child. As of 1995, she receives $913 per month, which includes a $57 'single parent supplement' and $448 to supplement monthly rent. This provides a yearly income of $10,956. Making ends meet on this amount, as I learned by attempting it myself, would challenge any citizen, especially when the smallest indulgence is judged an offence by onlookers. As recipients of public charity, these clients are expected to be careful, economizing, and thankful for the money they receive.

The difficulties of budgeting are exacerbated by the context of dependence, which ties people to the state and is expressed as the perception that 'it's impossible to get ahead.' The restrictions placed on recipients engaged in paid work subject them to scrutiny and identify them as potential frauds. Those engaged in formally paid work must report their earnings, which are then deducted from their assistance cheques. For example, Robert, an unemployed young man, earned $20 for delivering papers, $10 of which was taken from his welfare cheque. Similarly, $100 was deducted from a cheque that Bonnie had earned for her participation in a local theatre production.

Recipients develop everyday strategies to make ends meet, some of which are rooted in informal reciprocities discussed further in this chapter. Wanda, a single mother on assistance, grants herself minor luxuries once expenses of rent and phone are mentally calculated. For Wanda, who is going through a difficult personal crisis, the puff of a cigarette is a costly but necessary relief from anxiety. Upon visiting her house one evening, I am reluctant to accept her hospitable offer of a beer, aware that I will exceed her allotment for the weekend. Beverley economizes by purchasing turkey necks and chicken backs to add flavour to her weekly 'jigs dinner,' a traditional Sunday afternoon meal. June and David, a young couple with an infant, are continually reworking their tight budget. By shopping late on Saturday afternoon, they are able to take advantage of meat marked down for quick sale before the all-day closure on Sunday. With at least two second-hand furniture stores and two second-hand clothing stores in town (Salvation Army and St Vincent de Paul), those on a fixed income can find low-priced clothes and furniture. Moreover, most stores in town, such as Bi-Way, Wal-Mart, Zellers, and the Met, target a low-income market and a few offer lay-away plans which are extensively used by the women I knew. Such restricted incomes do, however, generate considerable tensions between mother and child and between couples, as well as testing individual will power. One week June and David argued over whether both cigarettes and fresh vegetables could be purchased.

Regimes of income redistribution structure the daily lives of welfare recipients and extract from them details of their lives that others are permitted to keep to themselves. Social workers like Peg compare their roles to that of priests, because 'we have access to people's deepest, darkest secrets. They tell us everything, because they feel they have to. The Department of Social Services has guidelines that restrict the amount of money a beneficiary can hold in the bank and the hours per week they may work. The requirement 'to report' often provokes recipients to 'tell all' and divulge minute details of their lives that may then be evaluated on a moral basis. To cite a case, one single mother who won a small amount of money at the bingo wondered whether she must report this to her social worker. Not only do these earnings constitute additional income, but to report them may provoke a social worker to ask, 'Why were you spending your money on the bingo anyway?'

June and David are convinced that they are not allowed to save any money while on assistance and feel obliged to report all additional income to their social worker, including gifts such as a baby carriage and small sums of money given to them by his parents. Social workers have access to bank accounts and pay monthly or infrequent visits to their clients' households. While some social workers simply talk to their clients, others, a few claim, arrive unannounced and feel free to sift through cupboards, fridges, and bathrooms. Moreover, a district manager in the Department of Social Services states that cases in which the system is 'abused' are most often reported by neighbours and relatives.

Beverley is acutely aware of the social stigma attached to single mothers 'on assistance.' She complains that these mothers are stereotyped by local residents because of where they live and because they are easily identified as welfare recipients. Several of these women live in low-rental housing units which are clustered together and viewed as undesirable by many. Welfare cheques and yellow drug cards signal their status as welfare recipient to grocery-store, drugstore, and bank clerks. For example, some single mothers complain that once a certain store owner saw that you had a 'drug card,' you would be the last served. Children are provided with school supplies (which other children must purchase) if they fill out the appropriate slip. Several teachers openly group these children to one side to collect their slips and pass out their schoolbooks. Single-mother clients are subjected to the surveillance of social workers and the 'snoopy' scrutiny of concerned neighbours.

The informal reports of 'busy-nose' neighbours (as one friend put it) and the social pathways of everyday transactions underline the fact that the way of life for these people is rooted in more than the lived experience of bureaucratic mechanisms. Rather, it unfolds in a spatial context, through a history of social relations that are culturally encoded. It is within this broader historical context that recipients are constituted and strive to maintain, not just a living, but personal dignity.

The cultural and historical association of women as mothers, the fluidity of contemporary heterosexual relationships, and the vagaries of employment inform the different experiences of men and women 'on assistance,' the strategies they employ, and the way they are viewed locally. An ideology of family mediates the interplay between domestic and state reproduction and provides a moral justification for gendered identities and divisions of labour (Beechey, 1988:50).

The Ambiguity of Paternity

The Department of Social Services strongly encourages women to obtain child support for their children because it reduces costs for the provincial government. Child-support payments, if steady, can permit women to seek paid employment and escape the confinements of state support. Karen and Joan are two of the 30 per cent of women who receive child-support in the province. Karen's ex-husband's payments are regular and his job is secure while Joan's payments are automatically deducted from her husband's monthly paycheque.

Although the Women's Council upholds the enforcement of child support payments, it calls for a flexible system that recognizes the wider social context in which women become mothers and the relations of power that might inhibit a woman from seeking child support from the father of her children. A case in point is Bonnie, who is reluctant to claim child support from her former husband because, in her view, it reinforces the control he had over her during their marriage and her dependence on him. Liz is reluctant to receive child support from her former partner because he was abusive.

Moreover, attempts to enforce a man's responsibility for paternity are directed towards the single mother, not the man, and can affect her livelihood. When the Department of Social Services requested Christie, a twenty-five-year-old mother of one boy, to name the father of her child so she might sue for child support, she refused and her welfare payments were abruptly ended. Christie was ambivalent about naming the father, a forty-five-year-old married resident with children, because she was reluctant to embarrass his family and at the same time feared that he would try to gain custody of her child at some point in the future. It should be noted that, in these circumstances, there is little incentive to obtain child support. Since 1989 child-support payments have been deducted from the amount of social assistance a woman receives, but the system provides her with no means to gain additional income.

Maureen

In Newfoundland the mobile and fragmented nature of the male workforce renders child-support payments low, intermittent, and difficult to monitor, according to local workers in the Department of Social Services. Consider Maureen, a single mother with two children who lived a short while with her first child's father, her 'fiance.' When the relationship did not work out, he left, and she asked for and received social assistance and was granted child support.

I was eighteen when I had Mark. I was in school, taking dicta-typing and

I was pregnant the whole year. I moved in with Mike and I spent time looking after Mark. I never seen Mike 'cause he was always off somewheres. I didn't know it until after we broke up, but he was out fooling around. I just got tired of him coming home all hours of the morning and one night I just told him to leave and not come home.

But Mike was a good father. He never ignored Mark after we broke up. He was the best type of father. His new girlfriend told him not to see Mark, but he'd come anyway. He put his child first. Now he's in Toronto.

[Q: Doing what?] I haven't the slightest idea cause we haven't heard from him since he's gone. [pause] Now, I just said what a good father he was and now I'm saying we never heard from him! Well, his mother heard. He just started a new job last week. [Q: Does he pay child support?] No. I went to court once and he had to pay $35 a month until Mark turned one year, then he didn't have to pay nothing else. He was only making $5 an hour. I lived good on that! [laughter] I had some wild times on that!

The experiences of single mothers on assistance, moreover, are shaped, not just by their relationship to the biological or socially recognized fathers, but by the partnerships they form once 'on assistance.'

Liz

Liz is a single mother of three who was awarded child support from an ex-husband who has relied somewhat regularly on short- and longer-term work in Ontario, supplemented by unemployment insurance. Currently Liz lives with her boyfriend, John, who also works for different periods of time in Ontario, sends money to Liz, and returns during lay-offs to Newfoundland where he collects unemployment insurance. Liz makes a living by alternating between social assistance and the unemployment insurance she receives when she can get work on projects. It is difficult for Liz to predict her yearly, even monthly, income because her husband has failed to send child-support cheques for months at a time and they can be deducted only if he is on UI or formally employed. Liz is unsure whether or not her current boyfriend, John, is allowed to live with her during the periods when she is collecting social assistance. At the same time she argues that, without the income he brings in, she could not survive. Liz's status is that of a single woman in a semi-permanent relationship with a boyfriend who has not claimed legal, paternal responsibility for her children. The system of income distribution does not easily permit someone like Liz to draw on different forms of government support when her living arrangements appear to be ambiguous. Yet that ambiguity arises from a series of choices, decisions, and negotiations with John that, given the circumustances of her life, make sense to her.

> It's like getting UI and getting welfare, there's no getting ahead. Sometimes, it's very depressing. Just the other day, I didn't know whether I'd get a project, I was having headaches for weeks, thinking – my unemployment's running out, what am I going to do? Now, nobody knows about John's UI. I should find out what you're supposed to do. I been telling John to pick up his things – boots and coats everywhere- if I started a project, would that be fraud? If I'm on welfare, is that fraud? I don't see what I'm doing is wrong because if you look at my income and his, it's not a great deal. When he was working in Ontario, he made good money. Now, on UI, his check is $200 dollars a month less. I mean we're not really hurting anybody. I mean, right now, it's my UI and I worked to get it and so did he. But it's just getting social services that's a problem. The way I look at it, it's for me and the kids. I mean, John is with me, but he don't have to be, and there's no guarantees he'll be there tomorrow.

Liz expresses the difficulties in meeting livelihood needs in a household where the dependence of children is fixed but the means of livelihood, the participation of adults, and the meaning of partnership are considerably more fluid. Several months later, her former partner had failed to pay child-support for several months, and in addition, Liz and her boyfriend separated for a brief period.

In Bay St George, childcare is a responsibility that women are socialized to assume and a right they claim. Yet the ambiguity of paternity, particularly outside legally constituted heterosexual unions, renders fatherhood a fluid social category. Although men can exercise their paternal right, they can also abrogate responsibility. Furthermore, while there is no legal obligation for a live-in boyfriend such as John to assume financial responsibility for his live-in girlfriend and her children, notions of family and the social meaning of cohabitation signifies to government officials that some income sharing should and, therefore, *might* occur.

For women 'on assistance,' however, state mechanisms do not just structure their economic choices and flexibility. Rather, they reach into the heart of the household, defining women as mothers and implicitly restricting their personal lives and sexual relations (Durst, 1994:213). This is most dramatically evidenced through the 'waves' of welfare investigations that occur intermittently in Bay St George to uncover single mothers living with men in 'family unit relationships.'

'We can go to someone's house at 9 am and invite ourselves in'

Members of the Women's Council question the legitimacy of social services to enter the homes of area residents unannounced. 'Even at the RCMP we often give notice – and we knock!' jokes Kathy, an RCMP officer. Indeed, the investigation of single-mother households subjects women to scrutiny and financial penance under the assumption that men living as boyfriends share income, just as they are expected to do within a nuclear-family context. According to one district manager, 'if she's living with a guy, you must prove that the guy she's with is getting money from some other source, but you don't have to prove that he's giving any of it to her. He's viewed as a leech, but she is the one who is suspended.'

Such was the case with Sarah, when one morning a Social Services investigator 'dropped by' her house without prior warning to enquire about the living arrangements of her current boyfriend. Sarah declared that, although he often slept over, he was not living with her. Nonetheless, the agent cut off her payments, leaving her without an income for two months.

The policing of these female recipients is, furthermore, informed by moral assumptions that underpin sexual relations and motherly behaviour (Lord, 1994:191). It implies that a single mother receiving assistance cannot have intimate relationships with men unless they are modelled after conjugal relationships. According to Sarah, 'the impression I get is you're not allowed to have a boyfriend. If they're over at your house in the afternoon, you're living with them; they can be there in the evening but they can't be there overnight; they can't eat meals with you. They can't have any belongings at your house. Now what am I, a nun? When am I supposed to have sex? I have feelings too. I don't know when sex is going to happen and it's hard when you have kids. I told the agent that Tom spends nights here, but he doesn't live with me.' In Sarah's view, people may indeed stay together before deciding to make a permanent commitment. Bureaucratic processes do not allow for a relationship to evolve, forcing women to live as chaste mothers or lie.

On the other hand, Beverley, has taken advantage of the nuclear-family bias that informs such welfare investigations. Although she receives social assistance at various times, Beverley has managed thus far to make ends meet by living with her brother, a single, seasonally employed woodcutter who contributes financially to the household. The social worker who pays a visit to her home every few months has failed to realize that her brother is a permanent cohabitant. Beverley laughs, 'She's so busy lookin' for the man I got hid in the closet, that she don't even see my brother sitting right there watching TV, his shoes and boots in the doorway and his tobacco tins all over the table! "Oh, he's just visiting," I says!'

The renewal of Beverley's placement in assorted projects is hardly guaranteed and is subject to the broader politics of redistribution in which fiscal constraints and local competition for project funds limit the number of jobs from year to year. If a placement is not offered (and this does occur), Beverley is instantly transformed from deserving worker to dependent recipient of social assistance. It is the shift from unemployment insurance to social assistance which positions women such as her and Liz as potential frauds or state dependants. Yet, from Beverley's perspective, a single mother cannot make ends meet without informal arrangements.

Indeed, many women such as Beverley draw on and are embedded within broader kin and informal networks where relations of reciprocity are reproduced at the fringes of the market. Here, an ideology of family dictates a sense of responsibility of kin towards each other. This can be a powerful, albeit last, resort for single mothers to meet both their emotional and their material needs.

Local Reciprocities and Extended Family

The reconfiguration of subsistence and informally commodified practices as a strategy of livelihood within state-mediated market economies is well documented both in Newfoundland and within the anthropological literature. Studies on livelihood in outport and rural Newfoundland have consistently noted the extent to which subsistence activities and informally commodified reciprocities form a crucial bridge between incomes determined by the labour market and the demands of reproducing a household. These studies detail the extent and potential market value of such exchanges in the reproduction of the household as well as the social and gendered relations in which such exchanges are embedded.[16] In Bay St George, informal and familial reciprocities link both the well paid and the unemployed in relations of exchange, which seem not just to meet material needs for subsistence items but to reinforce social relationships of kin and co-worker.

Residents of Stephenville anxiously await the beginning of autumn, when the moose rut begins and the opportunity to hunt a cow, a bull, or a calf is granted to those fortunate enough to have 'drawn' a licence. At this time of year, it is common to see men, rifle in hand, walking the roads outside town, or along the flat barrens that separate Bay St George from the Trans-Canada Highway, in search of moose. Adrian, a mill worker, was fortunate to get a licence for the area behind his house. After a ten minutes' walk into the woods, he and his 'buddy,' another mill worker with whom he shares the licence, had killed their bull, which they hung in his garage until it was ready to be butchered into steaks and roasts.

Joan, who has always loved moose meat, was guaranteed a few steaks from her sister and brother-in-law, who returned to Stephenville from the east coast to hunt. Joan was less sure that her husband's brother would offer a few roasts this year. Although she was divorced from his brother for a few years, she deserved, she said, some portion of his cow, because her son regularly visited his paternal uncles and grandparents. Fortunately for me, he did drop by one afternoon, and Joan gave me a few of the steaks she had received. In a region where fish is now a scarce resource, the annual moose hunt is an important feature of subsistence production that functions on the fringes of the market and provides numerous residents with the opportunity to visit relatives and acquire a large portion of meat for the winter.

For example, many men at the mill apply for a licence in twos, which increases their chances of acquiring one licence and, therefore, of killing a moose that they will share between them. Doug and his buddy, who are part of the maintenance crew, and John, a manager, and his buddy Bill, hardly 'need' the meat, given their salaries; rather, it provides a context for socializing and a low-fat tasty meat which is preferred by many. Also, although many men with whom I spoke showed little interest in hunting, others seem to enjoy the male comaraderie and the performance of masculine activities.

For many residents, however, the moose hunt provides both a substantial contribution to a winter diet and an opportunity to share with extended family. For instance, Anne was reluctant to give away much moose because, as she puts it, the meat provides Sunday dinners for her family of five for most of the winter. Betty awaited the arrival of her son. Although he resides in St John's, he applied to hunt in the area around Bay St George with his cousin so he can return to visit his mother and extended family. Darren, who was born and raised on the east coast but currently works in Stephenville, flew home for a weekend of hunting with his brothers in the woods not far from the Avalon peninsula. John, a Mi'kmaq raised on the Conne River, the only state-recognized native reserve on the the south coast of the island, frequently returns to his parents' home where he hunts moose and fishes salmon.

Moose hunting is only one of many subsistence-based activities that sustain family-based households and reproduce kin-based reciprocities and a gender division of labour. For instance, Constance and her husband bottle salmon and moose for the winter. Within her large extended family, quilts, sewn items, and jams are exchanged. Her husband, who has worked as a welder and fisherman, does carpentry work for area residents and extended family.

Many of these activities are partly or informally commodified. In Joan's case, her brother-in-law gives her moose meat, but he sells small amounts to neighbours. Tina visits her extended family and friends in the rural community in which she was raised to get salted cod, herring, and salmon at what she considers to be a low cost. Bottled moose and moose-meat pies are permitted to be sold at craft sales, which flourish in the area from September to December. Similarly, women sell their home-made crafts, including quilts, decorative pieces, and jams. At the same time, the sale of fish and moose is for the most part illegal and considered 'poaching.' Residents who have long relied on these items for their diet, and who gain small sums from their sale, do not view this as poaching but as a customary right.

The gender division of labour that underpins these activities structures the access of single mothers who rely on male kin to perform odd jobs and provide fish and moose. Some women do participate in traditionally male activities. Donna, a single mother of two children, joins her brother on a moose hunt, less for the pleasure of the kill than for the opportunity for a 'boil-up' in the woods. Anne completed shooting lessons only a year ago and now, instead of joining her husband in the woods 'to make the tea,' she is anxious to shoot her first moose. Wendy, a twenty-six-year-old single mother of two, who lives 'on assistance,' is one of the few female licensed guides in the province. She proudly recounts her skills in shooting and measuring points (antler-rack width) and bear skulls. Moreover, she has, she claims, invented efficient ways to carve up her animal, in spite of her small size: 'I used to watch the boys in the woods cutting up their moose with a handsaw – hard work! It takes forever. So, you know what I did? I just oiled my chainsaw with vegetable oil – that way you don't spoil the taste of the meat – and my moose is quartered in fifteen minutes!'

The boundaries that distinguish such subsistence practices from commodified exchanges are somewhat blurred by understandings of historically rooted customary practice and the attempts of low-income families to make ends meet. For 'clients' on assistance, these activities provide crucial income but their participation is coupled with the hope that social workers will turn a blind eye. 'Clients' are permitted, more by customary practice than official regulation, to make additional money, for example, by selling loads of wood they have cut. Many social workers disregard this additional income, particularly from work that is historically rooted in subsistence practices, including moose and rabbit hunting, fishing smelts, cutting wood, or helping to repair houses. However, Wendy does make some income (up to $1000) taking parties, mostly Americans, to hunt for moose and bear. She is required to report the money she makes from these trips. Many hunting parties, she claims, do not want the meat, 'just the rack' (of antlers); she cuts, distributes, and bottles the meat for family and friends.

For women, reciprocities within the extended family include a range of material, emotional, and social supports which provide single mothers with a few moments of leisure or with luxuries for her children that she can ill afford. Single mothers are cast in these relations as unequal recipients who are compelled to incorporate extended family in their lives to meet basic needs. Women on social assistance, in particular, rely on family for goods and services that must remain unreported so they will not be deducted from monthly cheques. Dorothy, a young single mother, frequently babysits her sister's daughter and is paid with either cash or groceries. Margaret, a fifty-six-year-old woman, 'helps out' at her sister's business and is given small, lump-sum amounts of cash which are not tallied according to an hourly wage. June receives numerous items of clothing (some used, some new) as well as food from her four sisters, whose children are now grown. Bonnie and her children are fed at her mother's on weekends. Upon the death of her husband, Elizabeth received social assistance and returned to her parents' home for the winter because she was lonely, afraid, and no longer able to afford the heating costs.

Numerous residents are connected to family or friends through these reciprocities. Yet the status of welfare recipients places them under special scrutiny. In Elizabeth's case, the social worker discovered her move and told her that she must move to an apartment she could afford or live with her parents and lose her assistance. Reluctant to give up the home near her family that she and her husband owned and built, Elizabeth felt compelled to conceal the details of her living arrangements. She joined her parents frequently on cold winter nights and continued officially to live in her own home. On the other hand, many informal arrangements are unreported, or overlooked by social workers and district offices already too busy to invest resources in dealing with these matters.

Single mothers who do paid work also draw on family support for social resources and making ends meet. Marie, a public-sector manager who is raising her son alone, states that she was able to establish herself as an independent single mother by living with her parents for the first five years of her daughter's life. Then she moved into a home owned by her parents which they leased to her at a low rent. Eventually she saved enough money to buy the house from them and now lives on the same street with her parents and two of her five siblings.

Beverley lives next door to her sister and brother. They frequently exchange babysitting and participate in joint child-adult activities. Similarly, Joan lives near her mother and often calls upon her for short periods of babysitting; when babysitting services are needed for more extended periods, she turns to a few nieces and nephews, whom she pays. In addition, her son frequently visits his uncle's and paternal grandparents' homes where he is included in activities with his cousins. Bonnie, however, is reluctant to presume that her mother is available to babysit and often calls upon close friends instead.

The importance of extended-family relations and exchanges in the reproduction of single-parent families is further evidenced by women who return home to Stephenville from across Canada once they are divorced. Joan lived in remote communities in northern Manitoba but returned to Stephenville where her mother and brother both live. Once separated from her husband, she was isolated and sought family members for emotional support, a sense of security, and short-term residence, until she was able to set up her own household. Although she lived with her mother for a short period of time, her experience of domestic control as a wife generated minor tensions there, which eventually erupted into larger conflicts.

Soon after her divorce, Doreen, who worked for many years in Calgary as a nurse, returned with her daughter to Stephenville where her extended family resided. She was fortunate to find full-time work in the hospital and considers herself to be making an acceptable wage for her family of three. According to Sharon, a fifty-five-year-old mother of two, the difficulties of working and maintaining a decent family life in Toronto finally compelled her to return to Stephenville and reside with her parents and her brother. Commuting from Brampton, Ontario, to downtown Toronto to work in an office gave her little time with her children, and the absence of extended family increased her sense of isolation and loneliness. Still, a return to the home of her childhood forced Sharon to give up the autonomy she had acquired; although she had little choice when her children were in school, she has since left her parents' home, anxious to regain her autonomy.

'The only thing single mothers are good for is lying on their backs'

This assessment, by a local politician, reflects that single mothers, particularly those 'on assistance' or those never married, are most often denigrated through sexist stereotypes which depict them as lascivious, promiscious, and irresponsible. Yet virtually every single mother with whom I spoke, regardless of her social location as worker or state dependant, emphasized the difficulties in actually forming any serious or even momentary sexual relationship. The demands of raising children and feminine presciptions convey that the responsibilities of motherhood and the attainment of emotional and sexual desires are irreconcilable pursuits. A trip to any local club underscores the difficulties single mothers face in meeting men who might make suitable partners.

These women include emotional and sexual interests as the needs that are often put aside. Most women indicated extreme reluctance, or adamantly refused, to 'bring home' men for fleeting sexual activity. Bringing home a man signifies to neighbours, children, and extended family his potential status as a household and family member. Thus, his potential as a father equals, if not overrides, his merits as a sexual or emotional partner. While many women have found short-term or extended relationships that eventually ended, they emphasize the amount of guilt this often generated. As well, it is difficult to distribute their emotional energy to children and partner while, at the same time, maintaining a family-based household where the conventions of redistribution and decision making presuppose some long-term commitment.

For Marie, the responsibilities of motherhood come far ahead of her interests in men, to the point that she no longer actively dates. Desiring male companionship Bonnie makes the occasional foray to a club, only to reject most of the men who come her way. Although one man did meet her sexual and emotional needs, she quickly ascertained that he was not 'the fathering type' and was compelled to meet him, very infrequently, away from her home. Although Joan and Rhonda display a more focused interest in remarriage, and have made efforts to circulate in clubs and engage in various local activities, they have found it difficult to find men sufficiently interested or, in their words, 'decent' enough to warrant serious consideration. The realities of dating mean that, although some women may aspire to a partner sometime in the future, they accept their single status and maintain the networks necessary to provide them with social, emotional, and material support.

Personal Plans and Feminist Visions

Joan, Karen, Bonnie, and Beverley all identify in some way with the label of single motherhood, a label frequently imposed on them. Yet each recognizes that, as their children grow, they will have to give their future some consideration. Recently, Joan decided that she does not want to take care of children for the rest of her life. She is now beginning what may be a lengthy return to the nearby college to complete high school. Bonnie, too, has just completed her university degree and, in anticipation of having her children full time, is reluctant to resume child support from her husband. Karen received high scores on her high school equivalency courses and then completed computer training. Unable to find full-time work that paid a decent wage, she has since, as she puts it, 'moved up along' to New Brunswick with her son. Lack of training and education is the commonplace explanation in contemporary discourse for the underemployment and poverty these women experience. Yet, as Karen's experience conveys, the only possibility for single mothers who achieve training and education is to move away with dependants in tow, a choice with an uncertain outcome that is rarely depicted in dominant constructions of the mobile worker who is 'free' to roam the country and settle where the jobs are supposed to be. Except for those trained in a profession, in the current context of government restraint (in which few new jobs are created), it is virtually impossible to make a single-parent wage in Bay St George, especially without the help of paternal support payments (Lord, 1994:195).

The importance of women's personal stories in contesting dominant constructions of dependency is that they convey the way current circumstances arise from a series of life responses and contingencies that unfold within family households. In this context, men and women are distinguished by divisions of labour, social and domestic responsibilities, and cultural categories of masculine and feminine that define and give meaning to their experience.

Beverley: 'When Mom died, everybody had a turn raising everybody'

Consider Beverley, who was raised in a family with thirteen siblings. Growing up, her family relied on the paycheque of her father, a construction worker, whose employment sent him across the island for weeks and months at a time. When Beverley was fourteen, her mother died, leaving her the eldest at home with six younger siblings. Beverley finished high school and began to attend community college when she met John, a factory worker who had returned from Toronto to join his father in the lobster fishery. Beverley became pregnant and gave birth to a son, just before other family members asked her to take a turn raising her younger siblings. Beverley describes how she eventually became a foster mother to her three younger brothers:

> When Mom died, my sister had just got married and her husband had gone to Labrador, so she came down to stay with the family for a while. But it didn't work, so my other sister tried. Everybody had a turn raising everybody. It was hard though, because I think Dad fell apart when Mom died. She was the one who kept the family together I think. When Mom died, Dad didn't know how to handle anything. So in a couple of years, he didn't pay his bills. He lost the house – then everybody was scattered all over the place. I didn't even notice my father drunk until after mom died. But he wasn't home when he drank. He would go off for days – so he wasn't abusive – I suppose in fact that he was neglectful. He tried to take the youngest ones, but then, when I had the baby, I got a place of my own, so I took my three brothers. I had them in a way since I was fourteen so I never felt like a sister to them.

In retrospect, Beverley reflects that her responsibility towards her siblings informed her decision to decline the marriage proposal from her son's father, who had once again returned from Toronto. She says: 'John came back from Toronto when my son was two, and asked me to marry him and I think that of all the time I had my brothers, that's the only time I hated having them. I turned him down – because it wasn't fair for him to take all those kids plus his own son.'

Beverley highlights certain forces that limited the range of choices and underpinned the decisions she has made. She implies that she was ill-prepared for a sexual relationship with John:

> When I was younger I wanted to be a nun. It's the truth. I was planning on going into the convent after high school. I thought I could help people, and you know, nuns do that. I had the idea of going down to other countries and helping people – such silly stuff – I guess. I wasn't interested in sex then. I thought I'd never have sex. It's something that never occurred to me – me and my friends, we'd say, we're going to have 20 layers of clothes so they can't get to us. But John convinced me. I started fallin' for him, I suppose. He was alright. I felt alright. He never put no strange demands on me. Sex had nothing to do with the church in a way – but the church may have had something to do with me not even thinking about sex before marriage.

Residual ideologies of family and church, the gender-coded structuring of contemporary institutions, and local constructions of appropriate feminine behaviour associate female identities with motherhood. Beverley reflects that, although she loves her son, she would have chosen to have an abortion when she became pregnant if the possibility had been raised with her. As she remembers, 'if someone had suggested to me to have an abortion, I think I would have. But it never crossed my mind. But then it wouldn't, because I was brought up Catholic. Dad, he just said, "well, you're not the first and your not going to be the last" – he was glad not to hear about it in the bar. But when I baptized my child, do you know what the priest said to me? 'Don't let me see you here again,' he said.'

The brothers she raised are now grown. Unwed and untied, they are somewhat self-supporting through low-paying, seasonal jobs in the area and in Toronto while Beverley, their 'foster' mother, lives on social assistance. Beverley has acquired skills that are socially embedded in responsibilities and relations with family members. It is a personal history that hardly lends itself to individual mobility and the risks of resettlement in an anonymous urban environment.

Moreover, it is difficult for Beverley to imagine an alternative when I ask her how she envisions her life in ten years.

> Now, I look back at my life as a child, and I say, well, Jesus, I was poor – at the material things. I mean, we didn't have anything, but it never bothered me. We never had a fridge, or a phone for the longest time – Now, I have a $10,000 student loan that I'll never pay off. I'll have a debt for the rest of

> my life. I'm poor – and now *you* know what poor means! In ten years time, I'll be further in the hole, I guess. I'd like my son to get an education. I'd like to get work. I would like to see myself in a house, but I don't know. I don't like to plan ahead. I never have. I find, if you plans, something always goes wrong.

Beverley suggests that poverty is more than the absence of material goods. Yet, although her narrative conveys a resignation to a future determined by fate or happenstance, her participation in the Women's Council suggests that she has found some way to articulate her interests in a social context which allows for her experiences to be shared and politicized.

Social Identities and Political Activism: The Single Parents Group

In many cases, 'family' provides the networks and emotional and financial support these women need to parent alone. Their difficulties, as single parents, however, leave women like Karen and Beverley with an emotional and economic investment in, and ambivalence towards, family and locality. Although they are members of families and of the community, they are frequently positioned as marginal within these domains. Nor are these experiences and the ambivalence they engender limited to marginally employed women who form the focus of this chapter. Rather, single mothers, some of whom have drawn on social assistance in the past and who are now employed in Bay St George as nurses, clerical workers, government employees, teachers, and employment counsellors, recount common difficulties in meeting emotional and social needs. They focus their after-paid work hours on their children and on extracurricular activities such as bingo and involvement in churches, choral groups, and parents' groups – activities that make living in Bay St George worthwhile to them.

For women like Beverley, attention to state policy and the experience of single mothers in general can be shared through the 'single parents group' which she currently organizes through the council. This group is a fluid body where women and some men meet to exchange information, socialize, share experiences, and challenge local stereotypes and political decisions, such as the 'welfare investigations' of single mothers. As a group, they advocate the creation of a rigorous but flexible system of support payments. Beverley and other members gain insights, resources, and support from other women on the council, like Maria, a former member of the single parents group who also draws on her connections to the francophone association which operates from a nearby rural community. In 1989, the Women's Council led protests against the government's decision no longer to allow women 'on assistance' to collect both child support and 'assistance.'

Occasionally Beverley is invited to speak to teenagers in area schools. In front of the classroom she details her monthly budget and enumerates the restrictions on her life. She openly criticizes her church and community norms on birth control, abortion, and sexuality. In so doing, she communicates an alternative narrative, one that depicts a local trajectory of female experiences unsanitized by the framework of nuclear-family idealization.

Through its support of single mothers, council members developed over time a more sustained critique of the way gender asymmetries are reproduced and built into the fabric of community and family life, as well as the state. Hence, my focus here has been to show how a critical perspective emerges from grass-roots activism – through the long-term understandings and interactions that council members bring to the organization.

In current national discourses where the dismantling of the state figures prominently, feminist critiques of state policies may, however unintentionally, reaffirm claims that state systems of redistribution engender debilitating social dependence and should therefore be dismantled. Moreover, the importance of kin relations and informal reciprocities in meeting the material, social, and emotional needs of residents may feed into this dismantling process if 'the family' as an institution is viewed by dominant policy makers as a haven of caring, a replacement for state services, and a justification for low state-income support. Local feminists are only too aware of the importance of the state in providing services and supports that can alleviate the work and responsibilties of area women and mediate conflicts within families.

By linking women's experiences of the state with their responsibilities to dependants in the family, feminists provoke a reassessment of the context of dependence itself in an effort to dismantle the ideology of individualism that informs current social relationships and labour-market assumptions and severs the exigencies of reproducing family from the individualized basis of waged work (Ginsburg, 1989:18; Fraser and Gordon, 1994:333).

The 'single parents' group and the Women's Council provide a context where life experiences and understandings of the matrices of power in which they unfold can be shared. However, the experiences of single mothers are shaped not just by the codification of gender difference within state policy and the insertion of those women into the labour market. Some women leave marriages and partnerships because of the particular and often violent behaviour of husbands or partners. It is the historical constitution of women as dependent that also renders them subject to forms of male dominance. Articulating this experience disrupts the ideal image of family, bringing into focus the exercise of male dominance by specific men. This has implications for the way in which the council has addressed the issues of violence and sexual abuse, as the following chapter illustrates.

CHAPTER FIVE

Sexual Abuse and Violence: Contested Meanings and the Politics of Narrative

Abuse ... is a part of our culture. (Mary, age 38)

On 11 June 1992, CBC[1] Newfoundland presented a documentary on the dinner-time news which was later shown across the country. The documentary, which recounted the sexual abuse of children in the Bay St George region, stemmed from the recent conviction of a man who had sexually abused twenty children from his neighbourhood. The program characterized the region as one of high unemployment and poverty and included numerous personal and professional accounts along with those of a Catholic school board official. One of the women recounted a personal experience of incest as a child and the sexual abuse of her son by the convicted man. The second woman, Mary, was a resident of one of the local francophone communities. Mary not only recounted the incest experienced by her children, but she went on to describe assorted abuses that pervade her entire community of White Brook. On TV Mary stated that 90 per cent of the people in White Brook had experienced abuse. In fact, she declared, 'Abuse in our community is a way of life; it is a part of our culture.'[2]

This incident occurred shortly after my arrival in Bay St George and it provoked immediate and long-term responses of anger and support in the region. On the one hand, the documentary gave prominence to issues that local activists had lobbied the government to address, and it precipitated the implementation of a Sex Abuse Counselling Service in the region. On the other hand, embittered residents of White Brook staged a series of protests to challenge Mary's statement and denounce the Women's Council for its support of her claims. Indeed, reaction to Mary's television appearance was so great that she was soon compelled to leave her community and has not since returned.

The documentary and its aftermath drew my attention to the way public confessions of social problems might affect local activism by reproducing or challenging pre-existing stereotypes and social cleavages. This was particularly important given that the Women's Council had supported Mary's claims and that sexual abuse and violence against women and children were two issues on which the Women's Council had increasingly focused its attention since the late 1980s. Moreover, 'breaking the silence,' making public the private experiences of abuse was a central strategy for addressing this particular problem in Bay St George and across the country. And narrating experiences of abuse was a part of local feminist consciousness-raising. To what extent could this method effect personal change and prompt public response and debate?

This chapter draws upon this incident to explore the ethnographic and discursive contexts in which sexual abuse is manifested and to consider the contested meanings which public narratives generate. I examine different settings in which experiences of abuse are debated and recounted to consider the social and political implications of narrating experience. Specifically, these stories are recounted in a context of power and are interpreted through historically rooted conflicts and local identities. The case of Mary in particular exemplifies the way feminist activism in Bay St George feeds into local politics, creating moments of consent and contention within communities and the region that tests the limits and expands the possibilities of this council to effect changes.

My analysis begins with Linda Alcoff and Laura Gray, who ask whether the narration of experiences of abuse such as Mary's can be an empowering and critical practice. Do the stories of 'survivors' challenge gendered relations of power or do they simply reproduce gender asymmetries and reinscribe the speaker within the hegemonic domains in which they are constituted? (Alcoff and Gray, 1993:260). In the following section I trace the emergence of sexual abuse as a social problem in local institutions and the media responses that Mary's television appearance generated. I contrast these public debates with the personal experiences of four women, one of whom is Mary. Culture informs the charged response to her public claims and the contested meanings over sexual abuse.

I suggest that feminist interpretations of survivor discourse can facilitate personal transformations in the lives of individual women and can expose the relations of power in which they are embedded. But I also show that, in this particular case, it takes the strength of a feminist collectivity – an organized politics – to effect institutional change and transform local practices.

The Discourse of Sexual Abuse in Bay St George

In Newfoundland the problem of child sexual abuse gained provincial prominence and entered popular discourse through the widely publicized trial of the Christian Brothers at the Mount Cashel orphanage in St John's, when they were convicted of child sexual abuse against young boys in their care. In Bay St George, the issue of child sexual abuse gained local prominence through the sporadic convictions of local men, three area priests, and, most recently, a video storeowner accused of sexually abusing twenty-three neighbourhood children.

The growth of social services in Newfoundland from the early 1970s generated an increase in the monitoring of conduct within the family. Child sexual abuse first appeared as a separate category within Child Welfare in 1981, and from this time reported cases rose throughout the 1980s, by 5000 per cent.[3] Social workers describe how the discourse of abuse permitted victims and professionals to name experiences that had previously been subsumed within the private domain of the nuclear family. John, a child-welfare officer in the area for the last twenty-five years, recalls that when he arrived in Bay St George, child neglect was the greatest problem. Yet he became increasingly aware of issues of child sexual abuse and played a major role in the recent case of the video storeowner: 'When I first came here things were pitiful – it was a very poor place. The big issue was neglect – not out of malicious intent, but families were really big and they couldn't cope ... I noticed a change in the late 1970s. My first sexual abuse case was in 1982. Kids would say "Dad's mad at me now." "I don't want to go home." Now they have words for it and now they tell me exactly what's happening. Now I pick up on it right away.'

George, who has also worked as a social worker in the area for twenty-five years, recalls that fifty-two children were dropped off at the door of Social Services in 1971 with notes such as, 'I can't take care of my children.' He is now aware in retrospect that some children may have experienced sexual abuse, but, as he puts it, 'they had no language for it, no way to communicate it.' This is exemplified by a woman who recently came to see him. She recounted her experiences of child sexual abuse while she was living in the area. According to George, 'I remembered her. She used to come into our office all the time, and try different ways to get our attention. One day, she stuffed beans up her nose. Now I realize she was trying to tell us something.' While child sexual abuse generates the most dramatic and outraged responses, experiences of sexual abuse are often recounted by adult women and men who recall past experiences.

Numerous government workers report that experiences of child sexual abuse figure in the recollections of their 'clients' in correctional institutions, the probation system, mental-health institutions, and local schools.[4] Social workers, counsellors, educators, and doctors, some of whom are Women's Council members, became increasingly aware of this problem through their paid work, personal relations in neighbourhood and family, and, in some cases, their own experience. For those who were actively lobbying the provincial government to provide counselling services for victims of abuse, Mary's television appearance was a decisive event for it provoked moral outrage across the province and compelled provincial ministers to respond. In her own community, however, anger that residents expressed was directed not at the issue of abuse but at Mary's interpretation of their culture.

Media Responses

Soon after Mary's television appearance, her neighbours in White Brook wrote letters to challenge her claims and protest the marginalization of their community through its depiction as an impoverished place. Mary was accused of 'disgracing' her home and 'spreading vicious lies' about a community that possessed 'high morals' and 'strongly Catholic' values. One resident wrote, 'The CBC tore us down worse than anybody could. They put us down as a poverty area dependent on the fishery, unemployment and welfare, but right now in Newfoundland that's happening everywhere, not just here.'[5] Residents interpreted Mary's comments as a condemnation of their francophone community culture and challenged the terms on which this culture was now being defined and depicted on television. As one writes, 'The Secretary of State is giving us money to preserve and promote our culture, which is a culture of what – sexual abuse?'

Similarly, a local political leader and journalist who lives in a nearby community responded to Mary's charges in his weekly column. He narrowed the scope of the problem to refer explicitly to child sexual abuse only and sought to distance the focus of the issue from this region in particular. Informed by a class consciousness, his identification lies with rural male breadwinners whose experience he attempts to represent. 'I live in this area and I don't abuse children,' he began, before proceeding to condemn the Women's Council, Mary's 'exaggerations,' and the absence of scientific evidence to support her claims. He concluded: 'People from this area grow the tobacco in PEI, man the fish plants in Nova Scotia, and the drydock in New Brunswick. We cut logs in Cape Breton, and bake bread in Arctic mining camps. Against all odds, we have struggled to preserve our families and our homes. When someone accuses us of abusing our children, it is the last straw.'[6] In contrast, the Women's Council expressed its support for Mary in the media. Informed by feminist interpretations of culture, their spokesperson highlighted the systemic nature of power relations between women and men and explicitly conflated child sex abuse with all forms of abuse of women and children. In the local newspaper, the council wrote: 'Mary's comments should be extended to include all the communities in the area. It is culturally acceptable in society in general for women and children to be victims of abuse. It's acceptable in a culture that has so little value for women and children. Incest in our culture is not taboo – to speak about it is taboo.'[7]

The interpretations of sexual abuse implied in this position are rooted in historically constituted cultural processes through which local identities of collective victims are constructed. It is interesting that each speaker seeks to reposition the issue of sexual abuse with respect to a particular understanding of culture. The reason, I think, is that their interpretations are based on different political identities which emerge from discrete collective histories of exploitation rooted in structures of class, gender, and ethnicity.

Media representations tend to simplify complex historical processes and generate oppositions rather than integrate the multiple experiences of exploitation that residents live. In sum, speakers erect distinct categories of victims and in so doing oppose groups of people to each other in relation to the problem of sexual abuse. However, while the issue of sexual abuse is mediated at the public level through these 'chains of association and displacement,' (Nava, 1988:105), the political boundaries that surface are hardly maintained in everyday life or the personal memories of these individual women.

Narratives of Abuse

In my field research, narratives of abuse emerged through the telling of life stories and the everyday conversation of numerous women. This was in spite of the fact that I in no way prompted them to speak about the issue. Their stories are frequently recounted not in a coherent chronology but in an open-ended outpouring of mixed metaphors, multiple explanations, and unfinished stories that centre them as eyewitnesses, actors, and victims of their experiences. Specifically, these narratives reveal that women experience numerous personal crises throughout their lives, and their stories impart multiple relations of subordination, including rape, domestic violence, child sexual abuse, neglect, unemployment, and addictions. Although sexual and physical abuse is documented in professional and popular discourses, it forms only one of many experiences that women face as daughters, mothers, sisters, workers, and wives.

What follows are partial life stories of Heather, Liz, Mary, and Rhonda, women who draw on 'survivor discourse' to interpret their experiences and reshape their identities. In these narratives women convey shared experiences as daughters, wives of fishermen, and waged workers that are woven through everyday relations of family and community. They signal the wider context of exploitation, involving boys, girls, men, and women, which cuts across life cycles and blurs boundaries of complicity and coercion in everyday social relationships.

Heather

Heather is a twenty-six-year-old government worker, and one of ten siblings, who was raised in the Bay St George area. I knew Heather fairly well and sought an interview with her with the unspoken intention of learning about her experience as a well-paid, unionized government worker. I drew her family tree in our first meeting, which she then pointed to as she narrated her story in somewhat chronological order. Heather's experience of child sexual abuse, once recounted, is woven through her entire story. At times it is through her explicit self-analysis, elsewhere in an implicit way that is evident in face-to-face contact but must be gleaned from the details of her narrative. She draws on key words used in the context of feminist counselling and 'recovery' therapy, such as 'safety' and 'disclosure.' Yet her notions of being saved and protected are equally embedded within Catholicism, the religion of her childhood.

> When I was growing up we lived here in Stephenville, and my dad worked mostly in road construction on the island. He worked in Churchill Falls, and at the mill in Stephenville before we left ... Growing up the youngest had its good points, but I was always accused of being spoiled – which I hated – *and I wasn't* – as far as I was concerned! It was probably responsible for a circumstance in my life – that – this one here (she points to her deceased brother on the family tree). I don't mourn his loss too much. (Pause)
>
> When I was a kid, he was sexually abusing me. When we moved out of Stephenville, I was quite happy then. Being the youngest, I don't know, I was happy enough, but that was a major factor. It affects my whole view of this town. It was hard to come back when I did.
>
> [In Stephenville] we had lots of space behind our house and the fair used to come here every year. The neighbourhood, when I look at it now – I thought it was good then. We had a yard we thought was huge and we used to make a skating rink in the winter; we always had fun and we had a cabin out of town that we went to every weekend in the summer – which was a getaway too. I was always safe out there 'cause *he* was older and he didn't always come. A lot of my life back then, was a concern for my safety – who I was with and that, played a really big role. I have two older sisters,

then seven boys, then me, and from all recollections I heard, they basically raised me because Mom was working at that point.

When I disclosed [the abuse] to my sisters about three years ago, they weren't surprised at who did it, but more that it happened under everybody's nose. It was believable because of the type of person he was. I often wonder, would it have been so easy if it had been an uncle or a father – you know – a lot of people get caught up in that mess, and for me, it was quite smooth because of the type of person he was.

Heather analyses the effects of her experience on her personal development, specifically her sense of herself as a 'misfit' and outsider, a theme that pervades her narrative. Throughout it, Heather recounts the process by which her experiences were 'disclosed.' After university Heather applied for a government job which required intensive training outside the province. She describes this period as the greatest seven months of her life in spite of a highly structured day, rigorous examinations, and difficult course work. During this time, her brother was under investigation by the Department of Social Services for molesting children. Heather, with a new confidence in herself as a result of her job training, disclosed the truth when she returned. She recognizes that the trauma of her experience was mitigated by a supportive family and the death of her abuser. It is the effects of this childhood experience that have preoccupied her during periods in her adult life and compel her to remember. Upon graduation from the government-training program, Heather accepted a job offer in Stephenville. Her return to the town in which she was raised, and the possibility of an adult sexual relationship, provoked a personal crisis and the resurgence of emotions and memories of her childhood.

I always knew that I'd be supporting myself. I had never intended to get married. I have never wanted children and I still don't. I knew I was going to earn my own way and I wasn't going to be begging for money.

I met John at a Christmas party and I never thought twice about him ... after the first two months that we started going out, I was cruel to him ... I'd been out with people, but never anything that lasted. I ended up in therapy. Well, it was something that was brewing anyway. I was freaking out. When I was in St John's I got to the same point – it was stress time and

> I wanted to remember when the abuse started. I went to a counsellor and he said, 'Now why do you want to remember that – you should be getting on with your life!' This was nothing that I wanted to hear. But when I got back to Stephenville, when I met this guy that I liked but I was frightened to death of, I was – emotions started coming up again – I mean, I had to talk to somebody! – and I called the Women's Centre and they said they couldn't accept anybody for counselling then and I said, I just had to come in.

Heather emphasizes that her desire to remember during 'stress time' or moments of personal crisis was subverted by the counsellors she had visited and the lack of resources. Although she has never forgotten these childhood experiences, it is the surrounding circumstances that she cannot recall. She implies that this recollection must be shared with another who will help her to understand the meaning and impact of these experiences on her adult life: 'There's different aspects of my life that, you know, I'm discovering is affected – like my sexuality. My feeling of being uncomfortable and God knows where that's rooted. It's just all these things I don't know. Even now I'll get into situation where – my boss, he'll give me a hug or pat me on the head and I'll just say, "leave me alone." It's not a real big problem it's just that it bugs me.'

Heather speculates on the sources of her current attitudes to sex, including her 'lack of interest' compared to her boyfriend and her discomfort in detailing sexual activity and talking about her body. 'I have limits and I think it has to do with the abuse,' she says. At the same time, she attributes her discomfort not just to the 'abuse' but to the historically rooted cultural norms that have shaped her understanding of sexuality and sexual relations.

> My Catholic upbringing had made it worse. It gives you more guilt. You are supposed to be untouched until marriage and there's a tendency for indoctrinated mothers to make their child/daughters feel responsible for pregnancy and I thought I was responsible by extension. But I know it was wrong. He was in his teens and I was a small child.
>
> Sex before marriage is not allowed – I felt tainted. I didn't always know it was wrong – you feel guilty. In the end, I know what was happening to me was wrong. But, for a certain amount of time, well no, I didn't. Well,

> by that point, you're trying to get out of it and you're telling somebody to stop, but he says, 'you're guilty too,' and all these tricks he uses. I asked him to stop. I would threaten him, that I'd scream or I'd tell ...
>
> I really thought they'd take me away, and I always feared they'd take me away but I don't know I thought that, I don't know if he ever said that, but where else would have I have had that impressiom. At home, we were always told not to make a fuss. I usually gave in. It was at first a game, then coercion on his part, but more emotional than physical. He didn't hit me. But I was often left in his care.
>
> My mother still sends me Mass cards ... I told her when I called her – I don't like receiving them. I never go to church, ever since I got old enough to escape it. I gave up confession long before that 'cause I didn't know what they wanted to hear – it's all for sin. I believe in God, and I believe in Jesus, and I have my own faith, but I don't believe in the Catholic Church.

Catholic ideology marked Heather, the child, as a sinner, whether or not she had a choice or a moral understanding of her experience. In her recollection, she could not distinguish right from wrong, or complicity from coercion. There is no room for the ambiguity of the unknowing child who, in the early stages of socialization, is acquiring morality. Lessons of obedience and submission to authority precede knowledge and understanding of the sexual body. It is difficult for Heather to sever the 'experience' from the cultural processes that give it meaning, both in the past and in the present.

Heather seeks, not just recovery, but to live a 'normal' life in which even a survivor status is no longer a fixed identity. At the end of our talk, I ask her why she told me about the sexual abuse. She replies: 'I was unsure whether I would say, or whether I wouldn't. Everytime I talk about it, I discover something else too. Much more like sounding off people. I talk to my sisters about it when I can, but I can't afford long-distance calls. And there's nobody else. I'd like to get involved maybe in a group – That's kind of what I'm searching for. In a lot of ways, I'm waiting for the opportunity to let people know. I'd like to talk with kids – like, when they're being abused, everybody thinks they can't live a normal life.'

As Heather's story conveys, the experience of child sexual abuse is hardly peculiar to White Brook, the community depicted in the documentary. Nor are other forms of violence that women experience in their adult lives. Indeed, such stories are recounted not just within the Women's Centre but in everyday conversation among women. The aggressive and belligerent behaviour of husbands, partners, and fathers is explained in numerous ways.

Local Explanations of Male Violence

On a cool summer evening in July, I joined June and her two sisters-in-law at Musicfest, an annual concert that features bands from Nova Scotia and Newfoundland. They played traditional Newfoundland music, country and western, and contemporary rock to crowds assembled on the grassy flats of an old airfield. As we waited in line under the beer tent, conversation turned to Lilly, one sister-in-law, and the new house she had bought with her second husband, a millworker. When June noted how contented Lilly seemed, Lilly nodded and then went on to compare her house and her second husband (essentially her new life) to the twelve-year marriage she had previously endured. She recounted the 'domineering' and 'violent' behaviour of her former husband, a 'Brown.'[8] Lilly recalled how he not only 'beat her to a pulp' but controlled all her movements and eventually cut the telephone wires to prevent her from communicating with friends or relatives. In fact, Martin, her former husband, was not only domineering but a poor provider, who did not take his responsibilities as a father and husband seriously.

June sympathized with Lilly. She, too, knew of the violent behaviour of the Browns, a family name that extends beyond the Bay St George region. A mutual friend had left her husband, also a Brown, after his repeated threats with a shotgun. I was not surprised by the mention of the Browns. I found that residents often invoked a last name to illustrate a certain behaviour, as if 'oh he's a Brown you know,' was all that was necessary to convey or explain an action. Similarly, in describing her husband's tendency to fight, another woman added, 'But he's a 'Smith.' He and his brother – they're all fighters.' In explaining her own husband's behaviour, another woman described how her husband was hit with a rope and wire repeatedly as a child.

The invocation of family as an explanation for such behaviour signified to me the knowledge and personal histories that residents hold in memory. Reference to family-based behaviour may also reflect the popularization of sociological theories that emphasize the importance of familial socialization in shaping human conduct. Such explanations were, however, rivalled by and combined with more individualized and medical explanations that attributed violence to excessive alcohol and lack of self-control.

Numerous women recall a husband or father to be soft-spoken and passive when sober and physically destructive and denigrating when drunk. Debra recalls that the first time her husband hit her was outside the bar when she confronted him for spending so much money on drinking and gambling. Sandra's husband, who was 'quiet and easy-going' when sober, would 'tear the house apart' after a night of drinking. Mary, a sixty-five-year-old, recalls the alcohol-induced 'Jekyll and Hyde' behaviour of her deceased husband, a man who was 'kind to everyone about town – but not at home.' Alcohol-induced abuse is frequently dismissed as the 'atypical' behaviour of otherwise good men. According to Laura, a forty-two-year-old mother of two whose husband is now deceased, 'I had a wonderful husband – except he was an alcoholic. But other than that, he was a good man! But uh, he was good to me, and to my son. Except for he drank. When he got drinking, I was a 'whore' and a 'slut,' and all this kind of stuff – but deep down I know that he loved me. He never once rose his hand to me, never once in his life. And the next day, after his drunk, he'd cry like a baby when I'd tell him what he said to me.'

Some men invoke alcohol to explain their outbursts. Jeff, a twenty-eight-year-old woodcutter, admits that, now and then, he'll find himself in a 'skirmish' in the bar at the end of the night. He admits that alcohol usually spurs his response but is unable to explain why this happens; sometimes, 'it'll happen for no reason at all.' Other times, he might be provoked by someone he already knows and doesn't like; or the belligerence of another man is impossible to ignore. 'I can't just walk away, they come after me, they jump on my back,' he explains. Similarly, a group of men serving short sentences in the Correctional Centre in Stephenville attribute their violent behaviour to an excessive use of alcohol and drugs, which makes them feel 'brave,' or reckless ('outta my head'). It is under these influences that, as one man put it, 'something happens.' 'I'll just be out with my buddies, and a guy will jump me, or something happens, and the next thing I know, I'm in a fight.'

These explanations tend to displace responsibility from the male aggressor onto an external force by medicalizing and individualizing behaviour as alcohol-induced or by invoking a family-based determinacy (Tavris, 1993:175). Rarely is it explicitly connected to the social power men hold and exercise within the family and as wage earners (Kurz, 1993:98). Some recognize that expressions of violence are socially legitimated and connected to certain displays of masculinity. For example, Tom, a social worker in the region, derives his understanding of violence as an expression of male authority and male frustration from his clients and his own experience. The son of an army sergeant, he believes that his father's frequent physical outbursts and bar-room brawls were produced by the way his father translated a military ethic into everyday civilian life.

The discourse of recovery informs the narrative of Liz, a young woman who sought help from the Women's Centre after leaving a violent relationship. Liz shifts the focus of responsibility onto her husband and links his physical and sexual abuse to the wider context in which extended family members resignedly accepted, if not condoned, his behaviour (cf. Kelly, 1987:129).

Liz

Liz is a thirty-two-year-old mother of two who twice fled to a nearby transition house[9] before she finally left her partner. Liz draws on the discourse of abuse to connect her physical, verbal, and sexual relations with her husband to his exercise of dominance. In so doing, she depicts her own transformation from a dependent woman who could not see a way out to one who is capable of living alone. An ideal of family and expectations of feminine behaviour form an explicit frame of reference for Liz, who attempts to explain her reasons for remaining in this relationship. Her repeated decisions to give her husband 'another chance' is, in her telling, informed by the determination 'to make it work.'

> I was sixteen when I got involved with Bill. And I think more than anything I was looking for a way to get out of the house. And I was with

> him for ten years – not a good relationship. I think, more than anything, wanting to be in the relationship, I didn't want it to fail, no matter how bad it was, I didn't want the life my parents had, I figured at all costs, I'd make it work. But it didn't ...
>
> He was verbally abusive, pretty well constantly. I mean, physically abusive a lot of the time and that was from the start. But then, he always said I deserved it and of course, I believed it. And when my daughter was born, Well, Anna was – born – she was – Anna was – conceived out of a rape.
>
> You often think in a relationship ... that spouses don't rape. But they do. I can remember Bill putting his hand over my mouth because I'd be crying and screaming ... and for the sake of not waking up the kids. After things like that, I hated him ... He said I would never leave. I couldn't see it either – how I could manage it. He'd say, you'll be on welfare ... I didn't know myself. Even after I come back from Transition House the first time.

In Liz's account, male dominance over her body was mirrored in verbal denigration and techniques of confinement which limited her mobility and circumscribed her relationships with extended family members and neighbours. Liz describes a context of abuse that shaped her own behaviour towards others, including her own mother and daughter.

> Bill made good money sometimes. He's a boilermaker. And he'd go away for a couple of months – mostly doing shutdowns, in oil refineries. Ontario mostly. I enjoyed the time when he was gone – very much. But he didn't trust me. I can remember one time, he asked if a [certain] neighbour ever dropped in. Bill figured I'd be right gullible with that guy. Things didn't get any better – he'd be abusive to me, and in turn, I'd take it out on Anna. I mean, I would screech at her constantly and smack her for no reason. Or, I should say, it seemed like a reason, but it wasn't. I was under a lot of stress, I was trying to keep her quiet and keep her – like Bill was so verbally abusive no matter what I did. I was concerned about my weight. And I would lose weight and he'd say I was getting too skinny. And I'd gain weight, and he'd say that I was too fat. There was no pleasing him at all.
>
> And then I got pregnant for David. Bill had just went away to work and

that was my choice to have David. My mother told me to break up with Bill – and his family all knew what he was like. They thought I deserved better. But the biggest thing with me was I hated to see it fail. I figured there had to be a way to fix it. Like, anything I could do, I would do. And then, it wasn't good enough. He would always change his mind. I was never sure, never.

His denigration of her character was facilitated by her husband's real economic power and Liz's belief that, as the chief breadwinner, he had rights over his children. Liz recognizes how her dependence on him was shaped by her acceptance of an ideology of family which prized male dominance and protection.

He was older and the biggest thing was I wanted someone to take care of me. Grown up. But when I got pregnant for David he wasn't pleased. He said it was bad timing. By then, I wasn't even talking to Mom. I'd pass her on the street and wouldn't look her in the face. [Q:Why?] Bill would say she was no kind of mother and he'd remind me of things she'd done. And I got to thinking, yep – that's probably right. I blamed her for a lot.

After the kids were born, he'd be gone all the time and I'd be home with the kids. That was my job. That's what he thought. I wanted the children, the nice home. Sure, we had a nice home, but he wasn't nice. As they got older he'd say, 'well, you can leave, but you'll never get my kids,' and I thought he was right. Even when things were getting really bad I couldn't see a way out.

The circumscription of her movements, in her interpretation, was reinforced by the complicity of family members: 'I used to visit his mother. That's the only place I used to go, was his mother's – or his sister's. He didn't want me telling his family what was going on. But they knew. Sometimes, his mother would say, "Well, I'll talk to him." They all knew. My cousin heard just from rumours about town. I didn't even go about town. I was home. If I went out, I was out with the kids. He'd tell me to take the car so I could come back as fast as I could.'

Yet it was female family members on whom she drew for the means of her escape. Liz explains that it was her mother who both provided money and told her about the Transition House. Her mother-in-law, who showed little support in front of other family members, and who actually denounced Liz's actions, nonetheless helped her to pack her belongings.

> I can remember coming home from his mother's and he was sitting in his chair. He had a knife in his hand and he come and opened the door and he ran the back of the blade across my throat and he said, 'It'd be so easy.'
>
> Then one day he had gone out. And I phoned Mom. And I said, 'when I can, I'm going to leave Bill.' And one morning, I phoned the cops and I told them I was leaving and that Bill would be after me. I just wanted someone to be there so I could get out. I had asked Bill when he'd be home just to see how much time I'd have. And as soon as soon as he left I started grabbing garbage bags. I was like a madwoman throwing everything in that I could. And I said to the kids – 'do you want to go on a little adventure with Mom?' ... I had told his Mom and she come down and she was helping me get packed as fast as I could.

Bill was charged with assault after following Liz to the Transition House eighty kilometres away. In the midst of a skirmish over the children, he drove off in his car as she lay trapped with her head on the seat and her body extended out of the open car door. He continued to 'stalk' her, following her in his car as she walked along the road, uttering threats and obscenities. Eventually they reached an agreement over child custody and, although Liz rarely sees him, she reluctantly allows her children to spend weekends with him when he is in town.

Liz received counselling from Women's Council members and is now, as she puts it, aware of 'the signs' of male dominance, which include attempts to circumscribe a woman's movements and 'put her down' through denigrating remarks. She is cautious about entering a new relationship yet more assured in her own ability to choose men who will not inhibit her desire to socialize and enjoy a wider range of activities. She discusses the positive effects of counselling in overcoming her experiences as an abused wife. For Liz, change is reflected in her assertion of independence to live 'without need of men' and her determination not to judge herself.

> I went to talk to the Women's Centre for counselling because I knew a lot

> of things would be too painful to tell Mom – like the extent of what I put up with. And I didn't want to hear, 'I told you so.' I'd get counselling every week and I would ramble on – like trying to get it all out – over ten years with Bill. She [Joyce] didn't say it was my fault or it was his fault. Well, to a point it was his fault. I used to think I was responsible for what I got. She made me see that he was responsible for his actions and nobody else.
>
> I felt guilty about taking the kids away from him. But nothing would've changed for the better. He wouldn't let me do anything, go anywhere, see anyone – I guess I just missed being alive.
>
> I know a lot more about relationships now – enough to give a bit of advice. I don't preach like I know everything 'cause I know the pull and the tug to stay especially where there's children. I think now, if it comes to the crunch I know what I'm going to take and not take. If you're at risk and your children are at risk then that's not much of a relationship. Sometimes I think I've come a long way.

Liz tends to emphasize that she remained in this relationship because she had internalized an ideology of family and male protection. Her narrative more indirectly conveys the connection of this ideology to the local context of waged labour and the gender division of labour that fostered the exercise of male control within the privacy of the nuclear-family-based household and over her body. Such behaviour is in practice facilitated by the resigned acceptance of male and female extended family members and their belief, as Liz puts it, 'to leave well enough alone' – in other words, to respect the privacy of the nuclear-family unit. The existence of a hidden space such as a transition house provides an alternate route of escape and allows sympathetic female kin to help covertly a battered woman such as Liz while maintaining the normative values of family privacy.

As the stories of both Heather and Liz convey, women do share experiences of sexual and physical 'abuse' at the hands of male aggressors. While some members of the Women's Council have themselves shared these experiences, others discover them through their paid work and assorted social networks. In many cases, women who initially visited the council to confront or recover from an abusive relationship learned of the council through friends, extended family, or co-workers. Mary, the woman who spoke on the CBC documentary, was one of many women who entered the Women's Centre to seek information. It is the environment of acceptance and the wider context of power that informed her lived experience. That prompted Mary to claim abuse as a part of her culture.

Mary

Some women came to me after I spoke and said, 'you have no right to speak for us.' The women, they're hiding. They don't have a choice. Survival. The parents always rule. And it's the mother who has the most influence out there. But it's the father who's the boss. You know what I mean? These mothers are the best actresses in the world. You wouldn't believe it, they're perfect my dear, everything is perfect!'

Mary is one of thirteen siblings from a family who have lived as fishers in White Brook for several generations. Eleven years ago, she discovered through her doctor that her four-year-old daughter had contracted gonorrhea. Sexual abuse was suspected and Social Services almost took her daughter away. Soon after, the child's grandfather was charged and served two months in jail. Mary's experiences and those of her daughter, in the court, the community, and within her immediate family, precipitated her intense interest in the issue of abuse. She was impelled to seek information on the subject from grass-roots counselling and resource services in Bay St George and in New Brunswick where she and her husband worked in short-term jobs. She explains how the issue of sexual abuse became important to her, and how it transformed her attitude towards state services and community norms:

> I have to go back eleven years. That's where it began for me. It began before that, it began as a child, being raised into the community. The abuse was there then – if we're talking about sex abuse – it was there then. Growing up into the community, we were allowed [to go] certain places and not certain places. We didn't understand why. I'm talking about my family and as I grew up. It was part of something that you saw and it was accepted 'cause you didn't know the difference. I'm talking from the knowledge that I have today.
>
> Then I had children of my own and that brings me to eleven years ago

where my children were sexually abused. It became a very strong issue for me. I was supposed to give up my child because of that. She was very young. It was then I decided I had to talk and I approached the Department of Social Services, the RCMP and I gave them the story of my life as I saw it in an abusive situation in the area where I come from. I had to educate myself to help them. And it was a family thing, so it was really, really, really hard to do. And then, I thought that because I gave them the information, they would do something about it.

When I went on TV, I had support, but not from this area. How the kids were treated? How my child was treated by the system? She was completely abused over and over, OK? So I decided I would get it to the public eye, where I knew I would have support, that I as a person living in the community, who brought the abuser to court. I had proof. He got jail. But in the community, they didn't see my daughter as the victim, they saw him as the victim. He came back to the community – no problem for him. Now they won't accept us, just him. We weren't supposed to bring this to the public eye.

Mary's awareness of sexual abuse is rooted in her intimate knowledge of residents and in the lived experience of poverty and religious hierarchy that pervades community life.

Now even some of the men confess it to me. I say, you have to start your acceptance, you have to go into your mind, and see, were you abused? One man told me he didn't need to go into his mind for that – it was all there and let me tell you, it wasn't no sunshine! His rectum was all torn up even as a child. And now he says he can't help himself, he just goes into a trance and does the same thing to others.

We got people home who's sixty, who can remember being abused by the priest. You can see the connection between the church and the abuser in the community. One man, he's a real hard case, he was a real pirate. He told me when he was an altar boy his father beat him black and blue for telling what the priest tried to do! The church was as big an abuser as the parents.

[Q:Are there many offenders?] Yes, mostly men, but women too – if we're talking about all abuses – but with sexual abuse, it's mostly men. And their victims are children whose parents are on social assistance.

> There's no such thing as an allowance for a child. OK? The only way a child can get an allowance is to go away and let their body be mauled by a man. Now, older women do it too. If they want to go to the bingo, they'll go to this place and get laid then they go up to the bingo. That's fine. To me, you got your age. But when you see a man and a crowd of little girls around him and coming out of his house and going to the store and buying all kinds of candy knowing those people are all on social assistance, and their parents can't give them any money, you can't put a blind eye to it.

Mary links sexual abuse to control over children through denigration and smacking. She places responsibility on herself and other female residents.

> I made it plain [for TV] that if I talk about sexual abuse, I'm clearing the innocent. But if I'm talking about abuse, I'm involved too. I made it plain that I'm guilty too. A child is a person. It's nothing for a parent to smack a child across the face. Now, I'm not saying that I never did smack my children, 'cause I'd be lying to you. I reared up my first child giving her smacks. And then I did a program and learned what I was doing wrong. It's so easy to let that hand go and smack and then you get complete silence.

It is her awareness of the broader context of power, and her concern to transform and redefine social norms, that prompted her participation in the documentary: 'I saw the problem getting worse. Like, it was coming more out into the open. In the community. And little children would actually imitate what they were doing with their father, with their uncle. Like I was the witch 'cause I found something wrong with it. And I realized it was useless going to Social Services and the RCMP. Here, the system made you feel dirty. Social services made you feel dirty.'

Mary attempts to redefine a community morality and in so doing identifies residents as complicitous and potentially guilty within a changing legal framework and redefinitions of normative behaviour. It is Mary's experience as the mother of a sexual-abuse victim, within the courts and Social Services, that prompted her to call for a counselling service 'from the outside.' As her narrative conveys, pre-existing dynamics of power within her community, between residents and kin and between town and rural communities, shaped a victim's experience of abuse in a way that favoured the offender, dismissed the seriousness of the offence, and placed blame on the victim. A counselling service, in her view, would have to operate autonomously from these domains of power in which victims, women in particular, were judged in a way that reproduced local morality and asymmetries between men and women and within the community.

Sex Abuse Counselling Service

When I spoke out, my phone was unreal, the calls I got from women all over the area, not just my community. They wanted to put in place something that would help them. They didn't want to put people to jail. And that's not my idea either. They said, 'Don't ask us to go to social services. Don't ask us to go to the RCMP.' What they needed was a support group. And we need people from the outside, who's going to help no matter who you are – let you be a cop's wife, let you be on social assistance, let you be the biggest bag on earth! Somebody to help you as a human being, no matter for your status. (Mary)

Although Mary focused on White Brook in the CBC documentary, she recognized that the problem of sexual abuse is hardly confined 'to home.' Similarly, since its formation, Women's Council members have increased their awareness of, and developed resources for dealing with, 'wife abuse' and 'child and adult sexual abuse.' They began to offer ad hoc counselling for individual women and more organized groups for 'survivors' of these experiences. During the last ten years, public-sector workers in the departments of social services, mental health, and education also became sensitized to the needs of their 'clients' for a counselling service that would focus on facilitating recovery from experiences of sexual abuse. Not only did they lack the specialized training in counselling, but their administrative and client-centred tasks were too numerous and diverse to offer the time that sex-abuse counselling might entail. This service, formulated through consultation with government ministries and a local 'community response team,' was officially opened in the spring of 1993.

A small number of residents who have used the service are from

White Brook, including Rhonda, who was compelled to leave her community. Her story demonstrates how child sexual abuse and adult sexual abuse can coalesce in the life experience of a single woman. Moreover, her experience illustrates the difficulties an individual faces in changing her life's course while remaining resident in her home community.

Rhonda

> Since I spoke out I've been talking to some women from my community, and we were talking about the people who are abusers and you know, how better to bring out a memory than to reminisce. And I'd say, 'did you visit that house?' And then, the realization that it was wrong! (Mary)

The memories of which Mary speaks trouble Rhonda, who both condemns Mary's TV appearance and accepts her claims. Rhonda left a violent husband and family members in White Brook, who scorn her 'foolish' behaviour. She has not forgotten experiences of sexual abuse. Lately, the way Rhonda tells it, memories come often and in various forms. They appear, unsolicited, in nightmares and daytime flashbacks. At the same time, she consciously invokes details of her past through counselling and conversation with sympathetic listeners.

Rhonda draws on the discourse of abuse to reinterpret sexual practices that pervade her life. She repeats the key words, 'abuse,' 'rape,' and 'healing,' which mark shifts in her own knowledge and understanding. It is more difficult to convey, in text, the long glances, downward gazes, and frequent pauses. Because we were together frequently for a few weeks, I recount her story as it unfolded in our everyday conversation.

'Home,' as Rhonda puts it, is neither 'all good nor all bad,' nor are its residents. The community is a place where the intimacy of family relations and neighbourly visits are both reassuring and unwanted, friendly yet prying. Neighbours arrive unannounced and news of family conflicts passes quickly from house to house. Drunken holidays generate endless argument and conflict, which can erupt at family gatherings. In describing her home to me, Rhonda began to talk about her family and her reasons for leaving White Brook. 'They aren't all bad home,' she said. 'But it was just getting to be too much. I wanted a good life for my children. I didn't know life was any different. I didn't know you could do other things. Now I'm seeing things so different ... I used to hit my kids – that's what they did in my family. Now I'm learning to talk to them more. And I worry about John [her son] 'cause he's always getting into fights and the boys would be out after him all summer long.'

Rhonda then expressed concern for her adolescent daughter, a topic that prompted her to talk more extensively about sex and her discovery of the word 'abuse': 'You know, I never knew of the word "abuse." There was no pamphlets home, no information. I never heard of the word rape – I didn't know it was rape. It was just – bad. I never knew that you could say no. Some of them home don't think anything of sex. You just go along. I was like that too. I never said anything to nobody. It wasn't talked about. But everyone knew it was going on. It's just something you have to live through. Sex is just living to them. It's life!'

One day, during lunch, I joined Rhonda for a cup of tea and she began to tell me about her day. In so doing, she revealed her own experience of sexual abuse. That morning the social worker had dropped by to inform her that her brother was suspected of sexually abusing his daughter. The social worker wanted both Rhonda and her sister to state formally that their brother had abused them as children and Rhonda was anxious to help. She deliberated aloud as if to finalize her decision:

> I decided I have to say something. The way I see it, it started with Mary and she went one step, and that may have got her nowhere, but then, now there's me. And I'm here. And if I speak up, then maybe somebody will come forward, 'cause it's got to stop. It's got to stop. I'm going to tell my sister to help.
>
> I'm not going to worry about my family anymore. Mom, she just says to leave it alone, it's in the past, it's done. [Pause] He abused me and my sister, and my sister got it much worse than me. But she won't go public with it. She'll admit it to me, but she won't go public.

We talked extensively about her family and Rhonda's ambivalence towards leaving them. Of her eight siblings, she is closest to her middle brother, a woodcutter.

> I haven't told my brother yet, maybe at Christmas. But all they like to do at

> Christmas is drink. Maybe we'll solve it then! [She laughs] Christmas is always supposed to make things better, but it never does. And I'll be alone this Christmas. Just me and the kids. That's OK, I don't mind. [Silence]. But it hurts. I wouldn't have said that before. It hurts. I wouldn't have said anything. But now I can. [Silence]
>
> You know, if I was talking this way home, they'd look at me like I was crazy. And if I'd met you five years ago, and you were to mention abuse, I'd say you were foolish. And if you was to come to where I live, they'd just put you out.

Rhonda hints that she was also sexually abused by others.

> I never heard the word abuse. I didn't know what it meant. [Pause] And now, I knows. I know it can mean many things. There was just rape – but for me, it was just, you were in the wrong place at the wrong time. I thought it was just my fault ... You know, when you go in a place and it happens. [Pause] They starts tearing off your clothes. I hated it! There's some places I wouldn't go without a rope or a belt tied to me pants. And then, I goes home, and I was told I was just stupid for being in the wrong place.

The notion of abuse allows Rhonda to consider related infringements on the body and, therefore, to identify with her husband's experience: 'I'm just beginning to see that there are other things out there. My husband, he was physically abused by his parents. He got a lacing all the time and I don't know what that's like. But I knows sexual abuse. We share that. He's in counselling now. But sometimes he looks at me like I've changed so much – he can't understand what's happened to me. I've changed a lot.'

The next day Rhonda urged me to sit down and have some tea. She had returned from a counselling session that had put her in an upbeat mood. Perhaps this is what prompted her to continue her story, this time by focusing on her addiction. It was after the birth of her second child that Rhonda began to get 'the baby blues,' and lose sexual interest in her husband. Rhonda now realizes that her husband's frequent outbursts of swearing, put-downs, and physical violence, directed towards herself and her son, may have increased her depression. At the time, however, her family told her it was 'just nerves' and she went to a doctor who prescribed drugs, which she has taken for the last six years.

> I started with two pills. And then, I was up to twelve pills a day and I couldn't do nothing – they were to calm me. I could sleep twenty-four hours. I couldn't do my housework. I tried to quit them but I kept getting sick. It was like I had the flu and I felt sick to my stomach and the doctor gave me more pills. I went to that doctor 'cause I was depressed and I told him, I though it might be in my head, and he burst out laughing. I felt so foolish!
>
> But all the time I was just wanting someone to talk to. For six years I tried to find someone to talk to. I called Social Services twice, but they couldn't help. [She whispers so her son won't hear] Then, I tried to commit suicide. That's what it took. Then I got counselling. I wouldn't be here now if it weren't for counselling. I càlls it my medicine, that's what talking is.

Rhonda did not remain so upbeat once she came closer to openly accusing her brother of child sexual abuse. She was concerned that he would serve a short time in jail, receive little counselling, and threaten her upon his release. A few days later she had 'nightmares' and 'a panic attack' so severe that she was taken to hospital. It is the *feeling* of memories that resurface through touches, smells, and voices that affects Rhonda so profoundly but defies precise description.

A few days before my departure, Rhonda came to see me. She was very depressed. She sat down on the rocking chair beside me and began rubbing her 'sore stomach.' Rhonda asked if I 'knew about' the drugs she was taking and the effects on her body. Perhaps I could explain the cause of her anxiety? She was straining to speak without crying. Her sister had phoned to say that she would not go for counselling. This upset Rhonda, as did her sister's lack of interest in her well-being and that of her children. The ambivalence about leaving her family to live in town, where there she had no friends, returned.

> My mother only visited me once. Nobody calls. After next week, you won't be here no more. I don't want many friends. Just a few friends – just somebody who can be my family. I was on the verge of a panic attack all

> day. So I took a long walk to calm down. [Pause] But I gets a tight head and my stomach, it's so sore and I can't sit still. So I try walking – I don't know what to do.
>
> Sometimes I wonder if it's a disease I got. I wonder if it comes from my family, if we all got it. I wonder, is it the stress that makes my head so tight? Is it the drugs? Do you think it's the prozac? Sometimes I think it gets worse before my period. I gets a tight head. I get goose bumps all over and my body jumps as if it's upset and nervous.

When conversation turned to mutual friends, Rhonda reflected on changes in her character.

> Like I told my sister-in-law, today, 'Nobody deserves to be hit or talked badly to when their husband is drunk!' Now, that's my brother who's hitting her and even though he's my brother, he has no right to do that. I wouldn't have thought that before. I would have thought, 'Oh, she probably deserved that.' I don't think that anymore.
>
> I sees myself now – how weak I was. Now I sees other women who are weak. Men can pick 'em out! Men, home, don't know you can say no. You say it once and they don't hear it – they just keep going. My husband raped me more than once. [Pause] But he wouldn't call it rape. He didn't know it was wrong. [Silence]
>
> I says 'no' [to sex] and he's there, putting me down on the bed, accusing me of losing my feelings for him, that I love someone else. I tried to explain to him the other day, that it's wrong, that he can't do that. And my sister, she don't understand that you have a right to say no. She sees it as normal. It's crazy isn't it?
>
> I used to think it was my fault. Just for being there. And my family – they blame me. They blame me. Everyone blame me – for the way I am – for the way I were. I was always so cross and contrary. But they knew. It was just living to them. It's the way things are.

More than a year has passed since this meeting with Rhonda, who is now settled in town and in much better spirits. Such news is a pleasant reminder that her personal transformation, suspended in text, is nonetheless an ongoing process.

The Power of Talking: 'I calls it my medicine, that's what talking is'

In recording women's life stories I was struck by the number of women who expressed a great deal of satisfaction in recounting experiences that included abuse and personal crises. These women, including those featured here, emphasized that talking was an important component of personal recovery in that it made them feel better. Similarly, feminist counsellors in Bay St George emphasize the curative and empowering effect of talking in place of drug therapy. They challenge the medicalization of women's problems and work to implement feminist forms of counselling within the local arms of government services. Yet Linda Alcoff and Laura Gray argue that the detailing of sexual practices can 'inscribe' the speaker within hegemonic discourses of sexuality. The normalizing effects of the confessional are reproduced, evaluating the woman's behaviour through the medium of experts and compelling her to speak about her experience. The result is to subject the individual to mechanisms of domination (Alcoff and Gray, 1993:260, 281).

In a similar vein, Michelle, a counsellor in Bay St George, argues that the specialized language of the professional therapist can not only define but confine a client's experience. For instance, a professional can reproduce the gender asymmetries and pre-existing power relations between herself and a client, and between client and abuser or other friends and relations. This may occur by using 'jargon' such as 'co-dependency' which can blame the client who has been victimized (cf. Tavris, 1993:198). Also, feminists point to the limitations of a family-therapy model (which has been used in Bay St George) that does not take account of gendered power relations within the family or the authority and social power of men outside the family (Kurz, 1993: passim). Furthermore, the language of the educated professional can reinforce difference by making clients, many of whom are less educated, feel inferior. The most dramatic example of the dominating effects of narrating experience are illustrated in television, especially talk shows where a survivor's trauma is framed to titillate viewers, blame the survivor, or reaffirm common-sense understandings and gender stereotypes (Alcoff and Gray, 1993:276; Epstein and Steinberg, 1995:279).

On the other hand, survivor discourse can also transgress hegemonic discourses, that is, disrupt or transform, for example, the way we talk about the family as a haven. It can provide a frame through which the speaker connects her experiences to a broader context, thereby exposing relations of power[10] within families, religious institutions, and communities. This is reflected in the narratives of Heather, Liz, Mary, and Rhonda. These narratives also highlight the importance of broadening our analysis so as to acknowledge ambivalence and to consider a broad configuration of relationships. In this way, loyalty and anger towards family members, and struggles to maintain yet sever familial and social ties, comprise their lived experience.

In recounting their lives, Heather, Liz, Mary, and Rhonda centre themselves as victims and agents of past experience. In so doing, they refashion their identities in the repeated retelling of their lives (Behar, 1992; Reissman, 1992). The discourse of abuse helps women to effect changes in their identities as mother, sister, and daughter. It clarifies the meaning of ambiguous memories and ambivalent emotions that might facilitate personal transformation (Ferguson, 1991; Herman, 1992). The articulation of experience, the retelling of life-stories, is a means by which women control their own narrative and transform their identities from victims to survivors. The authority of their narrative is effected in a setting where interpretations are restricted to that of the recovering individual and the sympathetic listener. The latter introduces labels as a tool for understanding, not as an instrument of domination (Kelly, 1987:130).

These experiences are recounted for the personal transformation of individual women. However, when exposed or recounted within an uncontrolled public domain, the authority of interpretations is subjected to debate. The persons in the narrative are implicated and potentially subject to judicial process. It is to the public narration of personal experiences that I now turn, which tests the limits and boundaries of local feminist practice and exposes the social conflicts that underpin a single social problem.

The expression of personal memories is structured by cultural relations of power that favour the reproduction and expression of certain social memories over others within a public and collectively recognized domain (Laurie, 1988). The performance of femininity has been, until recently, an act of forgetting, of eliding the expression of self and experience with others, within the family unit (Greene, 1991; Swindells and Jardine, 1990). As Mary conveys, there are social pressures for women to speak for the good of the family as a unit, even when it may obfuscate relations of power within it. In the most dramatic cases, and as each of these narratives convey, to perform a feminine role is to be a good and uncomplaining girl like Heather. It is to be a good wife like Liz, or a good sister like Rhonda, who is told to ignore the past, submerge the memories, and, most important, refrain from giving public expression to 'private' matters.

These narratives also suggest that women certainly contest the social pressures to silence them and in fact (in Liz and Rhonda's cases) can be rejected by their family if they translate this into action. A feminist discourse provides a critical and political avenue for the narration of experience and a means to leave this oppressive domain. The subversive character of narratives of abuse is underscored in a context where social pressures encourage women who have not forgotten to 'let it pass.' Social conflict emerges when personal memories begin to contest collective understandings.

The Politics of Memory

> When she went on TV, I just said to myself, 'Oh, that's Mary!' She made things worse. It's the way she said it – she said it was our culture – she made us feel like we were the only ones, and by doing that, she included everybody, even me. But I didn't do anything sexual. It happened *to* me.
>
> But in a way it was good for me. I started thinking of all the things that happened to me and I didn't want it for my children. I wanted a better life for them. And then I started thinking about how I grew up and how bad my life had been and how things were with my husband. (Rhonda)

Rhonda's ambivalence towards Mary's television appearance reflects her identification with a collective francophone culture as an undifferentiated entity. Mary, however, identifies relations of power within that culture and provokes a reaction from her neighbours and kin.

After the CBC documentary, residents of White Brook demonstrated against Mary in their community. Marching along the main road that follows the shore, they carried signs denouncing her claims. This group of about thirty-five men and women demanded Mary's resignation from the board of the local francophone association and eventually forced its closure. Furthermore, numerous residents boycotted the annual celebration of Saint-Jean Baptiste Day.

Mary draws on the discourse of abuse to characterize many relations of power of which child sexual abuse is only a part. It is this context of power, 'the way things are' in Rhonda's words, that Mary labels 'culture,' in the sense of a particular way of life. However, Mary harnesses the discourse of abuse to redefine the local culture of White Brook, which in the last twenty years has transformed itself into a distinct, francophone community. It is Mary's public redefinition of francophone culture that effects dramatic change in White Brook. Mary historicizes her experience as a survivor and as a mother, situating herself as part of the history of relations in White Brook (hooks, 1989:110).

Six months after the documentary, the community centre in White Brook, which was owned and operated by the francophone association, was burned to the ground. The event was directly connected by different sources to the events surrounding the CBC documentary. Mary has her own interpretation of these events:

> They figures I would shut my mouth and everything would quiet down if they got rid of the French centre, 'cause all my volunteer time was given over there. Everything we work with, the women's group, everything was done through that centre. All our progress. If we can't get the French centre back on its feet, we've lost. Because it's there we had the facilities to contact people. I knows, me, as a volunteer, we'd have seminars on crafts and behind it we had another motive – to get the women together and get their support.

The community centre was a social space that embodied the construction of a new francophone culture, where relations of power among neighbours, between genders, and within families could be exposed through consciousness-raising and education. Mary and others brought resource people to the centre who provided education on assorted topics including parenting and abuse. Tragically, the destruction of this social space also meant the loss of their recorded history, of 200 tapes of songs, stories, and family histories.

Conclusion: 'The problem is, she acted alone'

Alcoff and Gray draw attention to the context of power in which narratives are recounted to demonstrate the way hegemonic processes are reproduced. Just as gender asymmetries are reproduced through the techniques of the confessional, so too are marginalized groups reproduced by the way their economic circumstances are depicted. As residents convey in their letters, it is not just the condemnation of their culture on the basis of sexual abuse against which they react. It is the depiction of this area as an 'impoverished place,' as if it were different from the rest of Newfoundland and somehow inferior.

Here it is the political economy of White Brook that forms the background against which the problem of sexual abuse is featured. It is perhaps one thing for Mary to connect the lines among poverty, family conflict, and abuses of the body. It is another for a national television producer to do so. The latter does not provide a forum whereby claims, even antagonistic claims, between and within exploited groups can be addressed in a way that might expand their understanding, effect change, or politicize a wider group of actors within the collectivity (Sider, 1991:230).

Moreover, it is tempting to erect cultural boundaries around the life experiences of Mary and Rhonda, to distinguish a rural, francophone culture from the lives of nearby English-speaking Newfoundlanders, who themselves are marginalized as earthy folk and 'have-nots' in national myths (Kelly, 1993). In this way we might mark the transformation of a socially embedded folk culture. To do so, however, would be to reinforce local stereotypes in which townspeople distinguish themselves as implicitly superior to those on the peninsula; nor could it account for the experiences of Heather and Liz. It would also mean reducing a complex history to a reified set of behaviours and cultural traits, and would assign blame for these traits to the local francophone culture while overlooking the constitution of social subjects within a wider hegemonic context. Together, the stories of these women reveal their cultural connection to a broader social universe, the Canadian welfare state, whose mechanisms of power in the welfare bureaucracy, the labour market, the judiciary, and the medical profession structure their experience of sexual abuse.

For residents of White Brook, however, culture is, both 'the way things are,' a history of lived experiences, and a bounded unit with political meanings rooted in the shared history of francophone experience and marginalization. It is also an identity that residents have proudly reclaimed. Perhaps the conflicting meaning of culture itself in popular discourse fueled the destructive response to Mary's allegations about abuse in White Brook.

As Rhonda suggests, ultimately Mary failed because she did not get the women on her side. She did not include them in her struggle to gain intervention and help and, in so doing, forced them to choose sides. Whatever Mary's intentions, the individualistic character of her response lends itself to the dramatization of personal experience on television but does not have the collective support to effect qualitative change in White Brook.

The issues surrounding sexual abuse and violence against women are an enduring focus of council activities. They exemplify the importance of sustained, collective, and multi-pronged activism at the grass-roots, provincial, and national levels, a subject that is examined in the next chapter.

CHAPTER SIX

Grass-roots Activism and Feminist Politics

Once a month council members would assemble around the kitchen table at the Women's Centre and map with coloured markers a multi-pronged set of initiatives on a large chart. They would assess the strategies that were already in place to address a range of issues – a policy change in social assistance, for example. Or they would consider their media response to a politician's sexist statement, or contemplate the most appropriate venue for an upcoming meeting with a priest, a minister, or members of an economic-development organization. This was a time for board members to air their views and frustrations, to draw attention to a case, a client, an event, or a conversation which might contribute to whatever strategy was up for discussion.

The attention I have devoted to single mothers and a particular aspect of violence and sexual abuse is a very partial illustration of the problems that area women face and that council members tackle. My focus on these specific problems, however, brings into sharp relief the complex relationship among locality, region, nation, and lived experiences. Moreover, it provokes two important questions: What can a single grass-roots organization do in light of such complicated social problems? How do the processes of differentiation that are illustrated in previous chapters inform the practices and values that comprise community and feminist politics?

In the months after the television documentary on sexual abuse, council members and other community activists made some progress in their efforts to have sexual abuse and violence against women and children addressed through negotiations with government and the establishment of an anti-violence coalition. One of their accomplishments was the development of a model for a sexual-abuse counselling service which would service the entire southwest coast. The model (which is discussed in chapter 7), required the participation of several branches of government, including that of justice and corrections, which were reluctant to participate. I attended several meetings, one of which I recount below, because it encapsulates key features of local feminist organizing.

'Take off your shoes!'

It was 9:30 a.m. on a sunny day in March when two officials from Corrections Canada arrived at the Women's Centre in Stephenville, some ten months after substantive negotiations for a sexual-abuse counselling service had commenced. 'Take off your shoes!' directed Cynthia, who was in the middle of sweeping the floor. The men, clad in suits and ties, shuffled uncomfortably in the hall but soon obliged. After all, it was a 'home.' Michelle, the president of the Women's Council, had turned down their request to assemble in the boardroom of the local hotel and offered the Women's Centre instead, as a 'more comfortable' meeting place.

Joyce, the coordinator of the Women's Council, cheerfully greeted these men as they entered the open dining room and offered them coffee or tea before ushering them into the spacious, fully furnished living room. One man was gestured towards a large, comfortable couch covered with pastel-coloured pillows and home-made quilts. The other, eager to sit beside his colleague, was directed instead to a cosy love-seat where a woman was already seated. Once all participants had taken their places – they included two RCMP officers, two sex-abuse counsellors who work in the departments of education and mental health, respectively, two single mothers, and two Women's Council members – the council president introduced an agenda.

The officials had agreed to assemble and respond to the concerns raised by residents in Bay St George over the implementation of an experimental sex-offender 'recovery' program that was to operate in town and place sex offenders in the local halfway house. Those administering the program were proclaiming, through media reports, an 80 per cent recovery rate for the men who undertook the ten-week treatment program. The council and other residents hoped this program would be a part of their multi-pronged strategy to address violence and sexual abuse. The Department of Justice (so it appeared to locals) was concerned to remain quite separate from the integrated commmunity-based model which activists had proposed. Hence, the proposed sex-offender program became a focus for debate regarding the relationship between the community and different branches of government involved in addressing violence and sexual abuse at the provincial and federal levels.

Minutes after the introduction, domestic hospitality was eroded by intense and, at times, confrontational discussion over the program. The Corrections Canada officers began aggressively by defending their proposal with a lecture of explanation. One informed the audience that residents of the town had simply misunderstood the major elements of the plan and the scientific results of the study. His attempts to summarize these results were, however, interrupted by a series of questions from others who displayed a thorough familiarity with the program in question. Soon after, these two men were faced with assorted, well-informed arguments from all sides of the room. Kathy wanted a detailed account of how surveillance and protection would be maintained. Jim, the sex-abuse counsellor, cited other reports that questioned the utility of this therapy model and the possibility of 'cure.' Ruth, a single mother who lived across from the halfway-house, recounted experiences with other halfway house residents and stated somewhat angrily that claims of 'recovery' in the media might provide false comfort for neighbourhood mothers.

It is difficult to convey how the soft texture of a baby-blue quilt or the enveloping contours of an overstuffed couch can dismantle the trappings of male power. Ironically, these very accoutrements provided reassurance to female participants at the meeting, like Ruth, who would have refused to attend or been reluctant to speak in a hotel boardroom, a more typical setting for political negotiations. Enfolded in such domestic comfort, the officials, separated, and flanked on both sides, began to squirm rather awkwardly from side to side while fighting to keep their socked feet planted firmly on the floor. After two hours of heated discussion, they became thoroughly disarmed and nodded in agreement to many of the suggestions and criticisms presented. The meeting was called to an end and, once the officials had departed, participants sat around the kitchen table, recreated their favourite moments over tea and toast, and declared their meeting a success.

Anyone familiar with political negotiations will surmise that such declarations of victory are momentary in a process that is rife with confrontation, stalemate, and, sometimes, consensus. But the event exemplifed for me two important features of local organizing which demonstrate what this grass-roots organization can do. I was intrigued by the way council members had once again drawn upon gender ideologies and the practices associated with the domestic arena in the implementation of a political strategy. And yet the meeting also revealed the complex ways in which women were linked to different branches of the state: as activists, workers, enforcers, citizens, and clients.

This chapter situates feminist organizing in the context of community politics and feminist politics at the provincial and national levels. In Canada, the focus of organized activism, particularly at the national level, has been to lobby government (Rankin and Vickers, 1998:341). At the same time, the institutionalization of women's organizations and of the services they have provided has complicated the political position feminists articulate regarding the state as a site for critical change or for the reproduction of hierarchies and inequalities (Brodie, 1998:24) Nor are states ahistorical entities; rather, branches of the state form an overlapping and at times contradictory assembly of discursive practices. This limits the utility of feminist typologies in distinguishing the character of feminist politics on a continuum of radical, socialist, and liberal models which have been called into question in the 1980s and 1990s (Brodie, 1998:25–7). Other distinctions, for example, between 'mainstreaming' and 'disengagement,' (Adamson and Briskin, 1988:177–94), that is, working within pre-existing institutions or creating spaces distinct from them, are analytically useful provided the fluidity between these boundaries is captured.

The character of activism in Bay St George embraces all these typologies depending on the situation. Individual women move between extra-parliamentary mobilization and organizing within government organizations. In Bay St George, feminist practices are incorporated into a wide range of arenas – the public-service sector, community-based organizations, and explicitly feminist fora. At times, the introduction of these practices generates debate and conflict, a transformation in approach, or concerted action and a degree of consensus. Council members are often ambivalent about introducing feminist approaches to other spheres of their work. It requires considerable experience to recognize those situations and persons that would welcome a feminist perspective and those that require more sustained negotiation or are open to only a limited change in orientation.

Hence, it is more useful to consider those aspects of feminist organizing that illustrate its heterogeneity and socially embedded character. These qualities allow for the expression of multiple identities which provide a basis for motivating people to make the kind of changes that council members advocate. Specifically, I explore the local construction of political issues, the articulation of council practices within national, provincial, and community politics, and different forms of leadership. These themes show how issues are made politically and locally meaningful and demonstrate that the expression of feminist, Newfoundland, and community-based identities is an essential feature of organizing at the grass roots.

One can point to the signifiers of 'feminism,' or the 'women's movement,' for example, in the decoration of the Women's Centre and in the deployment of key terms, such as 'patriarchy'; but many women do not articulate a feminist identity by defining the term or the theoretical principals and practices that it signifies. Rather, feminist identities are expressed by reference to specific events in one's life and through examples of one's participation in everyday council activities and particular events, especially those that make them aware of their membership within a larger movement. And it is the articulation of feminism alongside Newfoundland identity which in fact grounds the council's sustained critique in women's experiences.

This is crucial for understanding the character of grass-roots organizing and its relation to the broader context of feminist organizing in the province, where the (now) eight women's councils form an important site for activism, advocacy, and service provision to a variety of women. Moreover, as the following section demonstrates, the strength of grass-roots activism and the expression of feminist political identities in Bay St

George emerge from the articulation of socially embedded practices within feminist ideology and the forces of organized feminism at the national level.

Organized Feminisms

When we started the council, we wanted to be known as a group that had a different perspective. But it was a frustrating process! We'd spend half the time talking about how so and so left her husband ... and little by little, the issues came. Even as our awareness was growing we were connecting. And then two of us attended a NAC [National Action Committee] conference and we were amazed! We learned there are times that being radical and speaking out is important, and that's the strength of a collective. It's not just one or two sticking out their necks. And then, some of us said, we have to consult, we have to listen. We had to learn the art of diplomacy as well. (Joyce)

Over the last thirty-five years, engagement with the state has formed a crucial component of feminist activism at the grass-roots and higher levels of national and international politics. The First and Second Wave Womens' Movements found expression in Newfoundland and Labrador, where women have a long history of political activism as suffragettes, in social work, as nurses and nuns, and in charities. (Kealey, 1992). As elsewhere across the country, the Second Wave of the Women's Movement in Newfoundland expanded with the publication of the report on women by the Royal Commission on the Status of Women in 1972. The report generated the formation of informal and grass-roots feminist organizations as well as more institutionally rooted feminist organizations across the country (Kealey, 1992), including women's councils between 1974 and 1985 in St John's, Corner Brook, Labrador City, Happy Valley/Goose Bay, Gander, Port aux Basques, Bay St George, and Grand Falls. These councils occupy a particular position vis-à-vis the state and organized feminism, one that defies tidy classifications regarding the locating of political engagement as 'outside' or within existing political institutions.

The political character of individual women's councils in the province is shaped by their membership and their particular location vis-à-vis communities, the state, and organized feminism at the national level.

On the one hand, these councils were generated from the grassroots, that is, from the assembly of concerned, resident women who were interested in addressing issues as they were locally experienced. On the other hand, councils are connected to the state and national feminist organizations which have been differently characterized in terms of their political engagement with governments. Individual councils in the province are structured in similar ways and are comparable in their efforts to provide services and education, to raise local awareness, and to confront issues including unemployment, family violence, sexual abuse, and health as women experience them (Pope, 1992). At the same time, each council in the province may be distinguished by its position on particular issues, its priorities, its political strategies, and the means and extent to which it is integrated within the region it serves and claims to represent.

In Newfoundland and Labrador, women's issues are addressed at two levels within the Status of Women portfolio. The Women's Policy Office is an arm of the provincial government that advises the government. An arms-length Status of Women Advisory Council fosters the exchange of information between women's councils, integrates the experiences of women across the province within a comparative framework through short policy reports, and has documented, for example, 'family violence,' sexual abuse, and teenage pregnancy across the province.[1] The critical character of these reports is, however, partially shaped by the relationship of Status of Women Advisory Councils to the federal and provincial governments. Feminists have argued that it is crucial to situate spatially all nationally based organizations (Rankin and Vickers, 1998:241–352) in order to understand their political character. Regional and local politics have an impact on the way nationally based organizations are utilized by governments and by activists. The relationship between the Bay St George Women's Council and those bodies that fall under the Status of Women portfolio at the provincial and federal levels has changed over time; moreover, the relationship between grassroots women's organizations and these same bodies varies across Canada.

The federal Advisory Council has been disbanded since 1995. It has been argued that this body was increasingly supportive of government initiatives and not always sensitive to the expression of women's diversity or the range of problems different women faced throughout the

1980s and 1990s (Burt, 1998:129–39). In Newfoundland and Labrador, a Provincial Advisory Council continues to operate. In the past, feminists in the province experienced problems with the advisory councils at both government levels. Over the last fifteen years, however, Newfoundland and Labrador feminists have drawn upon the Provincial Advisory Council, perhaps more extensively than in other provinces, in part because this body has been increasingly receptive to the concerns of local women's councils.

At the same time, all women's councils in the province are also member organizations of the National Action Committee, a body that has been characterized as increasingly critical of government initiatives in the 1980s and 1990s, most notably in its vocal opposition to the Charlottetown Accord, the Free Trade Agreement, and the dismantling and redistribution of transfer payments and social and economic policies at the federal and provincial levels (Bashevkin, 1998:118–21).

The Bay St George Women's Council has been fortunate in that a few of its members have acted as representatives for the province on the National Action Committee. Both Michele and Joyce, for example, emphasize that their participation in this large arena gave them leadership skills and a national analysis and strategy to which they might not have otherwise had access. This was important for their understanding of numerous issues, including the Charlottetown Accord, and fostered a much greater sensitivity to the way relations of class, racialized ethnicities, and sexual orientation distinguish women across the country. Moreover, participation in national campaigns has given council members the opportunity to travel to Ottawa. Elaine, Maria, and Lori, for example, recalled one trip to a mass pro-choice demonstration in Ottawa several years ago as a defining moment in their activism, when they realized 'the importance of numbers.'

As I have indicated elsewhere, a female-centred collectivity is created through a series of networks which implicate and are rooted in family, kin relations, and locality. In general, feminist activism in Bay St George combines the local tradition of family picnics and parades with the principles of pacifism and sisterhood which members have learned through their participation in national and provincial conferences. These are crucial arenas that provide members with the opportunity to meet women across the country and gain a national and provincial perspective on social issues and strategies for social change. In this way, the individual experiences and the particular conditions of local life can be connected through strong leadership, broader alliances, and a national vision of social change. And yet, a sense of collectivity, of belonging to and acting as feminists, varies and is rife with its own debates, disagreements, and inequities.

The marginalization of women's experiences has at times been reproduced within national organizations which have not always been grounded in 'women's voices' (Findley, 1998:296). And, according to Janine Brodie, the 'spatial dimension of Canadian politics' rivals other social cleavages (Rankin and Vickers, 1998:346). In this context, the articulation of regional identities within feminist politics is crucial for developing a more sustained relationship between women's experiences and national feminist agendas. The provincial women's conference, which is held yearly in different communities across the province, is one means through which women assemble to learn, debate, and share experiences and strategies. This is a context where regional identities and social cleavages within the province are expressed and yet women also reaffirm their shared common identity as Newfoundland feminists. Newfoundland feminists do agree on the importance of particular issues and develop political strategies which encompass the entire province.

Provincial Conferences: 'Women and Power'

Provincial conferences exemplify the way provincial and national organizations provide council members with a framework for action and analysis as well as a context to exchange information and experiences. Two council members recall that the feminist perspective they developed in Bay St George was initially formed by their participation in a peace conference in St John's in 1985. Bay St George council members are a somewhat raucous group who send a large number of delegates to meetings. They frequently raise the volume of these collective gatherings not just through their music but by pounding the tables and ridiculing the sisterhood if an air of solemnity threatens to overpower enthusiasm.

During the Provincial Women's Conference in 1993, council members found ways to permit as many as women as possible from Bay St

George to attend, the annual conference in Port aux Basques. Council members pooled resources, shifted costs to permit low-income women to attend and arranged babysitting to free a few single mothers for the weekend. I was one of the many drivers designated to transport women on the two-and-one-half-hour journey 'up the coast,' where we attended workshops that focused on 'abortion access,' 'violence,' 'employment and training,' and 'feminist process.' On Saturday evening, the audience listened to Estasy's songs and the reflections of 'Dick Head' (an Estasy character) before Judy Rebick (then president of the National Action Committee on the Staus of Women) offered an eloquent and devastating critique of the constitutional changes proposed in the Charlottetown Accord.

In 1995 the council hosted the Provincial Women's Conference at the Holiday Inn in Stephenville. Choosing 'Women and Power' as their theme, those in attendance were invited to join workshops on challenging structures of power in the justice system, in health care, and through 'community and economic development.' A separate set of workshops organized by an activist from Montreal was designed to develop the skills of local francophone women, who are increasingly confident about expanding their use of French outside the domestic and local arena where it has historically been confined.

In my experience of these conferences, issues have most often been addressed, as locals put it, 'from the heart' or the personal experience of the speakers. They invariably begin by declaring 'they have nothing to say' before proceeding into an ad hoc comedy routine which generates fits of laughter from the audience. In one open session, four women, a member of parliament, a union organizer, a women's shelter worker, and an educator shared their experiences of working with 'da bys' (the boys) and, more particularly, within and against the power structures that employed them. In so doing, they exposed the overlapping relations of power which link government policy with corporate initiatives in communities throughout Newfoundland and Labrador.

By focusing on the expression of a collective feminist identity, I do not mean to suggest that women agree on all issues, or that they are equally positioned within society and community in terms of access to power, class relations, and personal circumstances. In fact, as I discuss later in the chapter, there are profound differences between women in the province and these differences inform the character of each individual women's council. Indeed, the Bay St George council was particularly vocal in promoting and distinguishing itself from other councils; members certainly participated in the ad hoc, playful competitions that emerged at these meetings and hence illustrated the way feminist and regional identities within the province coalesce. Moreover, although most councils were located in towns, regional distinctions within the province – the cultural and economic differences among Bay St George, Corner Brook, St John's, and Labrador City, for example – informed discussions regarding political strategy and the prioritization of issues. Certain councils become known for particular strengths and practices. Also, the strength of certain councils changed over time. During the period under study, Bay St George was certainly prominent in defining issues and providing strategies that other councils recognized and drew upon.

Provincial conferences are crucial given that women have been marginalized from national organizations across Canada. Consider, for example, the 'Future of Work' conference organized by the National Action Committee in Toronto which Joyce and I attended. We were excited by the participation of women representing both large unions and small organizations from Kamloops, British Columbia, the Northwest Territories, and coastal Labrador. A day of listening to talks on unemployment, training, and economic restructuring generated a great deal of camaraderie, anger, and energy among the participants, who were anxious to develop a strategy for action. Conference time was allocated for a discussion of the effects of the cod moratorium on Newfoundland women. Yet, in the informal workshops, women were equally astonished and concerned to hear about the way Newfoundlanders had long resigned themselves to the everyday tension and insecurity which underpins the demands of migration, reliance on unemployment insurance and social assistance, and the limitations of training programs.

Joyce and I were somewhat overwhelmed the next day by the way the 'feminist' political process of the three-day event was directed and managed to generate a particular set of political actions and strategies that were, it became clear, pre-set by the organizing committee. This 'feminist' process included the careful stacking of each working group with organizing committee members, as well as a highly controlled speakers' list and rhetorical displays lifted directly from the contested arena of the bargaining table, a problem that Judy Rebick has also recognized (Findley, 1998:306). This greatly intimidated less experienced women who felt they could not even open their mouths. Joyce, who is an assertive and challenging speaker in Newfoundland, was unusually silent. 'You know it's these women who taught me how to talk back to men and I value that greatly,' she explained, 'but they've lost sight of the fact that there's no men here in this room and that we're not competing against each other!'

This consciousness-raising activity was, we discovered, a process by which we were expected to arrive at a pre-set strategy, irrespective of the context in which it was to be enacted. One of the activities included a day of sidewalk protests targeted at certain institutions, including banks, a strategy that prompted Joyce to comment, 'Now what's Mr. M – [the bank manager] going to think of that, or Margaret or Joan [bank tellers] – that's going to set us back about two years of hard work.' She compared this action to one initiated a few years ago, when NAC told all women's organizations to launch their protest against free trade with a march on railway stations, apparently unaware that Newfoundland had lost its rail service several years earlier. 'Well, there were no railway stations, so we just said, the hell with it and came up with our own action across the province,' Joyce said. 'Only it hurt us to think NAC hadn't even bothered to consult us or was so unaware of our situation.'

I was confident then that the Bay St George Women's Council had much to share with other women, especially from rural parts of Canada, who, we could see from our informal discussions, had far less experience in community-based organizing and whose circumstances might call for different political strategies. Unfortunately, there was no forum where rural women in particular could exchange ideas and strategies or discuss the impact of regional differences on their politics. Moreover, the absence of this kind of exchange made Joyce cognizant of the fact that she identified with the experiences of these women *as rural Canadian women*. And yet, at the same time, she recognized that it was not rural location itself which generated the particular character of collective expression in her province or which shaped the strategies that Newfoundland feminists employed. On a certain level, Newfoundland activists expected to be left out of, or marginalized from, national visions and strategies. They had developed an extensive network over a long period of time and this ensured that their action was not confined to local communities.

The importance of a well-established and grounded network was also reflected in the way council members were able to utilize nationally organized and government funded initiatives, such as the Royal Commission on Violence against Women (1993). The report, and the process through which it was generated, has been heavily criticized (Gotell, 1998:passim) by organizations such as NAC, for, among other things, its limited utility for women who address violence at the grass-roots level (Gotell, 1998:56–63). Council members are cognizant of, and in agreement with, much of this critique; but, this did not prevent them from recognizing that they benefited from the commission, partly because they were already well established and positioned to use the resources and information-gathering process effectively and sensitively. The Women's Council provided the space for commission representatives to gather experiences of violence from women in the area. It not only prompted greater awareness of the problem in the community but provided a focus for the development of a group for survivors of violence.

The social issues that the council has promoted over the last twelve years, such as violence and reproductive rights, derive largely from their contact with area women. For example, feminists in North America have addressed a variety of issues that include the representation of women in politics, career choices, or daycare; however, for these issues, claims Joyce, 'the women in Bay St George won't come.' Workshops that focus on domestic violence, sexual abuse, and addictions attract the largest number of women. This illustrates that the politicization of social issues unfolds within a locality and responds to and against pre-existing values and interpretations (Ginsburg, 1990:218).

The Local Construction of Social Issues and Feminist Identities

I got involved in the Women's Council through a summer job in recreation. And I was with the Peace Committee for a few years. I got involved in specific things. I was a closet member. There was stigma attached to the Women's Centre and I didn't want to be associated with it. But I changed my mind in the last few years and now I'm more comfortable.

But the stigma is still there. There's a large group of people who still see it as a house which lesbians created to encourage women to leave and hate their men. And we're seen as shit disturbers. I've always been a feminist but I haven't known the label. I saw it as a bunch of radical women. I don't like to see people boxed. I'd like the whole world associated with masculine and feminine to be gone. (Susan, age thirty)

For individual women, acquiring a feminist identity is an ongoing process that involves a rejection of, a reconciliation with, or an incorporation of values, practices, and relationships that constitute their individuality and their femininity. It is characterized by their membership within the council and by the way their feminist practice and working roles inform and transform each other. Their location in the paid workplace provides different sources of knowledge, networks, and identifications, all of which can generate tensions, ambivalence, conflict, and hierarchies among women. In raising awareness of social issues and challenging stereotypes, council members emphasize that they must take account of the biases and the interests of residents as well as the different positions that they themselves adopt regarding a particular strategy or issue. Consider, for example, a few events that were organized by the council.

Solidarity with the Innu

The biennual return of war planes, which I twice witnessed, evokes sympathy at the Women's Centre for the Innu of Labrador who have had prolonged exposure to noise during low-level flight testing. A favourite story frequently recounted over lunch at the Women's Centre recalls how, on Easter Sunday in 1989, council members sneaked chocolates and Easter baskets into the Stephenville prison, where Innu women had been incarcerated for several days for protesting these tests.

Incarcerations such as these were difficult for Elaine, a council member and corrections officer, who would rather not be told when council 'antics' challenge prison regulations. Yet it was her experience working in the prison system that has developed her feminist identity into a wider recognition of unfairness. She has been expected to exercise authority over, and treat as criminals, women whose life experiences of abuse, poverty, and civil disobedience she has come to know on a more intimate level. For Elaine, 'feminism' is a label that opposes unfairness, particularly, but not exclusively, towards women. It provides 'a focus' and a 'label' for the unfairness she witnesses.

The opposition to the incarceration of Innu women was significant for Elaine and other council members. It exemplifies their approach to peaceful demonstration, their ability to rouse media attention, and the extent to which they can achieve broad-based support. Immense support was mobilized throughout the region, in part through demonstrations waged outside the prison. Funds were gathered, including donations by the local Catholic church, to house the imprisoned women's husbands and children, who had been flown in from Goose Bay. Residents brought food to the Women's Centre, where one family was housed until the women were released. The incarceration drew considerable attention as protestors, including council members, marched with children in tow along the steel fence that distinguishes this building from other former air-base barracks. The second time they were arrested coincided with the annual Women's Conference, which was held in Stephenville that year. Both times, council members were able to draw attention to the dominant role of the state, the circumstances of the Innu people, and the larger issue of militarization through peaceful protest and through mobilizing community support.

However, council members recall that their support for Innu women came not simply from a shared history of a military presence but from meeting with them at provincial and national conferences which provided a forum for the Innu to speak directly of their experience of low-level flight testing. Indeed, the council's awareness of issues surrounding peace, militarization, and the distinct experience of domination that other peoples in Canada face does not simply emerge from the collective memory, practices, and social relations of locality. Rather, its systemic analysis of particular social problems is informed by the perspective it receives from its participation in provincial and national conferences.

One issue that has generated tension between this council and other feminists in the province has been its informal position regarding sexual orientation. A few lesbian women who have been active council members claimed that homophobic attitudes inhibit their expression of a lesbian identity in Bay St George. Unlike an urban centre, Stephenville is too small to allow anonymity, they argued. This has actually prevented some lesbians, who do not want to be identified as such, from becoming actively involved in the Women's Council. And, lesbian women who have been active in the council have not made their sexual orientation an issue of top priority. For example, Joyce admitted that she was hesitant to name herself explicitly and publicly as a lesbian because of the negative effect it might have on the Women's Council. At times she wondered if her reluctance was rooted in her own homophobia. However, having raised a family for twelve years with her female partner, Joyce considered that her sexual orientation has not been a central feature of her identity for quite some time. As she put it, 'I am a neighbour, I'm a mother, an activist, a trained nurse, a lesbian ... why should I define myself politically only in terms of my sexual orientation?' In other words, a feminist identity embraces these assorted social identities in a way that a lesbian one does not.

Issues of sexual orientation and the dynamics of lesbian and heterosexual relations are somewhat muted and cautiously approached in the Women's Centre. However, the council regularly addresses issues surrounding sexual orientation as a 'human rights issue' and is not reluctant to raise these issues in the local media or ask questions in political meetings. Still, lesbians do not share or articulate a common or political identity in Bay St George and their 'positions' on issues surrounding their sexual choices and women's issues in general vary considerably. Council members have been criticized by more explicitly politically organized lesbians in urban centres in the province. The Women's Centre, then, is not a comfortable space for all women, a problem that underscores the limitations of an unreflective claim that a focus on 'experience' somehow means all experiences.

All the same, the council's strength thus far has been to provide a base where women's experiences in paid and unpaid work intersect to develop a critical politics. For example, in Canada, it is common to raise awareness for national issues through journeys which frequently begin in Newfoundland. A proud moment for Newfoundland feminists occurred in 1990, when St John's feminists held a sit-in to protest the suspension of federal funds to women's councils. This action triggered like responses across the country. Similarly, landmark changes in national policy are frequently challenged or advertised by travelling shows that are organized by the networks of union, environmental, and feminist activists across the province. In 1992 an 'Anti-Free Trade Caravan' rolled into Stephenville on its way across the country and parked at the Women's Council, where numerous community activists had assembled. The riders and residents were treated to an informal buffet lunch of moose stew and fried baloney which a few council members had worked all morning to prepare. The money for such activities was acquired through a creative use of government and local funds combined with resourceful scrounging for donations from nearby retail stores and grocers.

The council offers a context of comfort where some of women's experiences and the power women in professions have acquired can be utilized to contest male-dominated institutions. This is also reflected in the attempts of individual council members to introduce feminist practices within their workplaces, the organizations in which they are members, and the boards on which they serve. In this way, they give attention to the differential experiences of women and the impact of policies and changes on women. As well, they attempt to 'de-hierarchicalize' the structure of meetings and incorporate the experiences of individual women in policies, decisions, and actions.

This diversity is exemplified by some individual activists – such as Kathy, the RCMP officer, who articulates a feminist identity as she negotiates her place in male-dominated institutions, conveys her authority, and confounds the ideological association of femininity with fixed character traits and social roles.

From the Women's Centre to the Community

One day after a big lunch, a group of us were sitting at the table finishing our tea when conversation shifted towards Kathy, who was born in Nova Scotia and has worked in Stephenville for a few years. On this day, Kathy expressed her ambivalence over her job, which often involved frustrating altercations with inebriated men. 'I'm tired of drunks and the smell of liquor in my face,' she complained. Kathy then smiled. 'But I love diving through a broken window and surprising a thief!' She showed us how she had learned to flip a six-foot man by swinging her body and catching him unawares. Joyce, clearly challenged by Kathy's exciting endeavours, chimed in soon after with her own story. She made it clear that her experiences as a teenager left her far more critical of law enforcement and aware of the harsh treatment that incarcerated women experience.

Kathy's strong belief in law and order are rivalled by Joyce's routine contempt for such institutions. Their positions reflect the diversity of individual feminist identifications that inform local activism and signify potential divisions and differences within the council. Yet these women, who bring very different perspectives to the council, also work together in assorted community activities.

One such activity in which I participated was a series of classes organized by Joyce and Kathy (the latter acted as community-liaison officer in her RCMP detachment). Through videos, games, and group discussions, students were asked to create their own gender scripts, to reflect on responsibilities and constraints on young men and women, and to consider the boundaries between sexual consent and coercion. A video on date rape, for example, elicited a variety of responses from these sixteen-year-olds; a few agreed that there were "bys" they could name who 'acted that way'; others thought that there should have been a moment at which the teenaged girl said 'no.' A quick survey indicated that many of the boys felt it was acceptable for husbands to demand sex from their wives. Students also had difficulty distinguishing sexual harassment from nonconsensual, sexually charged play. Yet Joyce and Kathy also bravely introduced discussion on gay and lesbian sexualities and masturbation, despite the disapproving looks of some teachers.

I could not help but notice the authority that Kathy conveyed. Fully uniformed, with gun in holster, she personified law and order. For Kathy, it was one of the best features of a job that usually kept her in the underbelly of local culture. In spite of the authority she conveys to youth and residents, her own experience in the police force underlines the extent to which pre-existing gender scripts and constructions of gender underpin a male-dominated workplace where the perpetual denigration of women seems to be the means by which male solidarity is fostered.

Kathy: 'You need a good network of friends or you become cold, hard, and suspicious'

Kathy describes her childhood in rural Nova Scotia as being relatively free of what she considers gender-based constraints. Her 'feminist-minded' parents rarely confined her to feminine roles and instilled in her the pleasures of fishing and trapping and hiking in the woods. Kathy was also 'raised a lady' in a devout Baptist home where there was no drinking or smoking. 'I don't resent my childhood – I grew up strait-laced and Dad made me very independent, very opinionated and strong-willed.' Kathy attributes her interest in becoming an RCMP officer to 'some pie in the sky ideas of eliminating crime' and her fondness for an uncle who was an RCMP officer. 'I saw him as a good man, with high morals, who was fair minded. But I discovered it wasn't that he was a good Mountie, he was just a good Christian.' After several years of working as a draftsperson in Halifax, she finally joined the RCMP once they lowered their height restrictions. 'I loved Halifax, I encountered no sexism at school or at work. I went to a Baptist church, I walked to work, I felt free; I was happy!' In Kathy's experience, sexism began with her RCMP training.

> I thought my Corporal fitness instructor was a jerk! How could he be a Mountie? Isn't this odd I thought – a Mountie who was a foul-mouthed pig! At age twenty-nine I hit a wall. I was doing field training which felt like Army boot camp. I thought I could handle the paramilitary for six months. All of my instructors were domineering and sexist. They try to teach you to take verbal abuse; but I didn't like their methods. I lost my self-esteem and confidence. They treated us like dirt. I remember them lining us up, asking us to name the blackest day in the history of the RCMP. And you know what they answered? The day that women joined the force! There were thirty-two of us and ten were women! They stripped me of all my confidence. For two weeks, I cried all the time.

In Kathy's opinion, men adapt better to this lifestyle and a lot of men join the police force 'just to wear a badge.' She is now ambivalent about her work, and the male-dominated culture of the detachment prompted her to seek out a different and female-centred community. 'You have to realize my clientele. I had a very negative impression of Stephenville. I saw only the dark side. There are things accepted in this town that would be scandals where I'm from.' She enjoys crime prevention, helping somone in a crisis situation, and the 'thrill of capturing someone who's barricaded himself with a shotgun.' But she tires of the sexist and anti-female jokes.

> We women have caused them no disgrace! Yet some of these guys drink a lot, screw around on their wives – it's demoralizing! I had them on a pedestal. But some of them are burping, farting, nose-picking pigs! And they turn far too much to alcohol to handle the stress of their jobs.
>
> We work with negative things daily and people react to us negatively. We are feared and hated. People have spit on me and called me an old bag licking cunt! I've seen sexual abuse. I've held diapers with blood on them, and I've scraped up the remains of people off the ground. I've escorted a ten-year-old girl who's been sexually abused to the doctor, and I've shot three dogs! You get depressed, and you need a good network of friends or you become cold, hard, and suspicious. It has changed me. Even my mother said I've become extremely brutal.

Kathy met council members through her work and found the atmosphere at the centre very comfortable. She has always seen herself as a feminist and would have called herself one as a teenager. However, Kathy does not understand women who seem just like her but shy away from the label of feminist: 'I trust the women down there. It's a sort of release for me – if I want to bitch I can. But I want the centre to be looked upon positively. Some of the RCMP officers think the women here are just big-mouthed dykes and radical feminists who are never satisfied; but others are coming around. My partner, who's a really nice guy, realized that these women deal with human rights, just as much as he likes to think he does.'

Kathy is committed to bringing a feminist perspective to the detachment by raising awareness among male officers and, more concretely, by incorporating feminist insights into the police bureaucracy. This includes, for example, taking account of gender (among victims and offenders) when compiling local statistics on forms of violent crime in the region and including 'like-minded' officers in community-prevention programs. As Kathy's experience conveys, institutions, and the social spaces into which activist ideas must be injected, can inhibit council members from shaping an agenda and challenging existing practices. Such is the case with other women who have gained relative power and privilege through their paid work, community participation, and labour-union membership.

The Women's Council has introduced feminist practices into local institutions and community-based organizations through their formal participation as an organization and through the individual occupations and participation of various members. Community Futures, the Anti-Violence Coalition, the Sex Abuse Counselling Service, the Canada Employment Centre, the Nurses Union, and the Public Employees Union are a few examples. Equally important is the participation of council members in area-wide events and educational programs in which the Women's Centre's perspective and resources are requested. As well, the centre itself has initiated numerous events in town and outlying communities. The tone of the organizations with which the centre cooperates in these projects can be elitist and the agenda already set by alliances of which the centre is not a part. Women have needed to use 'diplomacy' and non-threatening rhetoric in their attempts to introduce new initiatives to a pre-existing set of practices.

For example, as a social worker within the management sector of the Department of Mental Health Linda has worked hard through her job and participation on hospital boards to de-hierarchize relations between clients and professionals and to challenge the structure of medical and mental-health services. She was instrumental in introducing feminist approaches to therapy. This includes a challenge to the medicalized approach to counselling through drug therapy and an attention to the social and gendered context of power in which clients are situated and which structures their personal crises. Well known in the council as a 'diplomat,' Linda argues that she would not have had the courage to introduce such practices on her own without the support of council members and the confidence in these initiatives that her participation in council activities has engendered. Similarly, Joyce has challenged the dichotomy between clients and boards, professionals and clients, by speaking from her own experience of living in a foster home. As a participant on various community boards, she claims that, 'when I started doing workshops, I didn't know it was about feminism. I was on the board of directors for a group home and I was director for two or three boards that were very hierarchical, that left me feeling that your voice didn't get heard. I always felt that nobody listened when I said I want to be on these boards because I was a juvenile delinquent too. People were just hearing me as an instructor at the college, or as an employment counsellor.'

Pauline has acted as the Women's Council representative for Community Futures, a federal-provincial development initiative. It is programs such as this one that attract local businessmen and political functionaries who can act as mediators in the distribution of government money for business ventures. There are a few prominent businesswomen in the area, one known across the province for her succesful craft store in town, and another for various activities including an art gallery. Yet Pauline has discovered that participants, if they attend to women's employment and business at all, tend to focus initiatives on traditional women's activities such as home-based craft production. Pauline, who is known for her assertive behaviour, is considerably more intimidated in this environment, where decisions come to the table already made and issues she has raised are too readily dismissed. In its attempts to raise awareness of women's issues, the council uses its most subdued rhetoric when addressing meetings of organizations such as the Chamber of Commerce.

Sharon was hired to facilitate the implementation of community-based education for the Catholic School Board. Her enthusiasm to increase students' choices and sensitize them to gender issues has been hampered in the past by a school board that has been concerned to maintain 'family values,' which are narrowly defined by pre-existing norms and which continue to favour male breadwinners and motherhood for women. Sharon has drawn on the limited support of some board members, other employees, and those involved in related activities to gain support for her programs. She has had considerably more freedom developing these programs through her work on council-sponsored employment and training projects which incorporate a 'life-skills' component in conventional skills training. This is a form of consciousness-raising that encourages women to reflect on the relationship between their personal and paid-work interests. It enables them to see the way in which their experiences 'at home' with husbands and children affect their choices in the paid workforce and their personal views of sexuality, health, and gender stereotypes.

For example, a 'Home Care Training Program,' one of the council's first training projects for which it received government funding, was organized in conjunction with the college; it was intended to facilitate the entry of women who had little formal training into the paid workforce to work as 'homecare workers' for the disabled. Another program was organized to train twelve young women, who lived throughout the region, as daycare workers, a six-month program for which they were paid.

Union Politics: 'We're timid on the line'

Although a district labour council was formed by local union activists in the mid-1980s, it never established a wide base of support and eventually disbanded. Whatever local elites Stephenville has cannot be categorized according to conventional class dynamics. For instance, the pulp and paper mill in Stephenville employs the largest number of unionized workers in the private industrial sector. They are viewed as a local elite who gain high wages and have relatively stable jobs. Although they did strike once in 1985, and again in 1998, one millworker explained that they rarely view management as a source of power because so many decisions are made either by the corporate owner or by the national union. Public-sector unions, which represent a large number of workers in Bay St George, have struck several times throughout the 1980s. The relationship of the council to the predominant unions in town has waxed and waned through its ten-year history, depending on the initiatives of individual council members. Some women in the council have been politicized by their participation in these strikes; others, however, remain ambivalent or negative towards unions.

Peg's union identity has formed from seventeen years of work as a social worker and her participation in three strikes in the mid 1980s. While she is committed to the bargaining process and labour issues, she has never been comfortable on the picket line or with the required heckling of scab workers. Rather, Peg prefers to have discussions on these subjects in the lunchroom at her workplace (a government office), where she debates contractual issues with her fellow workers and tries to persuade them to 'look at the bigger picture.' In contrast, Lorraine, a postal worker, 'isn't afraid to speak her mind' and enjoys the fighting spirit a strike can generate. For other council members, however, an understanding of labour issues is mediated by their working experience and the gendered context in which such activism has historically unfolded.

For example, Sharon's ambivalence towards unions derives from her experience as a general labourer at the Iron-Ore Company of Canada in Labrador City from 1976 to 1981. Since her move to Stephenville, she has been regularly employed for the last ten years in the field of education; her jobs have been short-term, contractually limited positions with a variety of employers including the Women's Council, the Department of Justice, and the Catholic School Board. Although Sharon is supportive of unions in general, her mixed feelings on the subject were shaped fifteen years ago.

> I worked in the mine in Lab City as a labourer, attendant, and janitor. I didn't mind it – if you wanted to make good money it was worth it. They were just starting to hire women then and there were 100 of us. At first they were only going to hire married women 'cause single women were considered a distraction. We got lots of cat-calls, and whistles. This was a man's town – there were hardly any women. I just ignored it. I had to put up with a lot of sexism but they weren't going to make me leave.
>
> I wasn't overly impressed with the union. I remember how the guys going down for drinks to talk and telling us women that we weren't allowed in the pit. It was a dumb rule – that's where the union met. I was a member of that union but I didn't have the same access. And the union didn't care ... But I love a strike. I always love a good fight and I am a strong believer in unions – you can be exploited and abused by bosses. But then, unions get so big, they feel just like a company.

In spite of her experience within the union, Sharon emphasizes that she makes far less in salary now, as a non-unionized worker, than she did in the mine. And she recognizes that her higher salary in the mine was partly a result of collective bargaining.

Some women in the council have expressed support for their unions and the issues that underpin contract negotiations but are not particularly active. Others, however, are more openly hostile towards features of union organization which they feel do not reflect their interests or the interests of 'clients.' Moreover, numerous women involved in the council perform tasks that are comparable to public, unionized work but that are created through contractual arrangements and therefore fall outside the union. For these women, unschooled in the positive gains secured by the union movement, unions have provided few benefits and can be obstacles to securing full-time work.

For example, although Marie, a teacher at the college, is a union member, she believes that the quality of teaching is undermined when rules of seniority place certain teachers in positions which others could better fill. Similarly, because a variety of workers are collectively organized as 'general service workers' within the province, Angie has been frustrated when the elimination of jobs means that workers from one sector are transferred into a completely different department in which they have no experience, 'bumping' those who are more experienced but who happen to be lower on the seniority list.

Kim is a thirty-year-old woman who has worked for the most part in contractually based positions which are generated as offshoots from government legal services. Never enamoured of unions, she has been directly affected by trade-union agreements when applying for jobs. For example, she was the first chosen for a unionized job with Victim Services, only to be told that another woman, in a different department, was guaranteed the position according to the collective agreement.

In an organized discussion on their paid-work experience, fifteen women, nine of whom work in the public sector, expressed the ambivalence that surrounds work with 'clients.' On the one hand, they are cognizant of the demands of such work, not just in terms of their time, but also in terms of the emotional and personal commitment that is often an outcome of their own socialization or self-imposed expectations to 'do a good job.' This is particularly the case for women working with clients who are trying to solve particular social problems or whom they see as more disadvantaged than themselves.

Women who have experienced strike action, or who play leadership roles in unions, seem to embrace a broader perspective. For example, Andrea, who has worked as a nurse in the hospital and in public health for fifteen years, has always enjoyed her work and participation in the union. As she puts it, 'Working life saved me. It's where I got my positive strokes, through caring and nurturing and contact with other people. And I was always concerned with issues around work. I was always an activist – union president, shop steward ... Working in the union showed me where women's strengths are, to develop ideas and supports. Initially, I was quiet, more a listener than a speaker. Now I balance them.'

Although her own local has fairly good leadership, Andrea argues that nurses in the province 'are wimps.' Many 'do not identify with the union movement' and prefer to 'see themselves as professionals, and their patients as clients.' In spite of the pleasure work gave her, shift work at the hospital led to conflicts between her and her husband, a millworker who also worked shifts. It was only when his behaviour turned physically aggressive that she sought help from the Women's Centre and eventually shifted her activism towards the Women's Council.

> I needed information and I needed support, and I realized I was now living in an abusive situation. I had no friends. If you're living in an abusive situation, you choose to lose them, because they wouldn't understand why you remain ... I was afraid to go into the Women's Centre, but when I walked in, there was this cosy, caring atmosphere – there are no words to describe it.
>
> Before, I thought a feminist was a radical and I wouldn't have called myself one ... I decided to get involved, after that and now I call myself a feminist. I work in the schools. I work with families in rural areas and I always give a feminist perspective.

As a public-health nurse, Andrea injects a feminist perspective by raising awareness of personal health and introducing new practices; she considers the broader context in which rural residents live and are socialized, and the way numerous social problems, such as drug and alcohol addictions, intersect with health and family responsibilities. This includes providing information on abortion in spite of negative attitudes towards it, and a recognition of the central role women play in caring for family members. Andrea, who has remained active in both the council and her union, finds continuity in addressing issues, most of which involve the provincial government and which, she argues, affect both 'clients' and nurses.

Although many of these women feel limited in their power to effect changes, they are also aware of their relative power and privilege, particularly with respect to their clients or in relation to their own previous experiences. Consider Joyce, whose experiences as a foster child and placement in an institution for 'juvenile delinquents' feeds into her understanding of marginalization. Because Joyce was able to negotiate her way through this institution, to complete her exams while incarcerated, she is, in retrospect, aware of her privilege vis-à-vis her fellow inmates, some of whom had psychiatric problems. Or consider Rhonda, who, some four years after her disclosure of sexual abuse, is now an active participant in council activities. The perspectives of women like Joyce and Rhonda are reflected in the social levelling that takes place at the Women's Centre. It is not a conscious policy; rather, it is an effect of the awareness that women have gained and of their recognition that women are differently situated on a relative continuum of power.

Social Levelling in the Women's Centre

Before the meeting over the sex-offender program began, Cynthia, one of the participants, chose to take a position in the room by sweeping the floor, so she could slip into the living room in an unobtrusive way. Feminists across North America note the difficulties in maintaining feminist 'egalitarian' relations in the everyday activity of running a women's centre or similar organization, particularly if paid work is involved (Popkin, 1990; Vickers, 1991; Radforth-Hill, 1986). And activities like sweeping are not always valued, given their association with the domestic sphere. Grass-roots feminists have, since the early 1970s sought to foster an egalitarian spirit in organizations by de-hierarchizing relations between women participants through formal structure and through decision-making processes such as consensus (Ristock, 1991:43; Vickers, 1991:79). More recently, feminists have attempted to recognize systemically rooted and personal differences among women within a non-hierarchical framework where reciprocities flourish but are not tallied nor prioritized (Ristock, 1991:51).

A recognition of the differential experiences of women according to their sexual orientation or their race/ethnic and class position has generated fragmentations within women's movements which potentially threaten the force of a woman-centred collectivity (Adamson, 1988:214; Briskin, 1991:30). While these social categories are the most frequently named for the divisions they engender, the manifestation of conflicts and divisions among feminists is also specific to a locality and the cultural means by which these relations of power are expressed.

In Newfoundland, conflicts and tensions among feminists have emerged over issues such as political process, decision making, and organizational structure, particularly in the early years of the Newfoundland women's movement in St John's. Specifically, regionally manifested social divisions reflect differences between urban and rural women and between Newfoundlanders and recent settlers, known as 'Come-From-Aways' (Pope, 1993:175). My own research and participation in the 1993 Provincial Conference confirms that such tensions are present between women's councils and within them. Urban, educated women often have had greater access to feminist resources (such as books and conferences), which can make them both effective leaders and networkers but which can also permit them to define the political agenda and political strategies in a way that may not reflect or incorporate the realities, sensibilities, and practices of rural life.

In Bay St George, women are structurally and socially distinguished through explicit hierarchies and relations of difference. The potential for certain divisions does exist, since women are differentiated on the basis of class, ethnicity, sexual orientation, and rural-urban locality and since they are also multiply situated, as clients, workers, and professionals. The membership of the council suggests that there is potential for the expression and manifestation of social conflicts and hierarchies within this organization. Participants are employed and unemployed; lesbian and heterosexual; single, married, and divorced; and have different levels of education. Membership lists indicate that the council has a constituency throughout the region. In 1992 the council consisted of 146 women from Stephenville, 116 from the Port au Port peninsula, 35 from St George's and Stephenville Crossing, 36 from Bay St George South, and 27 who lived outside the region. In 1998 membership has declined somewhat, although the distribution of members is comparable.

Francophone women, particularly those in the francophone associations, became involved in council activities and increasingly drew upon council resources. However, much more of their energy was devoted to their own organizations, which suggests that ethnic identity, and their particular location in rural communities, formed a significant basis for a social and political activism distinct from that of the Women's Council. One Mi'kmaq woman was an active council member, and some women associated with the local Mi'kmaq association have had ongoing contact with council members through various outreach and education initiatives. But they did not play a substantive role in the Women's Council.

With regard to the thirty-five active members with whom I was in contact on a regular basis and who were council participants, the most educated and employed women tended to assume the formal leadership roles. The knowledge they gained from paid work put them in a privileged position regarding the exercise and meaning of government policy, the experience of residents, potential solutions, and strategies. Board members tended to be employed and educated (grade 11 at least and usually a certificate or degree as well). Many were government-employed, service-sector workers (about 70 per cent). Other board members were unemployed and/or did not have grade 11. Roughly half of the council's most active members were raised in Bay St George, and the other half came from urban centres and rural communities across the province. Volunteers and non-board active members, in contrast, tended to be less educated, intermittently unemployed, and had lower incomes. Most, but not all, of these women were born in the area.

The relationship between women's roles within and outside the centre is manifested in an ambivalence that women have towards their own self-worth and the contributions they can make to council activities. Many women involved in everyday activities at the centre place themselves in a hierarchy, explicitly and implicitly, both within the centre and outside it. For example, a few women who are single mothers or on social assistance frequently mentioned their unfair treatment by social workers, doctors, lawyers, and business people. These women openly complained that their social position made them feel inferior, powerless, useless, or undervalued.

Furthermore, a few women, most new to the organization, admitted that they felt intimidated or less important than other members, particularly with regard to what they could contribute. For instance, two women who were newly elected board members expressed a concern that they could not contribute as much as other members, because they lacked the knowledge of women's issues, a feminist analysis, or the leadership and oral skills required to articulate their opinions or debate with other residents. There were a few council members who were unanimously singled out as leaders both within the council and in the community. At times, council members have been loathe to recognize potential hierarchies and many of their strategies do implicitly or explicitly mediate social divisions (cf. Ristock, 1991:46).

Yet, during all the time I spent at the Women's Centre, in council meetings, and with individual members, I found that the minor tensions and personal animosities which do exist (as they do in any organization) had little impact on the cooperative and collective spirit of the organization. There were no overt divisions that grouped one set of participants against others; nor were there issues that clearly aligned members into separate subgroups. Moreover, most council members were reluctant to name or consider relations of power or differences between women in the council or within the community which might reflect a hierarchy among women. Whatever differences were acknowledged were not viewed by any member as insurmountable or divisive. While this may be evidence of their implicit expression of an 'united front' against the anthropologist/mainlander, I suggest that it is rather rooted in local practices that pervade the Women's Centre. These are manifested through the social levelling which I describe below.

It is within the domestic space of the Women's Centre that social hierarchies within the larger 'community' were mediated, not through explicit codes of conduct, but in the continuous negotiation of everyday relations and activities. At a surface level, hierarchies of power were mediated by the sense of responsibility for others that women in service occupations seem to have. Moreover, feminist values and ideology, which highlight women's subordination within larger patriarchal structures, seem to reinforce a levelling of social status among women. Those whose occupations do give them power over other residents repeatedly argued that they simply do not feel this as power per se. Rather, they tended to view themselves as also powerless, in the sense of having little control within a larger social system.

Within the Women's Centre, social levelling was achieved in subtle, everyday ways that, I would argue, are implicit in local practices and the way residents in Bay St George interact. This is not openly expressed as official rules of behaviour. Exclusive, intimate conversation in the living/kitchen area was gently discouraged. Women who make regular appearances, regardless of their social position, were expected to lend a hand to dry dishes, to make tea, or lick envelopes. To cite one case, the occasional visit of one particular woman from a nearby city was met with apprehension and ridicule. Her refusal to join in during lunchtime clean-ups and her tendency to limit her conversation to those she deemed important were frequently mentioned. 'Throw a dish-towel on her head,' 'lead her to the sink,' 'stick some cups on her lap,' suggested a few.

Women who exhibited their distinctiveness as a virtue, or as a sign of their superiority, were cheerfully mocked for 'being uppity.' At the same time, the specific skills of individual women were noted and encouraged and all contributions were recognized without prioritizing their importance. One woman was informally reprimanded and ostracized for 'her bossiness.' Not only did she tell other women what to do, but she gave them tasks that she explicitly demeaned, such as cleaning the toilet. Although I did try to help in many ways, I confess that I frequently ignored the dishes and failed to remove my shoes or sweep up the dirt that followed my soled feet across the room, omissions that were frequently and loudly noted. I usually begged forgiveness with woeful tales of the unkempt and dishevelled conditions in which I was raised. 'Poor Glynis, we get her a PhD and we even got to teach her to clean a house!' I like to think that I finally got the message.

Some feminist collectives advocate circulating roles automatically so as not to entrench a hierarchical division of labour. Council members tried this in the past, but they found it artificial, frustrating and intimidating for some women. However, roles are exchanged as individual women develop certain skills through their work at the centre, at home, and in their workplace as well as through participation in conferences and other organizations.

Individual women are, for numerous reasons, differently equipped at a given time to address their own social problems as well as others. At the Women's Centre, there was no sharp distinction made between 'the helpers' and 'the helped.' Indeed, volunteers, board members, and workers, fell into both categories. Even those who were themselves professional helpers sought other members during a personal crisis.

It is the act of female, collective association itself which generated a female-centred perspective on local social conditions and relationships. This sentiment was conveyed by Jennifer, a social worker who was raised in Corner Brook. She recalls that, initially, her interest in forming a women's council came from her work in child welfare. 'I saw the need for a service, there was a lack of support services, for single parents, survivors of abuse and the incest issue – so the focus of my interest was client-oriented.' After she joined the council, Jennifer recalled,

> I saw no direct influence for me. I was involved in lots of other committees. The issue was not personal. But I had no way of knowing how spending so much time with only women could affect me. It was a safe, friendly environment and it helped me. We had a common commitment and a vision to benefit the community. And we had fun, which was really important. I had never worked with just women alone before. It was mind altering, the fact that I'd never realized my place, my abilities, my contribution, my value, my uniqueness as a woman, my role as a daughter, as a social worker. I've never thought same since. My knowledge base and way of looking at the world changed completely!

The strength of this council as a grass-roots organization has been its ability to draw on and validate different sources of knowledge and relationships that women bring with them. This became clear to me when I visited another Women's Centre in the province, located in an office on the town's Main Street. Its members complained that their council was not very successful in reaching a wide range of area women. I do not want to compare these councils or reduce the success of the Bay St George Council to its refashioning of a home. Nor do I advocate volunteerism as a solution to the dismantling of government services. As I have already indicated, women's working roles and participation in the community are crucial to expanding feminist activism. However, it remains true that, unlike the council in Bay St George, the other council not only did not use volunteers but it conveyed the idea that it would not be appropriate for just any women to sit in the office or do the daily work of feminist organizing.

Leaders in the Women's Council

A focus on social levelling should not overshadow the recognition of difference or the importance of leadership in women's grass-roots organizations. The success of the Women's Council in Bay St George in reaching 'the community' is attributable to women like Joyce, who was renowned both in the council and outside it for her creative interventions and the way she could move from sage diplomat to sharp-witted commentator and boisterous, 'trouble-making' rabble-rouser. It was through her activism that Joyce was among the ten Canadians chosen to observe the first election in post-apartheid South Africa in 1994. Her work there was significant not only for her. As a well-known community figure, she provided frequent reports on her experience by radio, across the province, in a way that raised awareness among Newfoundlanders.

Leadership, however, is socially constructed and takes many forms. Hence, it is crucial to note that the socially embedded character of the council is also a result of diverse forms of leadership that are grounded in local cultural practices. For example, throughout my residence in Bay St George, I frequently noted that even among well-educated people there is, if not an aversion, then a dislike for 'book learning.' Practices are embedded in context-bound conversation which is difficult to replicate here in a meaningful way. There is a strong oral tradition where intimate histories are communicated in the middle of some other activity, where social critique is expressed in sarcastic quips and social levelling is achieved by mutual but playful denigration and respect. This was common among both women and men inside and outside the Women's Centre.

Such was the case with John, a sixty-four-year-old millworker I came to know, who tried to explain why he was unable to learn from a book but could easily figure out how to wire a house and fix a car. He would invite me to join him and his wife, Lynn, for dinner and the occasional journey into the woods. He would tow us in the sled behind the ski-doo to cut wood, snowshoe, and have a 'boil up' on a bed of balsam boughs. As he cut the wood and made the tea, John would talk, non-stop, about the responsibilities of fatherhood, the decline of the fishery, working conditions in the mill, and his own childhood experiences in the outport where he was raised. When I requested an interview with him or sought to record his insights as he spoke, he firmly refused. 'If you don't want to sit and talk to me like a regular person, then I don't want to talk to you at all.'

His attitude reminded me of Peg, a 'founding mother' of the council who would convey in one-line quips, or short parables, her social critique, values, or disapproval of a council initiative. The daughter of an Anglican minister, she was raised in outports on Labrador and Fogo Island. Peg, too, refused to sit for an interview, claiming that she had nothing to say. What I think she meant was that she had nothing to say to me under artificial circumstances. These two do not typify the character of social interaction in the region, just an aspect of it. It is a form of interaction that was allowed to flourish in the Women's Centre but that, as the next chapters show, has implications for the construction of political space. In other words, feminist leadership in Bay St George can also be exercized by sarcastic quips, silent withdrawal, and the refusal to sit down to anything more structured than a basic conversation.

Still, the ability to inspire a crowd, to connect the problems in Bay St George with the wider context of social and economic change, has been crucial in expanding the council's initiatives. Consider the keynote speaker at the Provincial Conference in 1995. Dorothy Inglis, a former St John's newspaper columnist, spoke at that time on the dismantling of social policies that has occurred across the country and that, in her view, threatens the quality of life for Newfoundland women. These changes, she argued, signals a qualitative transformation in a Canadian way of life as governments are increasingly relinquishing the responsibilities of the state in the maintenance of its citizens and their protection from global economic forces. The audience of two hundred women was impressed by her analysis and indicated their interest in having fora where they could further their knowledge of this issue. The conference was one indicator of the increasing shift in council initiatives towards social and economic issues and the relationship between women's issues and people's issues – in conservative times of restructuring.

I have drawn attention to a few leadership styles to illustrate strengths and limits of the Bay St George Women's Council and to indicate that women who convey a shared identity as feminists, and as Newfoundlanders, are at the same time differently skilled and positioned in terms of their access to political power. During the period under study, this council's members developed and expanded their social networks, devised heterogeneous strategies, and, individually and collectively, expressed a common identity as grass-roots, feminist activists. At the same time, they did not always convey their issues in terms that could be easily translated into action at the provincial level; here, the role of provincial and national organizations proved critical.

Over the last ten years, issues on which the council focuses have expanded in response to changing economic circumstances and the discursive context in which 'experiences' are legitimated. Its attention to violence against women in particular has developed considerably. The awareness of military power, peace, and the physical assault that women experience in homes and communities is now enhanced by a more finely parsed recognition of the multifaceted dimensions of violence: the gender-neutral language which glosses male responsibility, the way violence is addressed in different branches of government. The sex-offender meeting which began this chapter represents the Women's Council's attempt to develop a community-based model, so that issues related to violence become central to the reformation of community development.

An important aspect of feminist organizing in Bay St George is the socially embedded character of activism, the way everyday practices that take place in this feminist home emerge from the network and relationships which sustain the region. And yet grass-roots organizing is not just a mirror of the region. Rather, it is the articulation of feminist discourse alongside lived experiences which permits activists to reconfigure home, to confound public and private dichotomies, or to reproduce these dichotomies in an effort to negotiate change and to address problems as they become locally meaningful. The expression of feminist identities, its articulation alongside Newfoundland, place, and gender, is also fluid and relative. This has significance, as the next chapter suggests, for situating feminist politics within the larger context of making change in the province.

CHAPTER SEVEN

Rethinking Community: Feminist Activism and Sustained Settlement

> There's strength in our people, strength that will bind,
> Stronger through hardship, stronger in time.
> It starts with tomorrow, it's passed hand to hand.
> It grows from the roots on 'the Rock' where we stand.
>
> 'The Rock Where We Stand,' by Susan Fowlow

Many of the songs that Estasy members write and perform are not devoted to serious social issues. Some are playful satires on everyday life. Others, like 'The Rock Where We Stand,' are more sentimental odes that show how important settlement in the region is to council members and residents of Bay St George, in spite of the realities of migration and the social problems that people experience. Such nostalgic yearnings, scholars argue, feed into a 'sense of place' and are engendered by modernizing forces. 'Place-based identity' (Harvey, 1993:3) has intensified, argues David Harvey, in spite of the dissolution of spatial barriers in the areas of exchange, communication, and the flow of capital and labour. Vernacular, selected traditions are revived in the selling of specific places and the creation of distinctness. This is an increasingly necessary adaptation to globalization within post-industrial regional economies (Harvey, 1993:3–10).

The expression of a distinct Newfoundland identity is, as Jim Overton has argued, informed by such modernist constructions of place. Images of Newfoundland folk culture and the outport life have increased although the basis for this livelihood – the cod fishery – is on the threshold of demise. Indeed, this folk culture is most often symbolized by the household cod fishery, which, Overton argues, signifies the rural way of life for city dwellers, out-migrants, and mainlanders (Overton, 1996). The icons, symbols, and images that sell Newfoundland to outsiders also signify essential symbols of Newfoundland identity (Overton, 1995:17) and reflect the intersection of contemporary forces: where resource management and depletion are debated in relation to alternate adaptations: emergent tourism, out-migration, and urbanization.

Constructions of rural Newfoundland have formed a 'therapeutic leisure space' for out-of-province visitors; freedom, honesty, and humanism, which have been eroded by the forces of modernity, are emblematic of this folk culture (Overton, 1996:58). At the same time, the folk culture fulfils the nostaligic yearnings of out-migrants and urban Newfoundlanders (Overton, 1996:38) through, for example, annual 'Come Home' celebrations.

As I have shown, folk constructs in Bay St George have been generated by specific historical forces – especially, the American air-force base. And, although the cod fishery was never important in the region, folk images do persist and intersect with the celebration of the 'Carefree Days' to create a distinct sense of place in the region that also increasingly draws on tourism. This is most dramatically evidenced in the annual festivals that precede and follow Harmon Day during the summer. Visitors – including those former residents who are now settled on the mainland – can enjoy a variety of events: blueberry festivals in St Georges or Acadian music at the francophone festivals. The annual Stephenville festival offers a variety of performances including irreverent satires, cosmopolitan musicals, and reflective dramas on the history of outport life. This festival, which is widely known in the province and noted for its diversity, exemplifies the way Bay St George and its residents exhibit, but are not bound by, a rigid construction of place or Newfoundland identity.

Indeed, my experience in the region, with council members and others, reinforces Doreen Massey's insight that such constructions of place and a commitment to rootedness are not necessarily a reactionary, conservative or reifying force unless 'place' is assigned essential, fixed qualities and identities. Sense of place can form a terrain of shared meanings, upon which changes are debated, to evoke a 'progressive sense of place' (1993:60–6) which attends to changing intersections of people, ideas, and livelihoods.

This chapter explores the role of the Women's Council in creating a progressive sense of place in Bay St George – one that is not limited to pre-existing idealizations of outport/community life and that forms a powerful counter-narrative to the larger Canadian context, where labour mobility is viewed as an adaptation to economic change. I examine the council's participation in the wider discourse of economic development and social change to consider the role of feminism in the articulation of a critical politics.

The critical force of the council lies in the participation of its members in coalitions, in government, and in feminist organizing. Moreover, the perspective they bring to these activities – one in which social and economic needs of women, children, and families are combined, not separated – is reflected in their understanding of community and politics. Specifically, an attention to community enhances participatory democracy provided that the particular experiences and problems that 'vulnerable populations' face within these locales are incorporated into the understanding of community. Problems specific to women, such as violence and sexual abuse, poverty and cultural marginalization, should be, in the council's view, *constitutive* of specific solutions and not auxiliary to narrowly defined interpretations of 'community development.'

In this regard, the council is a grass-roots example of the way feminists have sought to reposition and expand notions of community and sustainability. Although this latter discourse of 'sustainability' is most often associated with environmental issues and livelihood practices (Escobar, 1996), other scholars expand the term to consider the way economic and political policies permit social and lifecycle needs (more broadly construed) to be reproduced within communities (Eichler, 1996; Rangan, 1994; cf. Ristock and Pennell, 1996).

The council's attempt to make 'women's issues into people's issues' is, however, fraught with moments of consent and debate; it is an ongoing process that, when examined in specific discursive contexts, highlights the way 'gendering' remains a powerful symbolic, social, and economic marker which continues to bear upon the way changes are imagined and politics negotiated in Newfoundland and Labrador today.

'Community' and 'Development' in Newfoundland and Labrador

Although periods of financial crisis have always characterized Newfoundland's history – both before and after Confederation – the moratorium on cod fishing has intensified related social and economic problems. In Newfoundland today, the new stores, pick-up trucks, and renovated houses that dot the landscape are attributed to federal-government income support for those most directly affected by the moratorium on cod fishing. Such signs of prosperity notwithstanding, the statistics reveal an economy in crisis – in which residents are differentiated as much by their relation to various forms of state support and as they are by waged work per se.

More than 20,000 persons have left the province since 1993, the year the moratorium was imposed. There has been a 75 per cent increase in those who have sought short-term government assistance – or welfare – between 1989 and 1996. In fact, this translates into 20 per cent of the population, that is, 100,000 men, women, and children in a province of 500,000 people who receive only 50 per cent of Statistics Canada's recommended annual income for families. Unemployment rates are twice the national average, at 19 per cent, and 29 per cent among youth.[1] This has contributed to a loss in government revenue, which was already diminished by social and economic policy changes at the federal level – including reduced transfer payments and a reorganization and reduction in funds for social-assistance and unemployment-insurance funds. Households are equally affected by the loss of local and regional government revenue, which has generated social and economic policy changes in education, health care, and social and economic services.

It is in the context of economic crisis that the Newfoundland government exhibits a continued reliance on primary industry, tourism, and concomitent constructions of Newfoundland distinctness. The return of the *Matthew* to Conception Bay to commemorate John Cabot's 'discovery' of the 'New World' generated a large tourist turnout in the summer of 1997 in spite of aboriginal protest. And a fledgling tourist economy sells Newfoundland as a 'world of difference.'

That whales and puffins are promoted as much as people and fish is an indication of the impact of out-migration and the cod moratorium on the redefinition of distinctness. While the long-term economic benefits of Hibernia oil development are still unproven, the government turns increasingly to Labrador for the latent potential of this 'undeveloped' territory, which is widely known as the 'Land of Cain.' Attempts to reopen contracts with Quebec to generate hydroelectric dollars have failed, but the development of mining in Voisey's Bay now beckons. Clearly, people want to remain in province and they and their government have not given up on the possibility of sustained settlement.

In this regard, community has long been a context for social and political identity formation in Newfoundland, where one's 'home' signifies both the island and specific outports and villages even though places like Jerry's Nose and Campbell's Creek no longer support the fishing and farming that made them worthy of naming in the past. Today 'community' is part of 'way of life' discourses through which local experiences and livelihoods are represented in the larger political arena.

'Community,' and the 'way of life' it conveys, has been an important keyword through which Newfoundland residents have lobbied various levels of government and through which they have articulated a resistance to changes in their life. Attempts to intensify capitalist production in the fishery through the resettlement of fishing outports met with the resistance of numerous 'communities' across the island in the 1960s and 1970s (Matthews, 1976:passim). 'Community' forms the basis through which residents are now responding to the imposition of a cod moratorium on fishing – by finding new ways to maintain settlement in their outports. And, for example, at a recent conference directed towards changes in child-welfare policies in the province, the maintenance of 'communities' formed the means through which the management and organization of these policies was debated by local politicians, public-sector workers, and activists.

The importance of community for residents in the province, then, exemplifies the way 'community' and 'ways of life' discourses continue to generate subjective meaning; they form one of the few sites through which particular categories of marginalized people can agitate in the political arena (Nadel-Klein, 1991). Moreover, subjective understandings of community and the place-based identities to which they have given rise have political implications. The expression of Newfoundland identity is incorporated into political discourses – of community development and sustainability, for example; it forms one means available for articulating a regional perspective and is exemplary of the political discourses through which marginal regions elsewhere make political claims (Rangan, 1994).

These subjective understandings of community are reflected in the local politics in Bay St George, which is reliant on the state and affected by the persistent depletion of natural resources. Although the local economy is not determined by the abundance or shortage of the cod stocks, the gradual decline in the catch of fish, including lobster, capelin, and cod, is accompanied by a recognition that forests in the region will not produce unlimited quantities of usable pulpwood. Experts have routinely vacillated between depictions of the region as sustainable and as economically depressed. Moreover, the more recent influx into Stephenville of Newfoundlanders who have received government support as a result of the moratorium suggests that the collapse of the fishery will have an increasing impact on the region in the future.

Since the opening of the air base, the state has assumed the role of the former merchant class, largely setting the broad terms in which economic changes should be implemented. Local politicians, members of various organizations, and residents from rural communities and the town convey – both publicly and personally – a right to community. As a former mayor of Stephenville explained, by overcoming the closure of the base, Stephenville established a resilience to economic crises. Residents expressed a commitment towards, and claimed a right to, enduring settlement in the face of the tide of out-migration. This generated responses by local organizations from the late 1960s. Residents have gained access to the political arena and they negotiate the way funds are redistributed within existing political structures. They have responded to the periods of bust which followed the closure of the air base and the linerboard mill by extensively lobbying provincial and federal governments to establish new forms of industry and employment.

Periods of labour disputes and sporadic protests against government attempts to scale back social and economic programs have not generated a radical class politics in the area, as it is conventionally defined; nor does the region possess an industrial and manufacturing base for the formation of a cross-sector trade-union movement. Rather, working-class and regional identity inform each other (cf. Dunk, 1991:54) and coalesce in the articulation of Newfoundland identity. This is manifested in the celebration of practical knowledge and common-sense values by area women and men and by the reliance on do-it-yourself skills as well as their structural location within the labour market, as seasonally employed or migrant workers. Some residents perceive themselves to be exploited or disadvantaged by inequalities that stem from decisions made in central Canada, and in the provincial and federal capitals, rather than by local bosses.

The issues that concern the Bay St George Women's Council are not peripheral or auxiliary to this local political process. And gender affects political practice at the local and regional levels in a way that replays a central tension witin local feminist politics. One the one hand, the council seeks to centre women's experiences. On the other, it works to demonstrate that women's issues are relevant and even central to the larger project of maintaining and redefining community and family life. This is reflected in the participation of the council and its members in community politics. I draw attention to one incident in particular to consider the interplay between gender and political practice because it illustrates this larger tension and yet also reveals a strength in local feminist organizing.

'Our last resource is our people'

The Fox-Eye Environmental Association, a fledgling environmental organization in Bay St George, hosted 'The Last Resource Tour.' Held in the community college, the 'tour' was a presentation by several male activists from across Newfoundland on the political economy of resource depletion in the province. An inshore fisherman from Petty Harbour (on the east coast) summarized the decline of Newfoundland's cod fishery and the depletion of the stocks that led to the moratorium. Detailing his nineteen-year participation as an inshore fisherman within a cooperative, this speaker criticized the industry's 'romance with technology' and argued for the potential of a sustainable fishery where ownership and control over the management of production and sale would be located within the outport. He was followed by a forestry expert who chastized the provincial government 'for working too closely with industry' to permit the large-scale harvest of the island's forests.

'The province cannot sustain three pulp and paper mills much longer,' argued this expert, who then called for a program of community-based forest management. The third speaker argued against the province's attempts to attract newly emergent business such as the 'waste management industry' by accepting the 'garbage' from northeastern American cities.

This last speaker argued that politics should be 'feminized' claiming that 'our leaders are male and they are all co-opted within the power structure,' he went on to compare this to the political work of women, who 'do a lot of the work – who do all the activities.' 'We need a complete shift in the way political economic decisions are made in this province,' he argued. 'After all, our last resource is our people.'

These latter comments certainly reflected my own observations, that women are prominent in the middle and grass-roots layers of community activism and rarely positioned in the highest or most mainstream political institutions. Until 1996, women in Newfoundland and Labrador had the lowest rate of formal political participation at the provincial or territorial level, though they had some influence as 'femocrats' in the provincial bureaucracy (Rankin and Vickers, 1998:352–60). Men, on the other hand, are somewhat more rigidly bifurcated; they are well represented in local business and 'economic development' organizations, and they serve on decision-making boards. They hold formal power and hence can be socially and politically distanced from the working experiences of those they claim to represent and whose livelihoods are being transformed. There have been class-based mobilizations in the past (as I indicated in chapter 2), but men have not emerged as outspoken, critical local leaders in Bay St George.

It goes beyond the scope of this study to compare systematically the participation of men and women in community politics in this region. The central point is that local politics was not characterized at that time by disputatious displays although there had been numerous strikes, for example, in the late 1970s and 1980s within public-sector unions. During the period under study, local men did not demonstrate a prominent voice in local politics, particularly in community-based groups which were critical of community development and attentive to inclusiveness and inequality. By contrast, there was a perception that certain women were prominent activists and that they were outspoken and willing to challenge decisions in terms of their impact on specific groups of people within communities. But women on the whole were not necessarily more vocal than men. This is perhaps why the Bay St George Women's Council came to be perceived by many both as vocal and critical and as the social conscience of the community.

A local union leader, who was originally from Cape Breton, expressed her frustration at the absence of a 'collective' spirit in Bay St George: 'On the one hand, women seem more involved in activism in Stephenville than men. A lot of the local presidents were women, and the Labour Council was started and fired up predominantly by women. Yet they ask me to go the picket line and help them say 'scab,' because they're too polite! They're not fighters. People here aren't fighters, and those that are, are women! Sure, the women at the Women's Centre are fighters, but not on the line, not in the union.'

Numerous workers in community development and government ministries claim that it is difficult to get a large number of local men to attend meetings in formal settings such as the college. It is noteworthy that the men in Bay St George who might have direct experience of resource depletion were, as my friend noted, certainly not in that room for the presentation of 'The Last Resource Tour.'

What did the speaker mean by 'feminizing' politics? One council member called this an appropriation of the term and argued that 'feminizing,' as used in that case, did not refer to a concern for women's issues or a gender perspective. I suggest that it referred to the character of political activism with which women are popularly associated and which has historical resonance in outport life. Feminists in Newfoundland have noted the extensive and historically embedded participation of women in traditional and community-based organizations in outports and towns across the province (Porter, 1985b:80; Neis, 1988:42; Davis, 1986:135). And Porter has argued that women's activism is culturally embedded while men's activism is centred in political institutions which are severed from that of the community where people live and work (Porter, 1985b:86). The political organizing of women in Bay St George suggests, however, that it is important to move beyond the outport, to consider not just the grounded character of politics but its intersection at different levels: that is, arenas of family, community, and government and the role of gender in this political process.

A 'feminized' politics means a more socially embedded politics, where experiences of living in Bay St George are shared and incorporated into a broad critical vision of social change. Such activism lends itself to Newfoundland given its social organization and the fact that Newfoundlanders have long been active in the creative reproduction of certain traditions, social relations, and practices that inform Newfoundland identity. This kind of politics necessarily encompasses the reproduction of community and family life. Yet these are contested sites that might reaffirm long-time asymmetries or could qualitatively transform them.

For example, the necessity of fiscal restraint is softened by local politicians who promise residents economic development and warn that the region could become 'one big retirement community' without concerted community efforts to attract business and influence government. Numerous community initiatives are directed towards establishing employment and transforming education. In this discourse, family is invoked both as a set of values and as a site of mutual dependence and reliance. The Women's Council, which itself draws on family values and reciprocities, struggles to influence the means by which visions of sustainability draw upon these historically embedded relationships.

A reliance on family-based reciprocity and socially embedded networks is not by definition a progressive move, as I have tried to show in earlier chapters. But council members and women do draw on these networks, to negotiate livelihood, maintain social networks, and implement feminist practice. This is expressed by council members, who argue that a 'just' community cannot be realized without a radical restructuring of family as an institution, or without the reconfiguration of responsibilities between men and women and the social control that is exercized over them and over each other.

For example, one of the most important discussions within the Department of Social Services and community-development organizations is about the utility and meaning of implementing a 'guaranteed annual income' to replace current systems of redistribution, namely, social assistance and unemployment insurance. The council's perspective is not unlike that of other activists within larger anti-poverty organizations, who recognize the benefits of transforming the current system, given its gender bias (as discussed in chapter 4) (cf. Haddow, 1994:passim). At the same time, they are worried that it might be reformed in a way that would simply reproduce current gender asymmetries. This is certainly reflected in the proposals of local economic-development associations, which argue that men and women in rural communities should be given training in 'self-reliant' activities such as carpentry and craft-making to supplement their seasonal working wage.

Moreover, council members argue that women's experiences must be built into the way assorted programs are designed and implemented. Activists, decision makers, and program designers must take into account the relations of power and hierarchies that exist in households, extended families, workplaces, and communities. These hierarchies may inhibit women's participation in community development by preventing them from having access to, or knowledge of, available resources; or the programs may not take into account women's interests, the demands on their time, their sense of self worth, their values and expectations. This perspective is built into the programs they have developed, for example, with the local community college. And, consider, too, the sexual-abuse counselling service. For council members, a 'feminized' politics means more than a socially embedded politics: it includes a focus on women's experiences and a sustained attention to gender relations and inequalities.

Sexual Abuse Counselling Service

In May 1993 the Liberal MHA for the Bay St George region of western Newfoundland joined residents and the mayor of the town of Stephenville at the local hospital to celebrate the opening of the experimental sexual-abuse counselling service, which was intended to service the southwest region of the island. After a speech from the mayor and the MHA, the coordinator of the local Women's Council thanked the 'community' of Bay St George for recognizing the problem of sexual abuse and for claiming responsibility for the treatment of its victims. Once the ceremonial ribbon was formally cut, visitors were treated to light refreshments, a cake, and a tour of the facility, which consisted of counselling rooms, a resource room, and a lounge already filled with toys to occupy visiting children. For Maureen and Dorothy – two survivors of sexual abuse who attended the ceremony – the event heralded the creation of a safe space, where experiences of sexual abuse could be recounted and which would ease the recovery of residents whose lives had been shaped by such childhood or adult traumas.

As I indicated in a previous chapter, during the last fifteen years, public-sector workers in the departments of social services, mental health, and education also became sensitized to the needs of their 'clients' for a counselling service that would focus on facilitating recovery from experiences of sexual abuse. In consultation with government ministries, they formed a local 'Community Response Team' which laid the groundwork for the Sex Abuse counselling service. The service was designed to operate somewhat independently of the administrative structures of the three ministries (education, health, and Social services) which initially provided the resources, staff, and funding.

The service was designed to be integrative: that is, to make the links between victims and their families, victims and offenders, and provide education in schools. At the same time, the anonymity of the victim would be protected and the service subjected to evaluations by its users and representatives of the 'community.'[2] 'Feminist counselling,' which attends to issues that I mentioned briefly in chapter 5, is the chief model it advocates, as well as an attention to the gender of the counsellor and client. After one year in operation, the service had been used by 183 'clients,' 146 of whom were female and 37 male, who live along the entire southwest coast of the island. Of these 183, 58 were children and adolescents, and 100 were adults between the ages of twenty and thirty-nine. In 1997–8, 167 people were treated; the majority were women, the male 'clients' were between the ages of eleven and forty-nine, and both the women and the men came from all parts in the region.[3]

An integrated model means that community forms the locus for the articulation of different branches of government. Hence, broad-based education forums are designed to reach a wider audience – that is, neighbours, parents, children, and educators – to sensitize them to the wider cultural context in which sexual abuse takes place. This means making links between sexual abuse and hierarchies within families in which men have social and/or economic power over women. And it includes a challenge to stereotypes – of male breadwinner and female dependant, of male aggression and female passivity – which can shape experiences of sexuality, parenting, and decision making. In sum, the sexual-abuse counselling program is framed by a few important principles: that the community must take responsibility for the social problems of its residents; that personal traumas are gendered; and that dealing with such traumas should be an empowering experience.

As politicians and media representatives noted, the community was beginning to take responsibility for numerous social problems, including domestic violence and sexual abuse, which had, only ten years ago, been largely invisible. By this I mean that normative standards in the region have been transformed to incorporate, and make public, issues of violence and sexual abuse against women and children. This is not, however, to claim that there is a community-wide acceptance of feminist discourse or that normative community standards embrace a feminist perspective on these issues. It is to suggest rather that a feminist perspective as reflected by the council occupies an important place in the legitimation of these issues as social problems.

Feminists note the way the discourse of violence against women may reproduce gender asymmetries by constructing women as victims or by minimizing male responsibility through gender neutral language (Gotell, 1998:63–70), and these perspectives were at play in Bay St George.

Moreover, although I focus here on locality, it is crucial to recognize the intervention of ministers and branches of the state, as well as the impact on residents of the conviction of Catholic brothers at Mount Cashel. This reinforces my claim that 'community' as a geographic and symbolic site intersects with wider political and discursive shifts. Sexual abuse and violence have become a focus for the way normative changes in religious practice, authority, and sexuality are debated and effected across the province (cf. Langlois, 1997). While I cannot embark on a more sustained analysis of this broader shift, it is important to note that the debates regarding violence and sexual abuse are gendered: they implicate men and women and invoke gender scripts which draw upon feminine and masculine roles but which assign different weight to power and focus responsibility differently: on institutions and/or individuals.

The impact of these wider debates on Bay St George was reflected in several ways: events surrounding Mount Cashel were invoked in everyday conversation, in reference to local sexual-abuse issues and convictions, in ways that embraced different positions regarding gender and violence. One woman, for example, claimed that it was Mount Cashel which prompted her to recognize the significance of her experience of sexual abuse as a child. The scandal generated a crisis for the church as many residents began to question their beliefs and Catholic practices.

An integrative, community-based approach to problems such as sexual abuse necessarily involves residents and can generate considerable tensions which may pit sister against brother, child against parent, victim against offender, and residents against each other. Moreover, there are professionals working within the region itself who have not been supportive of this model.

Some residents who were involved in the Anti-Violence Coalition felt that the Women's Council placed too much emphasis on women. They perceived violence and sexual abuse as problems that both women and men experience and gave less focus to the larger context of power in which gender roles are taken up. Others placed greater blame and emphasis on the 'traditional' and 'backward' practices of certain families or communities.

Furthermore, because Stephenville was the site of the men's and women's correctional centres (the latter has now moved), some residents were more conscious of the presence of those who were convicted of these offences. An important indicator of the specific position of the council, however, is reflected in its approach towards women who were incarcerated for having committed physical abuse on children. For the most part, the council provided some ad hoc counselling for these women. The presence of two elderly women in particular, who were convicted of severe physical abuse against children, provoked a heartfelt ambivalence in some council members. More than one council member had experienced a physically abusive mother. Yet the council's public position called into question the cultural context in which these physically abusive women were historically located as mothers, foster mothers, and caregivers.

The cultural context of abuse remains an ongoing issue in Newfoundland and Labrador and calls into question the power dynamics that operate in families. The position of the council on this matter is to situate the family as an institution within the larger context of Newfoundland history – poverty, large families, and powerful churches – and to recognize the role that gender and power play in relation to the understanding of violence and sexual abuse more broadly.

This issue is exemplary of the problem that feminist activists have: to represent women's issues as specific to women, to avoid victimizing women, and to show that women's issues are worthy, relevant, and connected to men, children, and the vitality of communities. The council negotiates this dilemma in several ways, including the manner it argues for the importance of social welfare and the maintainance of government support in the reproduction of community life. This is also reflected in its strategic use of keywords and the way in which its political arguments are framed.

'Women's issues are people's issues'

The founding mothers of the Bay St George Women's Council have increasingly and bravely encouraged the use of feminist discourse throughout Bay St George, in particular labels such as 'feminist' and 'patriarchy' that mark the organization as part of the feminist movement and distinct from the community. At the same time, such terms are, on occasion, purposively submerged within a more general discourse of emancipation, in which notions of 'freedom,' 'choice,' 'justice,' and 'equality' are invoked to signify the council's commitment to a social good. This occurs when council members want to stress what they share with particular groups of residents who are inhibited by what they assume the feminist label signifies. The malleability of these latter terms – their gender-neutral character – permits the council to address issues that affect women and men, including their commitment to place. This is increasingly crucial given the transformations and restructuring that have occurred well beyond the local arena, and it is reflected in the council's approach to community development.

Council members bring together their experiences as workers, and the knowledge of other women's lives that they have gained, to challenge government policy whenever the opportunity arises. The following example not only outlines their critical perspective towards government positions but illustrates the way council members 'make women's issues into people's issues.'

Coffee with Clyde

One evening in May, council members and a few other residents attended a dinner at the newly opened Holiday Inn in town. After dinner and a few songs, guests slipped into the adjacent lounge just as Clyde Wells, then premier of Newfoundland and Labrador, entered for a late dinner. Wells was campaigning for the upcoming election, which he was expected to win once again. Joyce, the council coordinator, interrupted his entry into the dining room, introduced herself, and began to criticize his campaign for the dearth of discussion of social issues. Unhappy with his brief response, she and others began to plot a way in which they could take greater advantage of this coincidental encounter.

Council members organized a huddle of various guests and, as I had noted on many previous occasions, suggestions shifted from boisterous confrontations to more reasoned interventions once those women, known as 'diplomats,' assessed the situation. Council 'troublemakers,' a noisy 'crowd' of five or six women, stood glaring at Wells as he and his entourage ate, making various gestures with their faces against the French doors that opened into the dining room. A few women wanted to burst open these doors in a display of nationalist pride, to sing the 'Ode to Newfoundland' with two new words inserted – 'Clyde Lied.' This phrase had been coined by the Newfoundland and Labrador Federation of Labour, and the council members who wanted to use it now had encountered it through their union membership. Others, however, felt that the use of the phrase would not reflect the character of local council activism and preferred what they perceived to be a less confrontational approach. As Linda, the diplomat, reasoned, 'No, no, what's that going to do?' 'Maybe it'll make him lose his dinner!' joked another. 'Ok, we'll ruin his dinner – we'll just storm in and surround his table – and demand he address the issues,' suggested another. While these women plotted, a few others physically distanced themselves from the strategists. One woman, a somewhat restrained council supporter and Liberal Party member, hid behind a table. Finally, we (by this time I, too, was swept into the huddle, as the 'distanced outsider') requested an ad hoc meeting with the premier via the waitress.

Eight women, capable of addressing a variety of issues, joined Wells at his table; interestingly, none of the male guests who was present in the lounge volunteered to participate. Joyce began by suggesting that there was little forum in the election for the discussion of social issues or the implications of government policy such as deficit reduction on women's lives and working conditions. Judy, a nurse, criticized Clyde's relationship with unions. 'You legislated a cutback for me, in Bills 16 and 17 in spite of a collective agreement,' she declared. 'How can I trust you?' Judy then launched into a description of the working conditions of public-health nurses in particular; she suggested that money could be better spent by directing resources towards 'progressive community health.' She noted the absence of resources for dealing with men and women who need after-hospital care. Lynda, the social worker, nodded in agreement with Judy and added that preventive counselling could foster better health care, particularly for her own 'clients,' who have addictions or have attempted suicide.

Michelle, another social worker, emphasized the strengths of community activism in Bay St George by outlining their broad-based and 'innovative attempts' to tackle experiences of sexual abuse before 'victims' became labelled as costly residents of the pyschiatric hospital in St John's. Wendy asked why government money was spent to hire 'welfare cops' who focused on 'single mothers.' 'Government has to consider women's sexual and interpersonal dynamics without a predetermined morality towards them, when making decisions about social assistance,' she argued. Finally, Brenda, a teacher, chastised Wells for depicting teachers, who were in the midst of collective bargaining, as 'fat-cats,' just to displace the focus of social issues and the dismantling of social policy onto a single category of workers.

To all this Clyde responded in a patronizing tone, especially to Judy, the nurse. 'We must cut – we must represent the public good. You – you, represent private interests and we cannot concede to all of you. Remember, we are a have-not province the size of Germany,' he concluded. It is statements such as this that generated critical responses to government from the council. It also provoked the council to challenge the way social issues were fragmented through the corporate language of 'private interest' by stressing that these problems are community issues. And it mirrors the wider problem that feminists faced throughout the 1980s and 1990s – when feminist claims were increasingly positioned by those in political power as 'private,' 'narrow,' or the demands of 'special interests' (Bashevkin, 1998:189). How else can such claims be effectively made?

It is noteworthy that, when these claims are labelled as 'narrow' or 'private,' the issues they refer to can be marginalized. A parallel discourse is that in which claims are made on the basis of 'distinctiveness.' I suggest that the ability of Newfoundland activists to draw upon this latter discourse provides a counterpoint to the marginalization of issues through a discourse of 'private interest.' This is effected through a broad process of cultural production, in the way distinctness becomes attached to a sense of place – communities and the province itself. This need not give distinctness an essential, territorial character; rather, in the case of Newfoundland, its relative character is equally significant and I suggest can form a locus for debate and critique via the expression of Newfoundland identities.

This is reflected in the relative ways in which distinctness is manifested both across the province and in the Bay St George region. For example, council members participated in government policy making as representatives on various boards or through their paid work. This necessarily placed some members in a difficult position of implementing government policies with which they may not entirely agree. And it provided them with an awareness of the way notions of community were implicated in proposals for change and economic development. Council members drew upon ideas of place and a sense of distinctness to communicate their perspective on these issues to residents. This was not, in my view, simply a form of rhetoric; they did so because they were positioned, as grass-roots activists, to make and live the connections between policy, livelihood, and cultural meaning.

Gender, Culture, and the Expression of Distinctness

When travelling across the island, one becomes aware of the variety of local publications that are produced to document and celebrate specific histories. Stories that focus on single communities or geneologies, with titles such as 'Them Days' and 'Supposin' I dies in a dory,' are found in stores across the province. This indicates that Newfoundlanders do manifest a sense of distinctness and that Newfoundlanders depict their lives from the 'centre' as they live it.

Newfoundlanders describe themselves through poetry, novels, and nationally circulated newspapers like 'The Downhomer' where a cultural identity and selected cultural practices – such as a love for Purity crackers and hard-tack bread – are celebrated. Moreover, it is arguable that Newfoundlanders' sense of distinctness allows for their cultural expression of political satire, which now speaks to a wide audience. This includes latent nationalist sentiments: residents who can still recall the Ode to Newfoundland, and stories of failed nationhood, captured in films like *Secret Nation*, and the debate over Confederation.

Similarly, in Bay St George, a shared experience of Newfoundland distinctness was reflected in numerous ways. For example, a communicative style was at play both in the Women's Centre and in other community-based organizations. Whoever was present drew upon certain phrases and mannerisms that they considered to be distinct to Newfoundland. During Glee Club rehearsals that I attended weekly, Mrs B—, the conductor and piano teacher, shifted frequently from refined musician to bossy outport wife. As 'the Mrs' she could exercise discipline and generate harmony among these resident singers – teachers, RCMP officers, social workers, and the marginally employed – especially when the men, many of whom were playful and talented 'hams' – got rowdy.

I noted a similar pattern at the Women's Centre: council members regardless of their education or origin within the province slipped into this style when they entered the room. We marvelled at the way Joyce, for example, could switch from what they called 'CBC' English for media interviews to informal everyday speech. In these cases, 'Newfoundland talk' conveyed a shared identity in spite of whatever differences might be at play within a specific group at a given time. 'Come-from-aways' could and did at times participate in this. Yet a marked difference in communicative style between the Newfoundland-born and raised and the 'come-from-aways' was frequently noted. Occasionally, the difference suggested that 'Come-from-aways' were socially superior, but this could be highly contested. Moreover, Newfoundland distinctness was often attached by Newfoundland speakers to a set of social traits that were related to the way Newfoundlanders were depicted in a broader Canadian context. In this sense, the council members' speech and its cultural referents formed a locus through which identity and difference were expressed.

For example, during the Lion's Club Winter Carnival Dinner and Dance in 1992, guests were treated to moose stew and the stand-up routine of locally, well-known satirist Ross N— as he celebrated the frequent migration and emigration of Newfoundlanders to the 'mainland.' He remarked on the fortune Newfoundlanders amass in the collection of unemployment insurance, highlighted the marvels of life on 'the rock,' denounced the everyday congestion of big-city life, and wondered out loud why Torontonians have not yet discovered 'the good life' that Newfoundlanders have long known. He contrasted the resourceful Newfoundlander who rigs up 'thing-me-bobs' to fix 'wha'do-you-call-its' with 'bits-of-this-and-that' to the urban sophisticate and the array of specialized technology and services he has at hand but does not know how to use.

The audience laughed approvingly at the satirical manner in which these familiar themes and long-time stereotypes were replayed. The skit and the laughter reinforced my understanding that Newfoundland men and women internalize, mock, and reclaim such cultural appellations through humour and satire, which speak to some understanding of shared experience.

When the Women's Council was involved, however, the critique could be sharp and draw attention to power *within* Newfoundland communities. For example, although nationally televized shows like *CODCO* and the currently popular *This Hour Has 22 Minutes* may be the most well-known examples of Newfoundland satire at present, characters like Marg Delaunty and Jerry Boyle have their equivalents in Bay St George. Characters like Mildred the Midwife and Dick Head, whom I mentioned in previous chapters, critique local social norms and recount lifeways as they see them. Mildred appeared in many forms which were context specific and culturally meaningful for residents of Bay St George. And, as as one resident put it, 'she gets away with things that nobody else would dare say.'

Speaking with a francophone accent that is quite peculiar to this area, Mildred offered advice to audiences by occupying numerous social roles: sometimes she was an overweight aerobics instructor; other times a sore-winning bingo player or a nun. She appealed to a lot of residents, including francophone women, who looked forward to her performances. And, she incited debate, for example, when her appearance as a physically abusive nun provoked a range of audience response – from those who thought her irreverance towards the church went too far, to those whose memories of school were stirred.

Finally, it is important to note that these performances unfold within specific sites of activism and are connected to both political, awareness-raising activities and to everyday leisure events which I have discussed in previous chapters. For example, anti-violence bingo games held in rural community centres were like bingo on any other day, except that in this case information was provided through specially designed cards which drew attention to the issue.

Activists in Bay St George, like feminists elsewhere in Canada, argue that in order to create healthy communities in both rural and urban settings, we need to expand our understanding of 'sustainability' to include more than the economic progress and growth of the community as a whole. Rather, a 'sustainable' community is one that maintains and responds to the different social needs of a variety of residents who may at different stages in their lives require government resources and community support to maintain quality of life (Eichler, 1996; Andrews, 1992). This includes residents such as women and those who experience unemployment, ill health, disability, and/or immense hardship or responsibility within nuclear, extended, and single-parent families. Numerous residents across the country have been marginalized from the centres of decision-making power, and their needs and responsibilities, in raising children and addressing personal crises, for example, require economic and social investments and resources which have not been previously considered as necessary in the designing of plans for the economic growth or development of a community (MacGregor, 1996).

Having spent a considerable amount of time with activists in Bay St George in a range of activities, I suggest they provide a process, if not a replicable model, for building healthy, sustainable, and 'inclusive' communities which recognize the differences that separate residents and the ties that bind them (Ristock and Pennell, 1997:18). For members of the Bay St George Women's Council, remaking community means confronting social issues; it entails drawing on the skills women have already acquired and minimizing the hierarchies that separate women from each other – including clients and counsellors, the employed and unemployed, and rural and urban residents. It calls for maintaining and reshaping the cultural links – the values, symbols, labours, and networks – that make social and political issues locally meaningful.

Conclusion

When sun rays crown thy pine clad hills,
and summer spreads her hand,
When silvern voices tune thy rills,
we love thee smiling land ...
we love thee Newfoundland ...

'Ode to Newfoundland'

When I returned to Stephenville one year after having left, I was greeted at the Women's Centre with a chorus or two of the 'Ode to Newfoundland.' Standing at attention around the kitchen table, council members bellowed this tune as I entered the living room, then shouted at me for once again failing to remove my shoes. This was typical of the attention I sometimes received, and although it was somewhat embarrassing, I interpreted it as a contradictory expression of respect and irreverence, for me and that which I represented. The 'Ode to Newfoundland' distinguishes Council members and signifies their identification with Newfoundland and the particular history that preceded its entry into Confederation. In this sense, the performance reinforced one aspect of our relationship, specifically my status as an outsider. Council members frequently invoked symbols of Newfoundland to establish their difference and at the same time to challenge what they recognized to be a context of power that situated me, an academic feminist from central Canada, in a position of privilege vis-à-vis them.

Yet, within Bay St George, and during my visits there, it is the discourse of feminism and the gender asymmetries it exposes that united me with them, and against residents and social forces that contest their agenda for change. As a feminist 'from away,' who would, as they frequently noted, 'just pick up and leave!' I have been both a part of their community and distinct from it. This latter point supports my claim, set out in the introduction, that situating the ethnographer can enhance our analysis. The anthropological distinction between insider and outsider can be useful, if it is employed in a flexible and situated manner. It has made me much more conscious of the importance of distinguishing myself from women activists in Bay St George. And this has implications for my understanding of feminist politics and the meanings of culture and distinctiveness. But, in highlighting these dualisms, I do not mean to oversimplify the relationships in which I was embedded or to suggest that my position as a 'feminist' meant that we agreed or even had the same perspective on local and national issues. In fact, I want to draw attention to differences but avoid setting myself against Newfoundland women as if they were a homogeneous group. Rather, I draw attention to differences in perspective with specific persons and in different contexts, because I think that doing so enhances our understanding of the themes which frame this study of women's grass-roots activism: the construction and depiction of culture, the expression of identities, and the relationship of women's issues and activism to regional discourses.

It is the articulation of Newfoundland and feminist identities that contributes to the 'grounding' of feminist activism in issues that are relevant to area women. This is crucial, given the concern that women's movements have become institutionalized (Findley, 1998:passsim) and that grass-roots organizing is considered a crucial means of maintaining feminist movements in times of restructuring (Brodie, 1998:20). In fact, the success of the Women's Council in generating critical, locally meaningful political response is its ability to present itself 'in terms that its members and opponents can understand' (O'Brien and Roseberry, 1991:13).

In other words, grass-roots activism in Bay St George has been successful insofar as it has had made a difference in the lives of council members and residents and in the way social issues have been taken up in the region and even the province itself. This is largely a result of several factors. The socially embedded practices that have flourished at the centre have been crucial in sustaining activism during its growth, and this is even more noteworthy considering that these are times of political conservativism. However, the prevailing conservatism, which, as Bashevkin argues (Bashevkin, 1998), has marginalized women's political participation across the country, should be set against the specific context of economic and social crisis in the province. In fact, I would suggest that this crisis has necessitated a qualitative reflection on lifeways in the province. Women activists in Bay St George were somewhat well positioned to participate in this process as a result of their paid work, and because they had developed a strong political and social network to make issues politically and locally meaningful. At the same time, council members expressed Newfoundland and Bay St George identities which conveyed their right to sustained settlement in the province.

And yet the effects of activism have also been curtailed in two ways. First, the conservative wave has reproduced a timeworn problem – that is, the marginalization of women's issues – while casting it in a new quise as the concern of 'special interests.' A committment to sustained settlement can provide an alternate discourse, which, when combined with feminist activism, can have a greater impact in terms of developing coalitions. Second, the terms in which sustainability is debated are necessarily informed by pre-existing ideas about family and community, which, as I demonstrated in chapter 5, can generate social cleavages in a way that potentially marginalizes feminist activism. In concluding this book, I consider the impact of grass-roots feminist activism on Bay St George and examine the significance of this study for feminist politics and research and anthropology.

'If only men were more like women'

It is tempting to characterize feminist activism in Bay St George as a local manifestation of cultural feminism that has emerged in the last fifteen years and is noteworthy for its attempt to transform and critique patriarchy through a celebration and reconfiguration of socially constructed or biologically rooted femininity.[1] As life stories and activities within the Women's Centre convey, there is a clear tendency to celebrate the feminine, the emotional, and the spiritual and to draw on traditional female practices as the basis for new social relationships and the organization of society. On the whole, council members do not seek to emulate male behaviour. Rather, they tend to draw on the social practices and moral understandings of a traditional, feminine identity that highlights women's caregiving and nurturing roles (di Leonardo, 1991:214). This is reflected in the way they transform the liberal language of emancipation to express an alternate social conscience that celebrates justice through peace, and also in the way reciprocities within the community mediate and at times are favoured over more disputatious displays.

Occasionally, the spirit of this council evoked for me an earlier period within the Women's Movement when radical feminists combined their critique of family and marriage with a consideration of women's poverty and their under-representation within arenas of political power (Echols, 1989:6). But to classify grass-roots movements such as this one within the categories of feminist theory or activism from the centre is to reinscribe local activism within a hierarchy that favours theory and assigns a cohesiveness of outlook to grass-roots initiatives that ignores the contingency of local response. It would be to reinforce a history of the centre where political movements and the categories they generate become institutionalized. And to position organizations such as these on a continuum from right to left, or from integrative to disengaged, ignores the unexpected results that specific integrative strategies can have (Adamson, 1988:168). It sets a predetermined agenda for action that may not suit the local context.

I suggest that the location of the women of Bay St George within a regional context that has been constituted both from within and outside as a distinct culture informs their incorporation within the national feminist movement and the way their social problems are understood within a national context. Although Judy Rebick has formally apologized to Newfoundland feminists, St John's feminists still recall somewhat angrily the way their occupation of the secretary of state's offices in 1991 was almost completely ignored by NAC. Interestingly, British Columbia feminists were second to follow Newfoundland women, whose protests are now credited for the restoration of federal funding for women's councils.

At the same time, I do not want to romaniticize the 'local' or suggest that it is a panacea for feminist organizing. As I already indicated, it is organizations like NAC and the Provincial Advisory Council that have provided valuable resources, education, and insights into women's activism at the provincial and federal levels. The Provincial Advisory Council in Newfoundland has not always demonstrated as critical a perspective towards government policy or attended to the effects of policy on women. But, during my tenure in Newfoundland, and since, this body has made substantive efforts to participate in government policy making and to develop its links more fully at the grassroots. My relationship with Joyce has changed considerably since I began field research, and now that she has taken up the role as president of The Provincial Advisory Council, she is determind to bring with her the skills and community-based perspective she developed during her participation in the Bay St George Women's Council. Moreover, council politics does speak to issues, and it does have a perspective that is informed by and is situated within a broader feminist politics.

The Politics of Reproduction and the Impact of Feminism on Bay St George

The focus of this council from the early 1980s to the present has been on issues of sexuality, violence, reproductive rights and choices, and shaping the way key institutions – education, justice, health, and economic- and social-welfare services – attend to women's experiences as clients, victims, workers, mothers, daughters, and wives.

In this sense, the council's activities form part of a larger politics of reproduction, whereby it challenges the terms and conditions under which women and men are expected to reproduce themselves and raise their families. Its commitment to experience, and a framework of analysis that centres the sphere of reproduction as a gendered context, are crucial components of an alternate discourse and an active politics. Integral to this is the council's expansion of a politics of the body in which it emphasizes autonomy of the female body and exposes the connections between relations of dependence and subjugation and the exercise of male power. The attention to the body informs a variety of debates over birth control, abortion, sexual abuse, the right to motherhood, and sexual relations. This provokes a reconfiguration of responsibilities and rights between men and women and challenges pre-existing institutions in a region such as Bay St George (cf. Canning, 1994:386).

Like many grass-roots and national women's organizations in Canada, the council's politics are directed towards the state and the way state power is exercised in its locality. Bay St George feminists seek elimination of gender asymmetries and democratization of power. Specifically, this necessitates more adequate redistribution of, and access to, existing state resources, which include money, decision-making power, and the collection and dissemination of information. The political process must be transformed through ongoing community consultations and a consideration of women's individual and personal experiences. The control that is exercised over women by mechanisms of surveillance should be shifted from women to men through changes in the legal system and social services. This means, for example, increased sanctions against violence and surveillance of perpetrators and a rigorous but flexible system and collection of paternal-support payments. Council members promote programs that recognize women's historically rooted and differential role in the social reproduction of families and the larger political economy through their paid and unpaid work that is, their concomitant social roles as mothers and workers.

The critical force and practices of this council emerge from its attention to the experiences of particular categories of women who are, by happenstance and circumstance, subordinated by overlapping and gender-coded relations and distributions of power. These include women such as single mothers, discussed in chapter 4, and victims of sexual and physical abuse, discussed in chapter 5. They are marginalized within the family, community, and labour market. This structural marginalization is reinforced by the way their experiences are culturally encoded; they are reinscribed into narratives of reproduction as pathologized, deviant, or unfortunate individuals.

In the late 1990s, the council's activities have expanded to include a greater attention to the impact of 'economic development' on women. Moreover, aside from its important role in service provision and advocacy, it demonstrates a greater attention to living with gender and living as women by focusing on sexuality, partnerships, and women's health.

The first and most superficial indication that feminism has made a difference in the region is through media depictions and the participation of the Women's Council in public and community discourse. The mayor's declaration that this Women's Council has been the social conscience of Bay St George is reflected in the way reports on women's issues changed from 1981 to the mid- 1990s; the extent to which the Women's Council was called upon for comment; and the character of its intervention in community discourse.

For example, over two six–month periods in 1981 and 1983, there was relatively little attention paid to women's issues per se, nor were social issues considered for their potential impact on men and/or women in the regional weekly newspaper, *The Georgian*. The few articles that did identify themselves as of interest to women examined homemaking and 'family life' issues and hence focused on women as mothers. This changed dramatically with the formation of the Women's Council in 1985; since then, women's issues and the activities of the council have been featured at least twice per month, if not more frequently, and often more than once in a single issue. Further, the integration of the council's activities within the region is reflected on three levels in *The Georgian* which indicate its role as a key participant in community and provincial politics.

First, council elections, seasonal celebrations, and specific initiatives such as training programs, or Christmas events were announced in the newspaper in much the same vein as other community events were. Secondly, the council was called upon to comment on a range of initiatives and issues, including the particular sentences of those convicted of crimes of violence and sexual abuse and employment and training programs initiated by government or funding agencies at the college and through community-development organizations. The council perspective was also sought to determine the issues that were of relevance for upcoming elections. Thirdly, council members participated more directly in specific debates over contentious issues such as abortion and the implications of the Charlottetown Accord.

Their participation in media discourse reflected their sustained participation in community-based organizations, as I indicated in chapter 6. Moreover, the council played a leadership role in organizing all-candidates debates for provincial and federal elections and participated in the question-and-answer component of these fora. It played direct roles in the numerous community-based initiatives I have mentioned elsewhere, including public demonstrations, government programs, and coalitions. This allowed it to have some impact on specific programs, such as the Sex Abuse Counselling Service, courses and programs offered through government branches, and the education of students on a range of social issues.

To summarize, the council offered a perspective that was attentive to the experiences of women and 'vulnerable' populations and to the centrality of gender and life experience. This meant developing a framework of analysis and of practices which would ensure accountability.

The council also had consideral impact upon individual women. Although council membership is always in flux, a large number who are no longer active are still in contact with council and are called upon to participate in community-wide activities. And they draw upon the skills and analysis which their activism provided to engage in other community organizations. It is significant that several women who were formerly active in the council left for one of three reasons: to spend more time with family and in raising children; to participate in other organizations; or to develop their interests in more direct relation to their paid work.

Moreover, more than a decade later, different categories of women are now much more positioned to participate in political arenas. Francophone women in particular are exemplary of this growth. In spite of the conflicts that were generated with the public accounts of sexual abuse in specific francophone communities, the indications are that these women have actually increased their political participation. This was evidenced in their enhanced participation in provincial women's councils and increasingly through their own organizing efforts in the francophone organizations. The importance of ethnic identity for these women, however, underscores the way in which women are multiply located. And, although council politics are 'grounded, there are exclusions (as I indicated in chapter 6). This also has implications for the ability of feminist organizations to participate in community-based and provincial coalitions.

Feminists debate the extent to which women can uncover or create a critical space, a position of opposition within overlapping discursive frameworks or structures of power (Canning, 1993; Alcoff, 1988:420) Hegemonic forces can structure a subordinate group in a way that absorbs their critical force and effectiveness (Roseberry, 1990:14). My entry into this debate, which feeds into other long-time debates over structure and agency in the social sciences, is to illuminate the importance of material context and grounded anthropological research in considering the impact and articulation of a critical voice.

Confronting Culture

The debate over the meaning and prevalence of sexual abuse that Mary's television appearance generated reinforces Ian Hacking's observation of the malleability of this discourse in reaffirming or challenging normative morality and pre-existing institutions (Hacking, 1990:34). What is important here is the way Mary transformed survivor discourse by expanding it to give a name to more extensive and historically rooted relations of power. Both she and the council expanded the meaning of abuse and the moral framework in which embodied relations are evaluated and legitimated. Indeed, the council has enlarged and contested the discourse of the body and sexuality and introduced counselling measures that involve women and men, boys and girls.

This event also draws attention to the importance of narrative context in reinscribing social subjects within hegemonic frameworks or challenging the terms by which relationships and problems can be talked about. Mary's narrative reaffirmed stereotypes because it was produced in a media context where individual experiences are presented against a selected social backdrop, which, in this case, highlighted the poverty of White Brook and reinforced its difference (cf Alcoff and Gray, 1994). Without the activism of the Community Response Team, it is unlikely that such a progressive program as the Sex Abuse Counselling service would have been implemented.

To read narratives such as Mary's and others in this book only as texts would be, then, to ignore the 'context of power and resistance in which they are produced' and the social relations in which they are embedded (Roseberry, 1989:24). An awareness of the historical context of Bay St George sensitizes us to the double bind that severs Mary from fellow residents. Mary draws attention to her community in particular, and in so doing she inadvertently reaffirms its marginality. This was exemplified to me, when Doreen, a woman I interviewed who lives on the other side of Stephenville, measured her own sense of community in relation to that of White Brook. Doreen condemned her neighbour's daughter for having him charged with sexual abuse committed upon her as a child. Doreen did not believe this young woman's claim, and responded, 'Well, I know my neighbour well and he didn't do it, not like the French over there in White Brook.' Francophone communities have historically been constituted as local 'others' in this region, as I indicated in chapter 2.

Hegemonic processes can prevent exploited groups from generating oppositions and framing the terms by which residents negotiate claims and rights in the political arena. Will the secretary of state, indeed, give money to a culture of sexual abusers, as one resident asked? Feminist politics was preceded by a fledgling politics of ethnicity, one that has been legitimated and shaped by state multicultural policy. Gender and ethnicity were, as Gerald Sider has argued, the cultural means by which locals historically recognized difference and manifested conflict (Sider, 1991:231). This has been transformed by the formation of an ethnic francophone identity that is reliant upon state funds for a share of the pie but that has gained little in terms of long-term economic development. Feminist discourse unfolds within and against pre-existing languages of the oppressed, which have given locals a collective identity and consciousness that recognizes their historical marginalization. This compels women and men in White Brook to take sides as if the oppressed cannot themselves be abusers. Or as if to abuse is to undermine the moral basis on which rights are given to marginalized peoples. Somehow, the poor, the dispossesed, the marginalized must be better than good, better than the average citizen, to deserve the claims they make.

Similarly, to document experiences of physical and sexual abuse, and to highlight gender conflicts as I have done here, is potentially to reaffirm the marginality of Newfoundlanders as somehow different from other Canadians. It may, therefore, recast blame on Newfoundland culture and confine gender asymmetries and social problems within the province and away from the rest of Canada. Clearly my research does not support such an interpretation. By situating their narratives within a broader context, I have shown how women describe their lives in terms of family and community relations and suggested that their experiences are structured within a context of power in which dominant discourses of gender, sexuality, and church and state are reproduced locally.

Feminisms and Ethnographic Representation

In my reflections upon the construction of Newfoundland culture and identity, I have found it crucial to distinguish myself from council members and at the same time to avoid viewing them as a people apart. For me, to consider Newfoundland culture is to locate Newfoundlanders within a national context of power. This exposes the permeability of Newfoundland culture. It highlights the commonalities with other Canadians who face similar changes and social problems in very different settings that have emerged from the peculiar dynamics of history. From the outside, I see the flip-side of this culture. To subscribe to, in Eric Wolf's terms, the billiard-ball construction of culture, by maintaining boundaries around Newfoundland culture, by highlighting its distinctness, is to ignore its constitution within a wider colonial history (Roseberry, 1989:6). This would put boundaries around Newfoundland's social and economic problems as if they were unique to that province and therefore had nothing to teach or communicate to the rest of Canada. Newfoundland indeed has a particular history apart from the rest of Canada, yet its union with Canada in 1949 has made it subject to Canadian political and economic policies for the last forty-five years.

Similarly, to articulate 'women's' interests as distinct can, as Di Leonardo argues, engender a sense of homogeneity. It can essentialize women and gender relations and reproduce hegemonic processes by crystallizing peoples into distinct groups (di Leonardo, 1990). This process (of which identity politics can be a part), becomes, as bell hooks argues, an instrument of domination (hooks, 1990:32). Given the political context in which rights and claims are made, this process can reproduce the plurality of liberalism without challenging the foundations of inequality on which it is based.

However, if we consider the context of grass-roots organizing in Bay St George, then naming experience, drawing on historical female practices and feminist labels, does not serve to crystalize their politics into the expression of a distinct women's culture. It provides area women with a culturally specific means to create a grounded politics, one that fosters the exchange of experience and generates a dignity that can be transformed into political action that is meaningful and appropriate for the context in which it is enacted. It seems to me that anthropological methods and ethnography itself can capture this dynamic between social process and codification, as well as the reconstitution of meanings through social practices.

At the same time, it is the ethnographic record itself that may crystalize women's action into a timeless culture. For example, my focus on experience as conveyed through narrative may lend excessive importance to the narrative account. It may give the impression that women in Bay St George communicate in this kind of extended soliloquy. This is not really the case except when they are asked and, in particular, during consciousness-raising activities. Rather, conversation and the recovery of life stories more often proceed in an interactive setting, where no woman is given more than a moment to tell her story without continual interruption and interjection. This is difficult to capture or record in text, but it constitutes an important means by which social levelling is achieved and an openess towards the past and interpretations of events is maintained. This inhibits the crystallization of past experience into a single, unified account and allows for the transmission of social practices into political practices, from one event to another (Smith, 1993:11). As I try to convey, the narratives here are momentary reinterpretations from women who are comfortable about speaking of their experiences.[2]

Because I am an anthropologist, not a trained counsellor, my decision to record life-story accounts posed important ethical questions. I became aware quite early in my fieldwork that some women were more comfortable than others in narrating their experiences, both informally and in the somewhat artifical context of a tape-recorded interview. I learned not to approach women who were in the midst of a particular crisis. This was, at times, a difficult judgment call. I was often used as a surrogate confessor and, not having been trained in this area, I had to consider whether or not my questions or further probing were welcome. It emphasized to me the importance of allowing the 'subject' to direct the flow of the discussion, although the emotional outcome of narrating an event was often a surprise to them as well. (See also Bauer, 1993; Jacobs, 1993). Their responses appeared (from their own statements) to be cathartic rather than traumatic. I would like to think this was not an exploitative process. A few women gave me brightly coloured folders where I was instructed to put their life stories. Others argued playfully about which chapter of 'the book' would be devoted solely to them.

Similarly, my participation in council activities was to most members more important than what I write about them, unless it became the means of defining them within a Canadian context. This is what generated a tension between us. On one level, I was a mirror for them to reflect upon themselves, and once I had been accepted, they noted how valuable a 'distanced' perspective 'from the outside' was in challenging their own assumptions or in thinking reflectively about the way they did politics. At the same time, I was their symbol, someone they could cart around, as if to say, 'see, we're important enough to be studied.' I was a reaffirmation from central Canada that they were doing something worth looking at, a social fact they both admired and resented.

'Experience' has been somewhat favoured in recent academic discourses surrounding political action and the relations of 'subjects' to their class, gender, and racial positioning. It is also a central component of grass-roots feminist organizing. However, from an academic perspective, the 'experience' of social subjects is mediated by academic discourses and, as post-structuralists emphasize, constituted within overlapping discursive domains (Canning, 1994; Scott, 1992). In many ways these academic issues, particularly the deconstruction of experience, run counter to the spirit of a Women's Council, which centres the experience of women as an important truth that should be validated as a source of knowledge in and of itself, one that, once recounted, exposes relations of power and subordination.

My analysis and, at times, constructionist stance towards personal experience are in no way intended to de-legitimate or upstage the serious problems that are recounted; yet this academic tendency does generate tension between feminist activism and analysis which must be recognized (Ferguson, 1991). In any case, and to move away from the academic context, the women I knew best in Bay St George had no trouble responding to their awareness of my power to depict them, with their repeated 'deconstruction' of the knowledge and experience I brought with me. 'After all,' one would rebut after lengthy debate, 'you got no experience, or why would you come all the way to Newfoundland to find it?'

At the same time, Peg and Joyce would often claim that they felt they were somehow being tested, by me, my academic peers, and by feminists in urban centres like Toronto. It is this concern for testing that prompts me to highlight what council members taught me and to show they transformed my insights in a way that made sense to them. This is also crucial for understanding the importance of identity and those forces that underpin the cultural expression of grass-roots feminist politics.

'Speaking from the heart'

It is my commitment to the spirit of interactive research and what I learned by doing fieldwork, moreover, that informs the preceding ethnographic account and the way I have depicted women's lives. I had many debates with council members over the dynamics of counselling and the role of unions, for example, which I cannot address here. Our discussions on the national feminist movement generated a few initiatives which, I am told, council members found to be 'empowering' and helpful. For instance, we held a feminist retreat which allowed twenty women or more to speak and consider the meaning of feminism to them. Our discussions on power, which I initiated and which council members were quite reluctant to consider at first, prompted the council to make 'power' the theme of their annual provincial conference in 1995 (see chapter 6).

At the same time, it is important to note the way they transformed the notion of power because it highlights the differences in our understanding and analysis and is reflected in the narratives included in this book. I noted in Chapter 6, how women spoke 'from the heart.' They centred their experiences by describing how they felt and responded to minor offences to their dignity and to major roadblocks that constrained their mobility and their choices. Their narratives convey their own process of empowerment as a discovery, of how things really worked, as how people acted and what events really meant. There is a duality to their narratives which conveys a power from without and a power from within. This is generated through activities in which they engage and the discovery of new meaning (Ristock, 1991:46). The contested character of oppression is depicted in the way women situate themselves as both agents and victims of particular forces, circumstances, and people. It highlights the pervasive and discursive character of power and response, the quotidian nature of local activism and the articulation of agency through narrative.[3] Local activists contest power through ad hoc meetings, flip comments, and everyday interactions. Council members were at times relentless, occasionally intrusive, but more regularly persistent in a way that is difficult to capture in text.

Yet a focus on narrative does not bring out the extension of 'kin work' within feminist practice, an invisible and extensive labouring that goes into writing a letter, planning a rally, or making a lunch. The reliance of the council on voluntarism draws area women to the centre, but it also places additional demands on their time.

In sum, the life stories and case studies presented here demonstrate that women in Bay St George situate themselves as victims of power and as agents who find ways to respond to the circumstances in which they are engulfed. They recognize the incongruities in making a living within a family-based household, incongruities that are informed by central narratives of reproduction. By this I mean stories of what making a family is and should be, plans and visions of a home and a good life in Newfoundland, which are measured against and in relation to childhood, adulthood, and the social changes that distinguish women from their mothers (cf. Ginsburg, 1988:140). The ideal is to have a home, to do all that your mother did, and all that she did not. It is against this narrative that the reality of migration is set, so that people return when the economy booms or when they have made enough money somewhere else. My inclusion of so many individual women is an attempt to 'write against cultural essentialism' (Abu-Lughod, 1993), to maintain the heterogeneity of individual experience and, at the same time, draw attention to the specific intersection of power and exploitation in the lives of individual women.

Normatively, failure to conform to the way things should be places blame on the individual or on fate. This is inverted by area women, particularly those who have reinterpreted their experience through feminist discourse, who recast blame on society, on the community, and on individual agents of power. Feminism is their recognition of some shared experience; that locality is a gendered place where unequal distributions of power generates incongruities for women, distinct from men and, at times, because of them. This focus on their powerlessness was not in my view a creation of themselves as victims. And they are now more than ever prepared to use the power they do have effectively.

The problem that underpins this anthropological representation, then, is how to respect differences in the lives of Newfoundland women without this difference being set against them to reaffirm dominant Canadian narratives. It is one thing for me, the anthropologist, to recognize and depict their distinctness; it is quite another for them to do it themselves. My concern to confront Newfoundland culture, to dismantle its distinctness, comes in part from my consideration of the implications of representing these conflicts and from my location in central Ontario. This runs counter to the importance and meaning that maintaining a Newfoundland identity and its distinctness has for area women and men.

Political Identity and Right to Community: 'Torontonian moves to Stephenville: When the shoe is on the other foot!'

Living in Newfoundland sensitized me to the way in which a national consciousness is reproduced through cross-country journeys of assorted citizens. The first traveller I met was a man from Alberta who was compelled to reorganize his cross-country bicycle tour after a day's journey across the rugged and windy barrens of the Avalon peninsula. Another man, intent on walking cross-country to raise awareness for kidney disease, crossed my path in Clarenville, and again closer to Corner Brook. The two journeys in which I participated, to raise awareness around child sexual abuse and to protest the free-trade agreement, drew considerable media attention and featured organized activities at pre-determined stops across the Trans-Canada Highway. These trips made me more aware not just of the national landscape but of national narratives of prosperity, settlement, and migration because so often Newfoundland was the beginning, not the end, of the journey.

It is perhaps against this dominant narrative that I was profiled in the local newspaper not long after my arrival. 'Torontonian moves to Stephenville: When the shoe is on the other foot!' read the caption under my photo. Indeed, the article made much of my decision to drive eastward and residents who recognized me chuckled at the inversion of a national narrative that spoke to the reality of migration in the area.

Towards the end of my stay in Bay St George, council members insisted that 'they had grown on me' and that I would be sure to return. Other times they would say in exaggerated Newfoundland dialect, 'So, off you go, eh – put down somewheres else, then off again.' They frequently chastised me for leaving, as if to do so meant that I had no heart. My departures were treated with the same mocking fanfare as my arrivals. Once I was deposited in the back of a pick-up truck with ten or more women and paraded around town before they bid me farewell at the airport with another chorus of the 'Ode to Newfoundland.'

What unites the Women's Council to locality is, as I have suggested, a sense of right to community, a belief that this place is worth fixing, and that its people deserve the effort. In Bay St George, to articulate a Newfoundland identity is to reaffirm a right to sustained settlement. Is asserting a right to community simply feeding our romantic notions of the permanence or rootedness of place? I suggest that it forms a powerful counter-narrative to that which operates in the current political climate where the mobility of peoples is posited as the necessary or the only solution. Departures cause pain for those who do not have the choice to stay. A local politics is one that would create conditions that allow people to make a choice.

Notes

1 Between Home and Field: Feminist Activism at the Grass Roots

1 For a review, see Sacouman, 1985, and essays in Fairley, Leys, and Sacouman, 1990.
2 For example, Porter, 1985; MacDonald and Connelly, 1990; Barber, 1992.
3 Richard Handler makes related arguments in his ethnography *Nationalism and the Politics of Culture in Quebec* (1988).

2 Gender, Ethnicity, and Labour before and after the 'Carefree Years'

1 Population figures vary. This figure is taken from *'The French Shore' 1857*, Stephenville Archives.
2 *Census of Newfoundland and Labrador, 1921*, vol. 1, 283–9. Female labour force, 1935: 208 women were employed – 113 as domestic servants, 12 as saleswomen, 48 as teachers. *Census of Newfoundland and Labrador, 1935*, vol. 1, 115–17.
3 The origins of the name are uncertain. Locals say that it was the name of a son in a family. The name appears in the 1874 census as Stephenville Ville River Blanche (*Decks Awash*, 1984:5).
4 Of a male labour force of 2302, 365, or 15 per cent, were loggers; 640, or 27 per cent, were farmers; 453, or 20 per cent, were cod fishermen; 386, or 17 per cent, were unskilled labourers. Figures are approximate and calculated from the 1935 *Census of Newfoundland and Labrador*, vol. 1, 546–9. They do not include unpaid or subsistence work.
5 Briefs presented by Port au Port Economic Development Association to the Royal Commission on Employment and Unemployment, vol. 3. (1985).
6 See Information Bulletin 4081st, Strategic Wing, Ernest Harmon Air Force Base, Newfoundland, 1960, 6, Stephenville Archives.

7 *Civilian Orientation Handbook*, 'Your Job,' June 1951, 1, Stephenville Archives.
8 This provides a general idea and does not include all marriages in the area. Catholic church records in Stephenville indicate whether the male was a serviceman or not. As well, they include conversions to Catholicism. Figures for divorce can only be ascertained here on the basis of those women who sought annulments from the church, information that is also recorded in the Stephenville parish records.
9 *Evening Star*, 30 December 1966, 1.
10 See Brief to Royal Commission on Employment and Unemployment, 1985, vol. 3:2. Also, Goulding, 1982:203.
11 *Census of Canada*, 1986:243; *Census of Canada*, 1996.
12 Reports on Bay St George in the *Annual Reports of Public Welfare* from 1950 to 1966 show increases and decreases in the number of welfare recipients, changes that the government relates directly to economic shifts in the area, specifically, work on the base and in lumbering, fishing, and the limestone quarry. For example, the government anticipates an increase in 1960 once unemployment insurance runs out for the 1000 workers laid off by the base. Although the numbers of cases on the Port au Port peninsula remain high relative to the rest of the area, there was a marked increase in recipients with the closure of the air base, from 1129 receiving cash and kind supplements in 1960 to 2508 in 1966 (Godfre, 1985:70, 75, 85).
13 *Annual Report*, Department of Social Services, 1987–8:17.
14 There were 55–60 live births per 1000 persons compared to the Canadian average of 29 (Williams, 1966:3).
15 These include, for example, the ARDA division, Department of Economic Development, Government of Newfoundland. During the 1970s the Community Employment Strategy Association, a federal initiative, worked with the Port au Port Development Association. The Newfoundland and Labrador Rural Development Council fostered the growth of these development associations.
16 Port au Port Economic Development Association, *Souvenir Booklet*, 5. The association was originally called the Port au Port District Development Council and included Stephenville until 1971.
17 Introduced as the Local Initiatives Program.
18 It is important to note that these French-speaking Canadians settled in Newfoundland much later than the Québécois and consider themselves quite distinct from French-speaking residents in Quebec. They share more with Acadians, some of whom married into the region from the late 1800s, as I indicated at the beginning of this chapter.
19 Virtually all the population of the region adheres to a Christian denomination, predominantly Catholic. The 'lowest' proportion of Catholics to Protestants (63.3 per cent) is in Stephenville, while in smaller communities Catholics comprise 85 to 100 per cent of the population. *Census of Canada*, 1991:53.

20 Matthews claims that francophone communities were viewed by locals as less civilized and lawless (Matthews, 1976:85).
21 According to the association spokesperson, some residents of native heritage do have native status but they do not claim land rights in part because the government considers them to be fairly recent migrants (within the last 200 hundred years) from Nova Scotia.
22 This is highlighted in the *Community Education Pilot Project: Educational Needs Assessment Report*, 1992:65. For example, more than twice as many male workers classified themselves as 'labourers' than as fishermen, followed closely by logger, fish-plant worker, and carpenter. But these occupations are not all carried out in the region. Such workers return to the area during layoffs and off-season.
23 See Dunk, 1991, and Philpott, 1985, for a comparative view of class and work culture in areas based on extractive industries.

3 Re-creating Home: The Local Construction of Feminist Practice

1 Scrunchions are fried pork fat; doughb'ys are formed from flour fried in pork fat.
2 This is not, however, a 'Transition House' (for 'battered' or 'abused' women) and cannot offer the same kind of full-time security and protection.
3 Angela Miles notes similar features in rural feminist organization in Nova Scotia. She has labelled these features 'integrative feminism,' in which women's position is approached in its totality through their experiences and roles in community life (Miles, 1991:73).

4 Contextualizing Dependency: Single Mothers and Feminist Politics

1 Canada Employment Centre.
2 Written by Susan Fowlow of 'Estasy.'
3 Member of the House of Assembly, Newfoundland and Labrador.
4 Note that an article that examines UI and other government schemes in the province begins with the caption 'Newfoundland way of life vanishing': *Globe and Mail*, 6 January 1994:A6. See also more recently, 'Why Canadians resist budging from their home provinces, *Globe and Mail*, 20 June 1998: D6.
5 For example, *Globe and Mail*, 1 January 1994: D10; 6 January 1994: D6; 7 January 1994: D6; 25 February 1995: D5. Also, *Proposal for a New Income Supplementation Program and Other Reforms to the Income Security System* (Economic Recovery Commission, Government of Newfoundland and Labrador, 1993).
6 Department of Social Services (1979:30; 1986:103; 1990:19).
7 This information is taken from interviews with Canada Employment Centre, Stephenville. A recipient working under a 'Section 25' cannot use these weeks of work to qualify for additional unemployment stamps.

8 This does not consider impact of the cod moratorium on fishing. *Proposal for a New Income Supplementation Program, Information Paper,* December, 1993: 5, 25, 39.

9 The report indicates that, in general, education and employment opportunities are low, especially for youth and those under thirty-five, a target group. The survey percentages in general are based on responses from approximately one-third of residents from each community. However, the study notes that interpreters should consider that age ranges vary considerably throughout the area, and thus educational figures, for example, include both senior residents and youth. *Community Education Pilot Project: Educational Needs Assessment Report* (Port au Port Community Education Pilot Project Committee, July 1992), 36–40.

10 For example, over 600 respondents identify themselves as 'labourers,' followed by 254 fishermen and 212 loggers. Only 92 identify themselves as domestics, and 58 as babysitters. It is difficult to tell, then, whether men and women are overwhelmingly employed as 'labourers,' or whether a much larger percentage of men were considered as single representatives of a household. Based on interviews with employment counsellors, I am inclined to suggest that those who identify themselves as 'labourers' are overwhelmingly men. *Community Education Pilot Project,* 1992:46.

11 'Youth' unemployment is attributed in part to the inability of young residents to acquire the first twenty weeks of work necessary to be eligible for unemployment insurance. After this, ten ten weeks are sufficient (within a defined time period) to collect unemployment insurance.

12 The median incomes of $23,000 and $28,000 for these two communities are based on 193 tax returns and include incomes from salaries, investment, and social assistance (*Globe and Mail*, 18 September 1995:8).

13 See Ken Battle, Douglas Durst, Susan Clark, and Stella Lord in Johnson, McBride, and Smith, 1994.

14 This figure is taken from Statistics Canada, 'Low Income Cut-offs, 1994,' which is based on a two-person household in a 'rural' area of less than 30,000 residents. The figure is substantially lower than that of the Canadian Council on Social Development, which calculates this line at $22,950 for a two-person household. The more conservative Fraser Institute sets a poverty line at $9688 for Newfoundland. My income figures are approximate and do not include refundable tax credits, which are included in the Statistics Canada figures (Ross, 1994:15, 16, 20).

15 Fewer than ten of these recipients were male (*Annual Report*, 1993:30).

16 My own anthropological training sensitized me to the social embeddedness of reciprocities: see Polanyi, 1970; Sahlins, 1972; Lee, 1979. More recently, as historically embedded relationships within a capitalist economy: Sider, 1986; Smith, 1989. Attention to gender: Parr, 1990. Within Newfoundland, Sinclair and Feldt in particular examine debates over the social and class location of those who

draw on the 'informal sector' as opposed to the market. In their study on the Great Northern Peninsula, they argue for the importance of the informal sector in maintaining 'generalized respect' and localized social relationships (Sinclair and Feldt, 1992b:61). See also Wadel, 1973; Richling, 1985; Sider, 1986; Feldt and Sinclair, 1991, 1992a, 1992b. Similarly, in Bay St George, residents participate in informal and kin-based exchanges not just to meet material needs.

5 Sexual Abuse and Violence: Contested Meanings and the Politics of Narrative

1 The Canadian Broadcasting Corporation offers regional and national programming.
2 I have changed the names of the women and the community involved to protect their identity.
3 *Proposal for Bay St George Sex Abuse Counselling Service*, 1993:2.
4 This is documented in ibid. The abuse of clients was also conveyed to me in interviews with these workers in the departments of social services, corrections, and mental health.
5 *Western Star*, 27 June 1992:3.
6 *Western Star*, 27 June 1992:4.
7 *Western Star*, Saturday 27 June 1992:2.
8 I use the name 'Brown,' a pseudonym, to convey the importance that Lilly placed on the family and patriline in which her husband was raised to explain and illustrate his violent behaviour.
9 A shelter for battered women and their children located in another town.
10 Alcoff also points out that this confessional/therapy mode reinforces binary oppositions between 'experience and theory,' 'mind and body,' 'feelings and knowledge' (Alcoff, 1993:280).

6 Grass-roots Activism and Feminist Politics

1 For example, 'Understanding Wife Abuse: An Educational Manual for Community Groups' (1988); 'Child Care Arrangements in Newfoundland' (1989), and 'Experiences of Teen Parents in Newfoundland' (1992).

7 Rethinking Community: Feminist Activism and Sustained Settlement

1 Social Policy Advisory Committee, 1997:3–6.
2 Ultimately it is dependent on the politics of redistribution whereby funds for these ministries are funnelled into the service. However, the actual service operates by

consensus decision making and peer supervision as opposed to a management hierarchy, and is equally accountable to clients, community and the hospital. *Proposal for Bay St George Sex Abuse Counselling Service.* 1993:20.

3 Sexual Abuse Council Services, *Annual Report, 1997–8.* Stephenville Community Health, Western Region.

8 Conclusion

1 There are several strands here that implicitly or explicitly emphasize the social constructedness or biological basis of femininty; see Bohan, 1993:6.

2 I refer here to Nancy Fraser, 1990, and Ristock, 1991, who incorporate Foucault in their analysis but who maintain the importance of a grounded politics, through, for example, Bordo's emphasis on the practised body and Ristock's attention to the microphysics of power in which feminists as activists are embedded (Ristock: 50).

3 For example, there are no doubt numerous and conflicting interpretations of life in White Brook. Unfortunately, the events that occurred there prevented me from engaging in even the most basic fieldwork or asking questions in the community. It is noteworthy that to portray myself as someone who wanted to talk about women's lives was enough to generate in people an idea that I was a 'woman's libber.' In the case of White Brook, they would not talk to anyone, let alone me.

Bibliography

Abu-Lughod, Lila. 1991. 'Writing against Culture.' In *Recapturing Anthropology*. Richard G. Fox (ed.). Santa Fe, N. Mex.: School of American Research Press.

– 1993. *Writing Women's Worlds: Bedouin Stories.* Berkeley: University of California Press.

Adamson, Nancy, Linda Briskin, and Margaret McPhail. 1988. *Feminist Organizing for Change: The Contemporary Women's Movement in Canada.* Toronto: Oxford University Press.

Agnew, Vijay. 1996. *Resisting Discrimination: Women from Asia, Africa, and the Caribbean and the Women's Movement in Canada*. Toronto: University of Toronto Press.

Alcoff, Linda. 1988. 'Cultural Feminism versus Post-Structuralism: The Identity Crisis in Feminist Theory.' *Signs: Journal of Culture and Society* 13(3): 405–6.

Alcoff, Linda, and Laura Gray. 1993. 'Survivor Discourse: Transgression or Recuperation?' *Signs: Journal of Women in Culture and Society* 18(2): 260–90.

Alexander, David. 1977. *The Decay of Trade: An Economic History of the Newfoundland Saltfish Trade, 1935–1965.* St John's: Institute of Social and Economic Research.

Andrews, Caroline. 1992. 'The Feminist City.' In *Political Arrangements*. Henri Lustiger-Thaler (ed.). Montreal: Black Rose Books.

Anonymous. 1984. 'Stephenville.' *Decks Awash.* St John's: Memorial University of Newfoundland. 13(4):1–77.

– 1990. 'Port au Port Peninsula.' *Decks Awash.* St John's: Memorial University of Newfoundland. 34(2):1–75.

Antler, Ellen, and James Faris. 1979. 'Adaptation to Changes in Technology and Government Policy.' In *North Atlantic Cultures* Raoul Anderson (ed.). The Hague: Morton Publishers.

Armstrong, Pat, and Hugh Armstrong. 1988. 'Taking Women into Account.' In *Feminization of the Labour Force.* Jane Jenson and Elisabeth Hagen (eds.). New York: Oxford University Press.

Barber, Pauline. 1992. 'Household-Workplace Strategies in Northfield.' In *Emptying*

Their Nets: Small Capital and Rural Industrialization in the Nova Scotia Fishing Industry. Richard Apostle and Gene Barrett (eds.). Toronto: University of Toronto Press.

Barrett, Michèle. 1988. *Women's Oppression Today.* London: Verso.

Bashevkin, Sylvia. 1998. *Women on the Defensive: Living through Conservative Times.* Toronto: University of Toronto Press.

Bauer, Janet. 1993. 'Ma'ssoum's Tale: The Personal and Political Transformations of a Young Iranian Feminist and Her Ethnographer.' *Feminist Studies* 19(3): 519–48.

Bay St George Women's Council. 1983. 'Report on Youth Survey.'

– 1985. 'Information Sharing: Summer Project.'

– 1987. 'Youth Survey Follow-up.'

Beechey, Veronica. 1988. 'Rethinking the Definition of Work.' In *Feminization of the Labour Force.* Jane Jenson, Elisabeth Hagen, and Ceallaigh Reddy (eds.). New York: Oxford University Press.

Behar, Ruth. 1990. 'Rage and Redemption: Reading the Life Story of a Mexican Marketing Woman.' *Feminist Studies* 16(2): 223–258.

Bella, Leslie. 1992. *Christmas Imperative: Leisure, Family and Women's Work.* Halifax: Fernwood Publishing.

Benoit, Cecilia. 1990. 'Mothering in a Newfoundland Community, 1900–1940.' In *Delivering Motherhood* Katherine Arnup, Andrée Levesque, and Ruth Roach Pierson (eds.). New York: Routledge.

Bohan, J. 1993. 'Regrading Gender: Essentialism, Constructionism, and Feminist Psychology.' *Psychology of Women Quarterly.* 17: 5–21.

Brock, Debi. 1991 'Talkin 'Bout a Revelation: Feminist Popular Discourse on Sexual Abuse.' *Canadian Woman Studies* 12 (11): 12–15.

Briskin, Linda. 1991. 'Feminist Practice: A New Approach to Evaluating Feminist Strategy.' In *Women and Social Change.* Jeri Dawn Wine and Janet Ristock (eds.). Toronto: James Lorimer.

Brodie, Janine. 1998. 'Restructuring and the Politics of Marginalization.' In *Women and Political Representation in Canada.* Manon Tremblay and Caroline Andrew (eds.). Ottawa: University of Ottawa Press.

Brown, Cheryl. 1982. *Work and Unemployment in Stephenville.* St John's: Community Services Council.

Burt, Sandra. 1998. 'The Canadian Advisory Council on the Status of Women: Possibilities and Limitations.' In *Women and Political Representation in Canada.* Manon Tremblay and Caroline Andrew (eds.). Ottawa: University of Ottawa Press.

Canning, Kathleen. 1994. 'Feminist History after the Linguistic Turn: Historicising Discourse and Experience.' *Signs: Journal of Culture and Society* 19(2): 368–404.

Cardoulis, D.A. 1985. *A Friendly Invasion: The U.S. Military in Newfoundland.* St John's: Creative Publishers.

Clark, Susan. 1994. 'Mothers and Children: Ensuring Acceptable Standards of

Living.' In *Continuities and Discontinuities: The Political Economy of Social Welfare and Labour Market Policy in Canada.* Andrew Johnson, Stephen McBride, and Patrick Smith (eds.). Toronto: University of Toronto Press.

Cole, Sally. 1991. *Women of the Praia.* Princeton, N.J.: Princeton University Press.

Community Response Team. 1993. *Proposal for Bay St George Sex Abuse Counselling Service,* Stephenville: Interagency Committee.

Copes, Meghan. 1996. 'Weaving the Everyday: Identity, Space, and Power in Lawrence, Massachusetts, 1920–1939.' *Urban Geography* 17(2): 179–204.

Copes, Parzival. 1972. *The Resettlement of Fishing Communities in Newfoundland.* St John's: Canadian Council on Rural Development.

Dahlerup, Drude. 1987. 'Confusing Concepts – Confusing Reality: A Theoretical Discussion of the Patriarchal State.' *Women and the State.* Anne Showstack Sassoon ed. London: Routledge.

Davis, Dona Lee. 1983a. *Blood and Nerves: An Ethnographic Focus on Menopause.* St John's: Institute of Social and Economic Research.

– 1986. 'Occupational Community and Fishermen's Wives in a Newfoundland Fishing Village.' *Anthropological Quarterly* 59(3): 129–42.

de Toque, Rev. Philip. 1878. *Newfoundland As It Was and As It Is in 1877.* Toronto: John B. Magurn.

DeVault, Marjorie L. 1991. *Feeding the Family: The Social Organization of Caring as Gendered Work.* Chicago: University of Chicago Press.

di Leonardo, Micaela. 1987. 'The Female World of Cards and Holidays.' *Signs: Journal of Culture and Society* 12(3): 440–453.

– 1991a. 'Habits of the Cumbered Heart: Ethnic Community and Women's Culture as American Invented Traditions.' In *Golden Ages, Dark Ages: Imagining the Past in Anthropology and History.* Jay O'Brien and William Roseberry (eds.). Berkeley: University of California Press.

– 1991b. 'Women's Culture and Its Discontents.' *The Politics of Culture.* Brett Williams (ed.). Washington, D.C.: Smithsonian Institution Press.

Dunk, Tom. 1991. *It's a Working Man's Town: Male Working-Class Culture in Northwestern Ontario.* Kingston, Ont.: McGill-Queen's University Press.

Durst, Douglas. 1994. 'False Economies in Newfoundland's Social and Child Welfare Policies.' In *Continuities and Discontinuities: The Political Economy of Social Welfare and Labour Market Policy in Canada.* Andrew Johnson, Stephen McBride, and Patrick Smith (eds.). Toronto: University of Toronto Press.

Echols, Alice. 1983. 'The New Feminism of Yin and Yang.' In *Powers of Desire: The Politics of Sexuality.* Ann Snitow, Christine Stensell, and Sharon Thompson (eds.). New York: Monthly Review Press.

Eichler, Margrit (ed.). 1996. *'Designing Eco-city in North America: Towards a Non-sexist Sustainable City.'* Toronto: Garamond Press.

Epstein, D., and L. Steinberg. 1995. Twelve Steps to Heterosexuality? Commonsensibilities on the *Oprah Winfrey Show*. *Feminism and Psychology* 5(2): 275–80.

Escobar, Artruro. 1992. 'Cultural Practice and Politics: Anthropology and the Study of Social Movements.' *Critique of Anthropology*, 12(4): 395–432.

– 1996. 'Constructing Nature: Elements for a Poststructual Political Ecology.' In *Liberation Ecologies: Environment, Development, Social Movements*. Richard Peet and Michael Watts (eds.). New York: Routledge.

Fairley, Bryant, Colin Leys, and James Sacouman. 1990. *Restructuring and Resistence: Perspectives from Atlantic Canada*. Toronto: Garamond Press.

Faris, James. 1973. *Cat Harbour: A Newfoundland Fishing Settlement*. St John's: Institute of Social and Economic Research.

Felt, Lawrence, and Peter Sinclair. 1991. 'Home Sweet Home: Dimensions and Determinants of Life Satisfaction in an Underdeveloped Region.' *Canadian Journal of Sociology* 16(1): 1–21.

– 1995. *Living on the Edge*. St John's: Institute of Social and Economic Research.

Ferguson, Kathy. 1991. 'Interpretation and Genealogy in Feminism.' *Signs: Journal of Culture and Society*, 16 (2): 322–39.

Findlay, Sue. 1998. 'Representation and the Struggle for Women's Equality: Issues for Feminist Practice.' In *Women and Political Representation in Canada*. Manon Tremblay and Caroline Andrew (eds.). Ottawa: University of Ottawa Press.

Fraser, Nancy. 1989. *Unruly Practices: Power, Discourse and Gender in Contemporary Social Theory*. Minneapolis: University of Minnesota Press.

Fraser, Nancy, and Linda Gordon. 1994. 'A Genealogy of Dependency: Tracing a Keyword of the U.S. Welfare State.' *Signs: Journal of Women in Culture and Society* 19(2): 309–36.

Ginsburg, Faye. 1989. *Contested Lives: The Abortion Debate in an American Community*. Berkeley: University of California Press.

– 1990. 'Introduction.' In *Uncertain Terms: Negotiating Gender in American Culture*. Faye Ginsburg and Anna Lowenhaupt-Tsing (eds.). Boston: Beacon Press.

Godfrey, Stuart R. 1985. *Human Rights and Social Policy in Newfoundland: 1832–1982: Search for a Just Society*. St John's: Harry Cuff Publications.

Gotell, Lisa. 1998. 'A Critical Look at State Discourses on 'Violence against Women': Some Implications for Feminist Politics and Women's Citizenship.' In *Women and Political Representation in Canada*. Manon Tremblay and Caroline Andrew (eds.). Ottawa: University of Ottawa Press.

Goulding, Jay. 1982. *The Last Outport: Newfoundland in Crisis*. Toronto: Sisyphus Press.

Government of Canada. *Census of Canada*. 1986, 1991. Ottawa. Government of Newfoundland and Labrador. *Annual Report*, Department of Public Welfare. 1950–66. St John's.

– *Annual Report*, Department of Social Services. 1979, 1986, 1987–88, 1990, 1993. St John's.

– *Census of Newfoundland*. 1857, 1921, 1935. St John's.

– Economic Recovery Commission. 1993. *Proposal for a New Income*

– Royal Commission on Employment and Unemployment. 1985. 'Briefs presented by Port au Port Economic Development Association.' St John's. Vol. 3.

– *Supplementation Program and Other Reforms to the Income Security System*. St John's.

Greene, Gayle. 1991. 'Feminist Fiction and the Uses of Memory.' *Signs: Journal of Women in Culture and Society* 6(2): 290–321.

Gupta, Akhil, and James Ferguson (eds.). 1997. *Anthropological Locations: Boundaries and Grounds of a Field Science*. Berkeley: University of California Press.

Hacking, Ian. 1991. 'The Making and Moulding of Child Abuse.' *Critical Inquiry* 17: 253–88.

Handler, Richard. 1988. *Nationalism and the Politics of Culture in Quebec*. Madison: University of Wisconsin Press.

Hareven, Tamara. 1993. 'The Home and the Family in Historical Perspective.' In *Home: A Place in the World*. Arien Mack (ed.). New York: New York University Press.

Harvey, David. 1993. '*Mapping the Futures: Local Cultures, Global Change*. Jon Bird, Barry Curtis, Tim Putnam, George Robertson, and Lisa Tuckner (eds.). London: Routledge.

Herman, Judith. 1992. *Trauma and Recovery*. New York: Basic Books.

Hernes, Helga. 1987. 'Women and the Welfare State: The Transition from Private to Public Dependence.' In *Women and the State*, Anne Showstack Sassoon (ed.). London: Routledge.

Hill, Robert. 1983. *The Meaning of Work and the Reality of Unemployment in the Newfoundland Context*. St John's: Institute of Social and Economic Research.

hooks, bell. 1989. 'Feminist Politicization: A Comment.' In *Talking Back: Thinking Feminist, Thinking Black*. Boston: South End Press.

– (ed.) 1990. 'Reflections on Race and Sex.' *Yearning: Race, Gender, and Cultural Politics*. Toronto: Between the Lines.

House, John. D. 1989. *Going Away ... and Coming Back: Economic Life and Migration in Three Small Canadian Communities*. St John's: Institute of Social and Economic Research.

Jacobs, Janet. 1993. 'Victimized Daughters: Sexual Violence and the Empathetic Female Self.' *Signs: Journal of Women in Culture and Society* 19(1): 126–45.

Jenson, Jane. 1992. 'Gender Reproduction or Babies and the State.' In *Feminism in Action: Studies in Political Economy*. M.P. Connelly and Pat Armstrong (eds.). Toronto: Canadian Scholars Press.

– 1997 'Who Cares? Gender and Welfare Regimes.' *Social Politics* (summer): 182–7.

Johnson, Andrew, Stephen McBride, and Patrick Smith (eds.). 1994. 'Introduction.' In *Continuities and Discontinuities: The Political Economy of Social Welfare and Labour Market Policy in Canada*. Toronto: University of Toronto Press.

Kealey, Linda. 1993. 'Introduction.' In *Pursuing Equality* Linda Kealey (ed.). St John's: Institute of Social and Economic Research.

Kelly, Liz. 1987. 'How Women Define Their Experiences of Sexual Violence.' In *Feminist Perspectives on Wife Abuse.* K. Yllo and M. Bograd (eds.). Beverley Hills, Calif.: Sage Publications.

– 1988. 'What's in a Name: Defining Abuse.' *Feminist Review* 8 (January): 66–73.

Kelly, Ursula. 1993. *Marketing Place: Cultural Politics, Regionalism and Reading.* Halifax: Fernwood Publishers.

Kurz, D. (ed.) 1993. 'Physical Assaults by Husbands: A Major Social Problem.' In *Current Contraversies on Family Violence.* Newbury Park, Calif.: Sage Publications.

Langlois, Tish. 1997. *Fault Lines: Incest, Sexuality and Catholic Family Culture.* Toronto: Second Story Press.

Laurie, Margaret. 1987. 'Introduction: Women and Memory.' *Michigan Quarterly Review* 26: 1–8.

Lee, Richard. 1979. *The !Kung San: Men, Women, and Work in a Foraging Society.* Cambridge: Cambridge University Press.

Lewis, Jane. 1997. 'Gender and Welfare Regimes: Further Thoughts.' *Social Politics* (summer), 160–77.

Limon, Jose. 1991. 'Representation, Ethnicity and the Precursory Ethnography: Notes of a Native Anthropologist.' In *Recapturing Anthropology.* Richard G. Fox (ed.). Santa Fe, N.M.: School of American Research Press.

Lord, Stella. 1994. 'Social Assistance and Employment for Single Mothers in Nova Scotia.' In *Continuities and Discontinuities: The Political Economy of Social Welfare and Labour Market Policy in Canada,* Andrew Johnson, Stephen McBride, and Patrick Smith (eds.). Toronto: University of Toronto Press.

McCay, Bonnie. 1988. 'Fish Guts, Hair Nets and Unemployment Stamps: Women, Work and the Fogo Island Co-operative.' In *A Question of Survival: The Fisheries and Newfoundland Society.* Peter Sinclair (ed.). St John's: Institute of Social and Economic Research.

MacDonald, Martha, and Patricia Connelly. 1990. 'Class and Gender in Nova Scotia Fishing Communities.' In *Restructuring and Resistence: Perspectives from Atlantic Canada.* Bryant Fairley, Colin Leys, and James Sacouman (eds.). Toronto: Garamond Press.

McIntosh, Mary. 1988. 'Introduction to an Issue: Family Secrets As Public Drama.' *Feminist Review* 28: 6–15.

Mack, Arien (ed.). 1993. *Home: A Place in the World.* New York: New York University Press.

MacLeod, Mary, and Ester Saraga. 1988. 'Challenging the Orthodoxy: Towards a Feminist Theory and Practice.' *Feminist Review* 28: 16–55.

Mannion, John. 1977. 'Settlers and Traders in Western Newfoundland.' In *The Peopling of Newfoundland.* John Mannion (ed.). St John's: Institute of Social and Economic Research.

Marchak, Pat. 1983. *Green Gold.* Vancouver: University of British Columbia Press.

Martin, Biddy, and Chandra Talpade Mohanty. 1986. 'What's Home Got to Do with

It?' In *Feminist Studies, Critical Studies.* Teresa de Lauretis (ed.). Bloomington: Indiana University Press.

Massey, Doreen. 1993. 'Gender, Power and Place.' In *Mapping the Futures: Local Cultures, Global Change.* Jon Bird, Barry Curtis, Tim Putnam, George Robertson, and Lisa Tuckner (eds.). London: Routledge.

Matthews, Ralph. 1976. *There's No Better Place Than Here: Social Change in Three Newfoundland Communities.* Toronto: Peter Martin.

Miles, Angela. 1991. 'Reflections on Integrative Feminism and Rural Women.' In *Women and Social Change.* Jeri Dawn Wine and Janice Ristock (eds.). Toronto: James Lorimer.

Moore, Henrietta. 1994. *A Passion for Difference.* Bloomington: Indiana University Press.

Moraga, Cherrie. 1986. 'From a Long Line of Vendidas: Chicanas and Feminism.' In *Feminist Studies / Critical Studies.* Teresa de Lauretis (ed.). Bloomington: Indiana University Press.

Morris, W. 1988. 'Vignettes of the West.' *Western Star,* 30 June, 3.

Moss, Robert. 1956. 'A Salute to Stephenville.' *Atlantic Guardian,* June, 5–34.

Murray, Hilda Chaulk. 1979. *More than Fifty Per Cent: Woman's Life in a Newfoundland Outport, 1900 to 1950.* St John's: Breakwater Books.

Nava, Mica. 1988. 'Cleveland and the Press: Outrage and Anxiety in the Reporting of Child Sexual Abuse.' *Feminist Review* 28: 103–21.

Neary, Peter. 1988. *Newfoundland in the North Atlantic World, 1929–1949.* Kingston, Ont.: McGill-Queen's University Press.

Neis, Barbara. 1988. 'Doing Time on the Protest Line: Women's Political Culture, Politics and Collective Action in Outport Newfoundland.' In *A Question of Survival: The Fisheries and Newfoundland Society.* Peter Sinclair (ed.). St John's: Institute of Social and Economic Research.

O'Brien, Jay, and William Roseberry. 1991. 'Introduction.' In *Golden Ages, Dark Ages: Imagining the Past in Anthropology and History.* Jay O'Brien and William Roseberry (eds.). Berkeley: University of California Press.

Ochberg, Richard. 1992. 'Introduction.' *Storied Lives: The Cultural Politics of Self-Understanding.* George C. Rosenwald and Richard Ochberg (eds.). New Haven, Conn.: Yale University Press.

Orloff, Ann Shola. 1997. 'Introduction.' *Social Politics* (summer), 1:57–9.

Overton, James. 1988. 'A Newfoundland Culture.' *Journal of Canadian Studies* 23: 6–15.

– 1996. *Making a World of Difference: Essays on Tourism, Culture and Development in Newfoundland.* St John's: Institute of Social and Economic Research.

Parr, Joy. 1990. *The Gender of Breadwinners.* Toronto: University of Toronto Press.

Personal Narratives Group. 1989. 'Origins.' In *Interpreting Women's Lives: Feminist Theory and Personal Narratives.* Personal Narratives Group (ed.). Bloomington: Indiana University Press.

Philpott, Stuart B. 1985. 'The Anthropology of Primary Resource Industry.' Paper presented to a conference on Current Anthropological Research on Industry and Industrialization, Winnipeg.

Polanyi, Karl. 1970. *The Great Transformation.* New York: Beacon Press.

Pope, Sharon Gray. 1993. 'Change Within and Without: The Modern Women's Movement in Newfoundland and Labrador.' In *Pursuing Equality.* Linda Kealey (ed.). St John's: Institute of Social and Economic Research.

Popkin, Annie. 1990. 'The Social Experience of Bread and Roses: Building a Community and Creating a Culture.' In *Women, Class and the Feminist Imagination: A Socialist-Feminist Reader.* Karen V. Hansen and Ilene J. Philipson (eds.). Philadelphia: Temple University Press.

Port au Port Economic Development Association. 1992. *Community Education Pilot Project: Educational Needs Assessment Report.* Port au Port Community Education Pilot Project Committee.

Porter, Marilyn. 1985a. '"She Was Skipper of the Shore Crew": Notes on the Development of the Sexual Division of Labour in Newfoundland.' *Labour* 15: 105–23.

– 1985b. '"The Tangly Bunch": Outport Women of the Avalon Peninsula.' *Newfoundland Studies* 1: 77–89.

– 1990. *Women and Economic Life in Newfoundland: Three Case Studies.* Report on Project 482–87–0005. St John's: Institute of Social and Economic Research.

– 1991. 'Time, the Life Course, and Work in Women's Lives.' *Women's Studies International Forum* 14 (1/2): 1–13.

Radford-Hill, Sheila. 1986. 'Considering Feminism as a Model for Social Change.' In *Feminist Studies, Critical Studies.* Teresa de Lauretis (ed.). Bloomington: Indiana University Press.

Rangan, Harypryia. 1996. 'From Chipko to Uttaranchal.' In *Liberation Ecologies: Environment, Development, Social Movements.* Richard Peet and Michael Watts (eds.). New York: Routledge.

Rankin, L. Pauline, and Jill Vickers. 1998. 'Locating Women's Politics.' In *Women and Political Representation in Canada.* Manon Tremblay and Caroline Andrew (eds.). Ottawa: University of Ottawa Press.

Reissman, Catherine Kohler. 1992. 'Making Sense of Marital Violence: One Woman's Narrative.' In *Storied Lives: The Cultural Politics of Self-Understanding.* George C. Rosenwald and Richard Ochberg (ed.). New Haven, Conn.: Yale University Press.

Richling, B. 1985. '"You'd Never Starve Here": Return Migration to Rural Newfoundland' Canadian Review of Sociology and Anthropology 22(May): 236–49.

Ristock, Janice. 1991. 'Feminist Collectives: The Struggles and Contradictions in Our Quest for a 'Uniquely Feminist Structure.' In *Women and Social Change.* Jeri Dawn Wine and Janice Ristock (eds.). Toronto: James Lorimer.

Ristock, Janice, and Joan Pennell. 1996. *Community Research as Empowerment: Feminst Links, Postmodern Interruptions.* Toronto: Oxford University Press.

Roseberry, William. 1989. *Anthropologies and Histories.* New Brunswick, N.J.: Rutgers University Press.

Ross, David, E. Richard Shillington, and Clarence Lochhead. 1994. *The Canadian Fact Book on Poverty.* Ottawa: Canada Council on Social Development.

Rowbotham, Sheila. 1985. 'What Do Women Want? Woman-Centred Values and the World as It Is.' *Feminist Review* 20 (June): 49–69.

Sacouman, James. 1985. 'Atlantic Canada.' In *The New Practical Guide to Canadian Political Economy.* Daniel Drache and Wallace Clement (eds.). Toronto: James Lorimer.

Sahlins, Marshall. 1972. *Stone Age Economics.* Chicago: Aldine.

Scott, Joan W. 1992. 'Experience.' In *Feminists Theorize the Political.* Joan Scott and Judith Butler (eds.) New York: Routledge.

Sider, Gerald. 1986. *Culture and Class in Anthropology and History.* New York: Cambridge University Press.

– 1991. 'House and History at the Margins of Life: Domination, Domesticity, Ethnicity, and the Construction of Ethnohistories in 'The Land God Gave to Cain.' In *Golden Ages, Dark Ages: Imagining the Past in Anthropology and History.* Jay O'Brien and William Roseberry (eds.). Berkeley: University of California Press.

Sinclair, Peter R., and Lawrence Felt. 1992a. 'Separate Worlds: Gender and Domestic Labour in an Isolated Fishing Region.' *Canadian Review of Sociology and Anthropology* 29(1): 55–71.

1992b. '"Everyone Does It": Unpaid Work in a Rural Peripheral Region.' *Work, Employment and Society* 6(1): 43–64.

Social Policy Advisory Committee. 1997. *Investing in People and Communities: A Framework for Social Development.* St John's: Report of the Social Policy Advisory Committee.

Smith, Dorothy. E. 1989. *The Conceptual Practices of Power: A Feminist Sociology of Knowledge.* Toronto: University of Toronto Press.

Smith, Gavin. 1989. *Livelihood and Resistance: Peasants and the Politics of Land in Peru.* Berkeley: University of California Press.

– 1997. 'Pandora's History.' *Between History and Histories: The Production of Silences and Commemorations.* Gerald Sider and Gavin Smith (eds.). Toronto: University of Toronto Press.

– 1999. *Confronting the Present: Towards a Politically Engaged Anthropology.* Oxford: Berg.

Stimpson, Catharine. 1987. 'The Future of Memory: A Summary.' *Michigan Quarterly Review* 26: 259–65.

Struthers, James. 1996. 'Can Workfare Work? Reflections from History.' Caledon Institute of Social Policy.

Swindells, Julia. 1989. 'Liberating the Subject? Autobiography and Women's History: A Reading of the Diaries of Hannah Cullwick.' In *Interpreting Women's Lives.* Personal Narratives Group (eds.). Bloomington: Indiana University Press.

– Lisa Jardine. 1990. *What's Left? Women in Culture and the Labour Movement.* New York: Routledge.

Tavris, Carol. 1993. *The Measure of Woman.* New York: Simon and Shuster.

Thomas, Gerald. 1983. *Les deux traditions.* Montreal: Les Éditions Bellormin.

Tsing, Anna Lowenhaupt. 1993. *In the Realm of the Diamond Queen: Marginality in an Out-of-the-Way Place.* Princeton. N.J.: Princeton University Press.

Ursel, Jane. 1992. *Private Lives, Public Policy: 100 Years of State Intervention in the Family.* Toronto: Women's Press.

Vickers, Jill. 1991. 'Bending the Iron Law of Oligarchy: Debates on the Feminization of Organization and Political Process in the English Canadian Women's Movement, 1970–1988.' In *Women and Social Change.* Jeri Dawn Wine and Janice Ristock (eds.). Toronto: James Lorimer.

Waddell, Eric, and Claire Doron. 1983. 'The Newfoundland French: An Endangered Minority.' In *Two Nations, Many Cultures: Ethnic Groups in Canada.* James Elliot (ed.). Scarborough, Ont.: Prentice-Hall.

Wadel, Cato. 1973. *Now Whose Fault Is That? The Struggle for Self-Esteem in the Face of Chronic Unemployment.* St John's: Institute for Social and Economic Research.

Weedon, Chris. 1987. *Feminist Practice and Post-Structural Theory.* Oxford: Basil Blackwell.

Williams, A.F. 1966. 'Pilot Report: Overall Survey and Determination of Development Problems and Potentials.' *Comprehensive Rural Development Surveys – Port au Port Peninsula. ARDA Project 1050.*

Williams, Raymond. 1976. *Keywords: A Vocabulary of Culture and Society.* New York: Oxford University Press.

– *Marxism and Literature*, Oxford: Oxford University Press.

Wolf, Diana. 1996. 'Situating Feminist Dilemmas in Fieldwork.' In *Feminist Dilemmas in Fieldwork.* Diane L. Wolf (ed.). Boulder, Colo.: Westview Press.

Women's Policy Office. 1988. 'Understanding Wife Abuse: An Educational Manual for Community Groups.' Government of Newfoundland and Labrador.

– 1989. 'Child Care Arrangements in Newfoundland.' Government of Newfoundland and Labrador.

– 1992. 'Experiences of Teen Parents in Newfoundland.' Government of Newfoundland and Labrador.

Index

ANTHROPOLOGICAL HORIZONS

Editor: Michael Lambek, University of Toronto

This series, begun in 1991, focuses on theoretically informed ethnographic works addressing issues of mind and body, knowledge and power, equality and inequality, the individual and the collective. Interdisciplinary in its perspective, the series makes a unique contribution in several other academic disciplines: women's studies, history, philosophy, psychology, political science, and sociology.

Published to date:

1 *The Varieties of Sensory Experience: A Sourcebook in the Anthropology of the Senses*. Edited by David Howes
2 *Arctic Homeland: Kinship, Community, and Development in Northwest Greenland*. Mark Nuttall
3 *Knowledge and Practice in Mayotte: Local Discourses of Islam, Sorcery, and Spirit Possession.* Michael Lambek
4 *Deathly Waters and Hungry Mountains: Agrarian Ritual and Class Formation in an Andean Town.* Peter Gose
5 *Paradise: Class, Commuters, and Ethnicity in Rural Ontario.* Stanley R. Barrett
6 *The Cultural World in Beowulf.* John M. Hill
7 *Making It Their Own: Severn Ojibwe Communicative Practices.* Lisa Valentine
8 *Merchants and Shopkeepers: An Historical Anthropology of an Irish Market Town, 1200–1986.* Philip Gulliver and Marilyn Silverman
9 *Tournaments of Value: Sociability and Hierarchy in a Yemeni Town*. Ann Meneley
10 *Mal'uocchiu: Ambiguity, Evil Eye, and the Language of Distress*. Sam Migliore
11 *Between History and Histories: The Making of Silences and Commemorations.* Edited by Gerald Sider and Gavin Smith
12 *Eh Paesan! Being Italian in Toronto*. Nicholas DeMaria Harney
13 *Theorizing the Americanist Tradition.* Edited by Lisa Philips Valentine and Regna Darnell

14 *Colonial 'Reformation' of the Highlands of Central Sulawesi, Indonesia, 1892–1995.* Albert Schrauwers

15 *The Rock Where We Stand: An Ethnography of Women's Activism in Newfoundland.* Glynis George

www.ingramcontent.com/pod-product-compliance
Lightning Source LLC
LaVergne TN
LVHW090806070826
844660LV00022B/1098